Unexpected Love Tales

#1 Love From Afar
and
#2 All Their Christmases

Cenarth Fox

Unexpected Love Tales
Copyright 2025 Cenarth Fox

Love From Afar
All Their Christmases

The real events, places and people in this novel are used as a way of telling an invented tale. All other characters are fictitious and any resemblance to real persons, living or dead is purely coincidental.

All rights reserved. No part of this publication may be reproduced, transmitted, or stored in a retrieval system in any form or by any means without permission in writing from the publisher.

Cenarth Fox has asserted his right to be identified as the author of this work in accordance with the Copyright Act 1968.

First published in 2025 by Fox Plays
Melbourne Australia

www.cenfoxbooks.com
www.foxplays.com

ISBN 978-0-949175-75-5

Cover design by Oliviaprodesign

Love From Afar

Chapter 1
Does talent trickle?

Poverty ain't pretty and rural poverty's downright ugly. Meet the family McKay. George, father and husband, worked a smallholding as a tenant farmer with more rabbits than sheep. Alma, wife and mother, soft on the inside but tough as old boots, made meals out of home-grown veg and thin air. Her skills as a seamstress earned a little money. With son Hamish, and daughter Moira, the family lived in a basic stone cottage a few miles from the Scottish capital near the village of Crain. In 1877, Queen Victoria was over halfway through her reign.

Every day George thanked his elderly cow and fox-threatened chickens for their usually regular supply of milk and eggs.

Hamish, son and heir to nothing, left school with basic spelling and arithmetic and little else. He helped his father tend the sheep, planted potatoes and carrots, and took any odd job that came his way.

Daughter, Moira, helped her mother, loved her Da and worshipped big brother, Hamish.

Finding firewood became a daily task. Those Scottish winters only last about six months. One redeeming quality in all these struggles was a talent Hamish showed for art. His maternal grandmother loved to sketch birds and, if you believe such a thing, her talent trickled down the family tree to her grandson. Does talent trickle?

Finding paper for drawing was tricky. Any letters the family received, hopefully with one side blank, were saved for the young man to try his hand. His real gift was drawing faces. His family stared at the latest portrait.

'I'd like it more if was worth something. Can you try drawing wealthy folk?' asked George.

'Do you think art is worth money, Father?' queried Hamish.

His father sniffed and handed back his likeness. The idea of being paid to draw nestled in the artist's mind as his mother hugged him.

'Your grannie would be so proud, Hamish. Even in her dotage she would sit by the fire and draw pictures of birds.'

'Where are those pictures, Ma?' asked Moira. 'You talk about your mother's drawings, but I ain't never seen even one.'

'Shhhh,' whispered her father, frowning at his daughter.

The girl remembered hearing about the fire. The cottage where her grandparents and mother and her siblings once lived was consumed by flames. The humans survived but everything inside turned to ash.

Hamish too wanted to ask about the tragic event and more so his late grannie's artistic life. He was a child when she died, had questions but remained silent. Years ago, his father told him the event was painful for his mother and should never be mentioned.

Hamish thought about his grandmother and her art. *Where did she get the materials to sketch? Did she draw humans as well as birds? Did she ever show her art to other people, apart from family members? Does my art look like hers?*

'Supper is served,' said Hamish's mother and the family silently ate the homemade soup thinner than the letters Hamish filched to use for his art.

The Reverend James Dunbar, 46, bald, tall, and softly spoken, stood in the pulpit of the local kirk. He arrived in the parish more than ten years ago and, according to the congregation, was now a local, part of the furniture. He baptized, married, and buried them in this quiet part of Scotland where nothing of any importance happened, and where all was well with the world. Oh, apart from the poverty and incessant coughing and snivelling of pretty much everyone.

Mr Dunbar's wife made less noise than the family of church mice living beneath the floor of the kirk on which sat an ancient pedal organ. It must have been hell for those rodents when Mrs O'Brien pumped away on *Onward Christian Soldiers*. The instrument, being both loud and out-of-tune, meant one could only hope the mice were tone deaf.

People greeted the minister's wife asking after her three children yet knowing her response. 'Thank you, we are all well.' The offspring were placed in the department headed, *Children should be seen and not heard*, meaning ongoing chats with the minister's wife were rare.

The minister, fortunately, was the opposite. His mind housed thoughts and ideas and his lack of stentorian eloquence from the pulpit was compensated by his thirst for knowledge and genuine interest in his flock. 'What have you been up to, young man?' he would say to Hamish after morning service. Even details of vegetable growing and lamb feeding were sought after by the religious.

Having exhausted domestic details, Hamish changed topic.

'I finished a drawing of my father yesterday, Mr Dunbar.'

'A drawing of your father,' exclaimed the softly spoken minister. 'Why did I not know of your artistic endeavours? It sounds fascinating.'

Hamish tingled. He knew his artistic forebear told no-one outside the family about her avian art. He decided to break the family vow of silence.

'I've made a few sketches, sir.'

'A few, you say, meaning more than one. How long has this fine activity been your hobby?'

'Only a few months, sir.'

'I am favourably impressed. When may I view your handiwork?'

This stumped Hamish. The request surprised even flummoxed the budding artist.

'I'm not sure they are worthy, sir.'

The minister's hand rose in a disapproving gesture. 'Now, let us hear no more of such nonsense.' Hamish looked worried. 'Humility always serves the righteous well but let us not be hiding our light under a bushel. Please bring your family to tea at four this afternoon, sir, and do not forget your works of art.'

The minister's hand appeared, Hamish shook it and hurried to join his family all of whom wondered why the son and heir took so long to thank the minister for his sermon.

'What's happened?' asked father, George. 'Why were you so long?'

'We're invited to take tea with Mr Dunbar this afternoon.'

'But why?' asked Hamish's confused mother. 'Whatever for?'

'He wants to see my drawings.'

Hamish's mother made sure her family scrubbed up well. Bonnets for the females and caps for the males. It was a half mile walk to the manse and muddy roads attacked shoes, boots, cuffs, and dresses with gusto.

'Lift your hem, Moira,' ordered her mother as the family McKay headed to the kirk. Puddles prepared to pounce.

The family stood at the front door at a minute to four. Poor families promoted such qualities as tidiness, politeness, and punctuality. They cost nothing and promoted success and pride. The never garrulous Mrs Dunbar opened the door, nodded, offered a wisp of a smile, and beckoned them inside.

'Good afternoon, Mrs Dunbar,' said the head of the McKay family.

The minister's wife let her hair down, metaphorically speaking, and whispered, 'Good afternoon.'

The minister came out of his study and made up for his wife's alogia by welcoming everyone by name.

The McKays entered the empty sitting-room as the Dunbar youngsters, now the not even seen but not heard children, remained in their rooms.

With everyone seated and small talk exhausted, Mrs Dunbar rang a small bell, the sound of which matched the volume of her rare vocal utterances. The maid was listening at the keyhole. Silence settled before the door opened and the domestic entered knowing she must never speak unless spoken to.

'Tea, Agnes,' said Mrs Dunbar and the visitors exchanged glances at the sound of the usually mute lady of the house.

James Dunbar observed this situation and knew he was resigned to his lot in life. He harboured no ambition for high, even higher office. He worshipped his children and loved and supported his wife. The bible was constantly read in his home, particularly so because a former King of Scotland once ordered its translation.

One thing which gave the minister a spark happened when he saw talent in a person and especially an untapped talent in a young person. He knew nothing of Hamish's drawing skills but eagerly awaited details.

'Now young man, kindly reveal your artistic talent.'

All eyes focused on Hamish. Reluctantly he produced the letter his mother received from her cousin in Edinburgh. Handing said epistle to the confused minister, he spoke.

'It's on the other side, Mr Dunbar.'

The minister stared at the sketch of George McKay. The atmosphere froze. Hamish stopped breathing.

'Mr McKay,' said James Dunbar referring to George. 'This is your exact likeness, sir. It is brilliant.'

Hamish thought his heart would burst. George and Alma smiled, and young Moira reckoned her brother was the bee's knees.

'But what is this paper?' asked Dunbar waving the letter. 'Where is your sketchbook?'

Hamish wanted to reply but his mother got in first. 'We cannot afford the materials, Mr Dunbar,' she said. 'The costs are too great.'

There was a knock on the door and James moved. He took the tray from the maid, placing it on the small table in the middle of the room. 'I'll return,' he said and disappeared.

His surprised wife sorted the crockery and Alma stood. 'Please allow me to help, Mrs Dunbar,' she said and did. Unsurprisingly, the minister's wife remained speechless.

With tea poured, shortbread distributed, and the company seated, James reappeared. 'I knew I had this somewhere.' He offered a large artist's sketchbook to Hamish whose jaw dropped.

To accept the gift, the artist needed to place his cup and saucer and small plate with the finest Scottish shortbread, on the floor. His mother winced. *"The table, Hamish, the table!"* Hamish stuttered.

'I .. d .. d .. don't know what to say.'

'You could try, "thank you",' said his father in a soft voice.

'This is extremely kind of you, Mr Dunbar. Thank you so much, sir.'

'Mind you, there is a cost, young man,' said the benefactor, and a pause dominated. What cost? The family has no money. 'I will require a portrait of my wife and children, please.'

There was great relief with Hamish all smiles only to freeze when the normally non-speaking spouse spoke.

'Oh no, James. I could not possibly agree.'

The wise minister diffused the situation. 'Of course you are right, my dear. We will have a portrait of our three children.'

Peace returned but Hamish took heart.

'And you, Mr Dunbar. My family believe I did well with my father's illustration so I would be honoured to produce a portrait of you, sir.'

Spirits lifted and even more so when Mrs Dunbar went, well for her anyway, all garrulous.

'I agree, James. You must have your portrait painted.'

Nobody pointed out it was a sketch, not a painting.

The walk home featured non-stop chatter. Alma and Moira discussed the décor in the manse, the crockery and shortbread, whereas George added his pennyworth about the gift from the minister.

'There may be a shilling or two in this portrait business, son,' he said. 'Do a good job with the Reverend and who knows what may happen.'

Hamish grinned, said nothing, and felt all warm inside.

Chapter 2
Look at Me!

Countess Elspeth Buchanan and her beauty were frequently part of conversations in parlours and sitting rooms of stately homes, manor houses, terrace dwellings, cottages and elsewhere throughout the county, even as far as Edinburgh. A widow at 44, this English-born beauty happily married the wealthy Earl of Buchanan when the couple met by chance on the side of a road. Not an arranged marriage for the aristocracy but love at first sight by accident.

Her carriage suffered a damaged axle, and the passing Earl stopped to render assistance—well, his man and the driving contingent did the heavy lifting—meaning the Scottish Earl, Michael Ranald Buchanan eventually came away with the hand of an English beauty.

Her blue eyes and blonde hair when part of what observers would call a perfect countenance, saw the Scottish nobleman in seventh heaven. Already the daughter of an English Earl, the Lady Astley found the older Scottish aristocrat vastly different from her many English admirers who lined up to earnestly press their suit.

'Your decision, my girl,' opined her father, 'but do get a wriggle on, Elspeth. One gets bored with so many chaps lining up, cap in hand.'

Elspeth adored her mother who delivered sage advice. 'Forget all this "good match and damn fine family" business, my darling. Marry for love. Marry the man who gets you all hot and flustered especially when you're both fully dressed and he's not even in the same county.'

She did and in three years, Lady Buchanan presented her husband with two daughters. Many gents would have preferred a son and heir, but Lord Buchanan rejoiced in the good health of his two wee girls. Morag possessed her father's strong facial bone structure, minus the whiskers of course, whereas her younger sister, Bonnie, appeared as a mirror image of her stunning mother.

Twenty odd years after their wedding, this match made in heaven ended tragically when his Lordship found himself secreting blood from body locations not intended for such a purpose. The best doctors in the late nineteenth century were unable to accurately diagnose let alone cure the ailment. Laudanum and whisky in liberal amounts were swallowed daily with Lord Buchanan dying in his 60th year.

The females mourned his passing and the whole village attended the funeral, spilling into the graveyard where ceaseless rain made the mournful setting perfectly miserable.

Buchanan Hall became as loud as a nunnery. Servants crept about performing their duties. Firewood was chopped far from the house and creaky stairs avoided. Whispers were muted.

Weeks passed. When would Lady Buchanan venture forth into the world? Locals asked questions. Gossip centred on her Ladyship's attire and whether she would emulate Her Majesty and remain in black forever.

A month after the funeral, the widow and her daughters dined and when their meal ended, Lady Buchanan asked the girls to join her in the library. A fire crackled and Morag and Bonnie sensed an important issue bubbled close to the surface.

'What is troubling you, Mother?' asked Morag, the sensitive one.

'When will our mourning end?" added Bonnie, keen to be active as dancing and dinner parties thrilled her no end.

Under duress, their mother hesitated before speaking. She believed her words would cause the young women distress.

'Before your dear father died, he made me promise one thing.' Even the books became tense. 'He told me not to mourn but to get on with life and live it to the full. "Promise me you will do it, Elspeth", he said.'

'He was always a wonderful and wise father,' said Bonnie.

Morag pondered. 'You should not feel any pressure, Mother.'

The widow breathed deeply. 'Your father told me to attend functions and accept invitations from families we know. He said I was too young to remain a widow.'

The daughters froze. Not living forever in black and locked away on the estate was one thing but the idea of their mother re-marrying shocked the young women.

'Married!' whispered Morag.

'To whom?' demanded Bonnie, worried a tyrannical stepfather would put a stop to her active social life.

Elspeth raised her hands. 'Please. Stop!' She paused. 'I have no plans for even receiving callers let alone accepting any offers of marriage. I merely wish to tell you how your father was thinking before he died. And as a fitting period of mourning has passed, I want us to return to the activities we once performed. Attending the kirk this Sunday will be an appropriate first event.'

The daughters considered the announcement. Morag was pleased to learn her mother would not become a recluse. Bonnie was inwardly thrilled to know her previous life of gaiety and glamour might soon resume.

Next Sunday, their coach pulled up outside the village kirk and locals stared as the three Buchanan women stepped down wearing suitable clothing. Bonnie's bonnet announced her arrival as the lady from the Big House with style. If wearing a sign had been invented, Bonnie's would read, *Look at Me!*

Males doffed their caps and females bobbed as the wealthy women moved to the front door. The whispering among the onlookers took on the sound of bees buzzing or wind in the trees or both.

Despite being a small kirk, segregation ruled supreme and a special pew for the largest landowner and its only titled congregants awaited the Buchanans. An usher stood ready to open the little door to the pew—we can't have the poor people enter such hallowed ground—and Lady Buchanan led her daughters on this, their first public outing since the Earl breathed his last.

The minister in his small robing room—everything in this kirk was small—heard the news about the special worshippers and took an extra wee while to adjust his attire.

It was a normal Sunday morning service, but the kirk needed a *Standing Room Only* sign. Word ran through the village and people who decided to stay at home were now hurrying to witness the women in black from the Big House.

No black in sight meaning the whispering and pointing, more subdued inside, faded.

The Reverend Dunbar stepped from his private quarters with the congregation rising as one.

'In the name of the Father, the Son and the Holy Spirit,' he spoke with immaculate diction albeit a paucity of projection.

The rustling of ladies' voluminous dresses indicated the worshippers had resumed their seats. But not for long as the first hymn began being sung with modest conviction. They were Scots, not Welsh.

The minister knew his etiquette and spoke with sincerity and warmth in addressing the Buchanans.

'Good morning, m'Ladies, and may I say how delighted we are to see you back in your rightful place in our kirk. You are most welcome and long may you continue to worship and take fellowship here.'

Her Ladyship gave an imperceptible nod with Morag smiling and Bonnie wishing the service would soon end. It had only just begun.

The minister, in giving church notices and prayer requests for those poorly folk in the parish, finished by breaking from his usual comments and spoke from the heart.

'I have recently discovered a member of our flock has been blessed with a talent, an exceptional talent in the field of art.'

Worshippers concentrated. Hamish caught his breath. This was unexpected.

'Hamish McKay showed me a sketch he made of his dear father, George, and I admit to being mightily impressed. Hamish captured his father's features in a way any trained portrait painter would applaud. I discovered Hamish was without the materials to continue his art, and my wife and I were delighted to provide the young man with a sketchbook. We look forward to his further portraits.' He switched to his priestly duties and the service continued.

Mr Dunbar waited outside the kirk as his congregation departed. Lady Buchanan and her daughters led the way.

She smiled, shook the minister's hand, and spoke first. 'Thank you for your kind words, Mr Dunbar. I have missed your thoughtful sermons and we three look forward to resuming our regular visits.'

Other worshippers held back allowing the widow to have her moment with the minister. The daughters smiled and were helped into their coach. Lady Buchanan was no longer in mourning.

Hamish, with his family, took their turn to greet the minister.

'Thank you for your kind words, Mr Dunbar,' said Alma.

'Most kind, sir,' added her husband.

The budding artist accepted his benefactor's hand.

'Ah, the artist himself,' said Dunbar. 'Now sir, to keep your part of the bargain, may I suggest afternoon tea at 4 when we can discuss your first portraiture commission.'

Hamish's brain buzzed. His mouth went dry as his joy overflowed. 'I shall look forward to it, Mr Dunbar. Good day, sir.'

On the walk home, George McKay wondered aloud if the planned meeting between his son and the minister constituted working on the Sabbath.

'Oh, George,' scolded Alma. 'It's not work; it's a social event. Encourage the boy.'

'What's a portraiture commission?' asked Moira mispronouncing both words.

'Yes, Da' added Hamish. 'Is that what you talked about before? You know, making money from art?'

The pater sniffed. He once thought the possibility of his son being paid to draw or paint was pie-in-the-sky nonsense. Now he thought otherwise. What would happen with the minister this afternoon?

Chapter 3
Meet the villain.

Rory McGrath married into money. With little of his own, the handsome parasite landed on his feet as his father-in-law was loaded. Rory's wife, Orla, was attractive, but her best feature by a country mile was her father's estate and attendant wealth.

There were few, if any, people who would write a glowing reference for Rory McGrath. The best response he could elicit was *contemptuous* with *selfish brute* a close second. He used and abused his fellow humans with women his favourite class of victim.

When Miss Orla McGregor appeared on the scene, Rory didn't need a plan of action. He leapt into his seduction routine acting in what he thought was an honourable way. He fooled his future father-in-law —more fool him—and conned the would-be bride into believing he was her knight in shining armour—more fool her.

They wed and, at first, Rory swam in the cash his wife's father bestowed upon the new Mrs McGrath. Alas, selfish, self-centred and sponger Rory easily upset folk. He gambled his wife's money and lost. Creditors circled. The bully saw him mistreat his wife, and when she told her mother who relayed the news to her husband, Rory copped a beating having been dragged from a local public house by workers on the McGregor estate.

His wife grew to hate the pathetic McGrath, and they lived apart under the same roof. Only their daughter, Elsie, kept the mother residing in the family home.

The future of the marriage looked bleak with Rory racking his brain to find a way back aboard the gravy train. He held no fear of the Law and the only thing stopping him from having his wife murdered was the certainty his father-in-law would leave him nothing. More likely, before Rory was beaten to a pulp, McGregor would have his former son-in-law pay for the burial. Meet Rory, the villain of the piece.

Hamish placed his sketchbook under his arm and set off for the Dunbar manse. His mind buzzed, his heart raced, and his hands perspired.

The minister opened the door. 'Come in, come in,' he beamed drawing the budding artist inside with an extended handshake.

Hamish was shown into the study, its walls lined with floor to ceiling chock-a-block bookshelves.

Silence was the major characteristic of this house. Mrs Dunbar and the three offspring may have been visiting the man in the moon for all the sounds they made or didn't make.

'I am excited about this project, Hamish,' said the older man, his grin growing ever wider.

Project? thought Hamish. *What project?*

Instantly the mood changed. 'However, my dear wife leads me to believe creating a portrait of our young children may place too great a strain on their tender minds and bodies.'

Hamish nodded not knowing where this was going or how he should response.

'Mrs Dunbar,' continued the minister, 'suggested I should be the subject of your artistic endeavours. If it means you will further develop your talent, I am at your service.'

'You are most kind, Mr Dunbar. I only hope I can create a portrait with which you and Mrs Dunbar are pleased.'

The youthful artist did not consider the fact the man of the cloth remained troubled, his conscience wrestling with the sin of vanity. Making himself the centre of attention did not sit well with the reverend gent. Part of the *Book of Ecclesiastes* bounced around Dunbar's cranium.

Vanity of vanities; all is vanity!' he pondered.

Hamish surprised himself by taking control. 'Shall we begin, sir?'

Surprised and relieved, the subject of the exercise agreed. 'Of course, of course, where should I sit?'

And thus the first proper portrait, apart from the sketch of his father on the back of a letter, created by Hamish McKay, commenced. The subject proved an ideal "sitter." He remained still and mute and thought of where his portrait would reside and wondered if his God would be offended at what might be considered pride.

He took comfort in the knowledge he was supporting a worthwhile activity. One of his flock possessed a God-given artistic talent which could remain hidden. Nurturing this talent was a noble endeavour and he, the young man's minister, would nurture it however he could.

Orla McGrath tossed and turned. Past midnight, she hated her life and knew her misery caused this insomnia.

Her estranged husband, Rory, banished to another wing of the house, continued to torment her. Her father's loyal workers put the bruises and thus the frighteners on the loser. Getting him out, permanently, was the solution to her problems.

Her father spoke plainly. 'Say the word, my girl, and your beloved bastard will disappear forever, his horrible remains never to be found.'

Orla hesitated. What would she tell their daughter who doted on her papa? Would one of her father's employees get drunk and let slip their murderous activity? Would the Sheriff get involved? Would Rory cause more trouble dead than alive?

She eventually fell asleep but woke in a sweat. Why?

Grabbing her silk dressing-gown, she headed down the corridor to her darling daughter's room. Outside, she froze. Voices. Orla pressed her ear to the young child's door. Rory. He spoke softly but speak he did. What was he doing in this room? And why? Saying goodnight when their child would surely be asleep. Terror battered Orla's heart.

Instead of bursting in and demanding to know what was happening, she ever so gently turned the door handle and prayed the opening door would not creak.

Moonlight. The bed, bathed in a soft glow, revealed Rory lying on the bed covers beside his daughter, her hair stretched out on the pillow.

Orla froze in the dark and listened. Only Rory spoke. His whispered words came in snatches to his wife who trembled. She watched, listened and nearly died.

'But Daddy,' said the child, 'why does Mummy hate you?'

Orla tapped the door, once. Rory knew he was not alone. A hiss sounded. He bent in and kissed his daughter. 'Good night, my darling,' he whispered, rolled off the bed and walked towards his wife.

He left the room, and she followed. In the corridor he glared at her. 'So, spying on me, is it? Have you no shame?'

'What were you doing?' she demanded.

'Saying good night to our daughter as any loving father would do.'

'Is that all?' she hissed.

He caught her meaning and prepared to smash her face.

'Go on,' she said. 'Strike a woman. That's about your level.'

He froze knowing to attack his wife would be signing his death warrant.

Knowing she bluffed him, she kept going. 'Trying to turn our child against her mother. Persuade the young her father is a wrongly maligned victim. I bet you never mention your gambling, womanizing, and thieving.'

Her words became painful blows because they were true and meant he so desperately wanted to use force.

She piled in on him. 'If you're still here at dawn, I'll send word to my father and your life will be over. Get out while you still can.' She stared at him in the darkened corridor. 'Edwards can drive you to town.' She spat. 'Go!'

Orla brushed past him and entered their child's bedroom.

In the corridor, he knew the marriage was officially, permanently over. Rage and despair flooded his body. He packed a bag, stole what he could carry, saddled his favourite horse, and left the family home with his body intact and spirit smashed.

Chapter 4
And that driver looked dishy.

Lady Buchanan wrote yet another letter. Apart from her now regular church attendance, she remained at home keeping her daughters close. Her sister, aunt and a cousin on her late husband's side, were kept advised of her situation by post, and the widow faithfully replied to each epistle received. Correspondence was a way of life.

The daughters could not have been more different. Morag didn't need to think about her future. Her role was to support her widowed mother and would do so forever. Bonnie hated her situation. She loved social events and desperately wanted to be dancing, dining, and dominating. Not being brave enough to say as much to her mother increased her thriving frustration.

One day Bonnie's heart took flight. From an upstairs window she watched a carriage coming along the drive. No tradesman would own such a vehicle nor dare venture anywhere other than the rear of the stately home. For Bonnie, anyone, anything to break the monotony was a godsend. She checked her hair and attire and headed downstairs.

The butler tapped lightly on the library door and entered.

'Yes, Fraser?'

'A gentleman has called, m'Lady.' The butler held out a silver tray upon which lay a calling card. Elspeth collected and studied the details. Sir Richard Galbraith was once an associate of her late husband, and Lady Buchanan met the visitor at various social gatherings.

'Show him to the main sitting room,' she said and, like her daughter, prepared herself for company.

Sir Richard, bachelor, stood before the fireplace, hands behind his back, and fidgeted. Despite his wealth and status, dealing with a woman left him uncomfortable. And when the matter involved social etiquette, his discomfort crept towards discombobulation.

The door opened and Lady Buchanan swept in. 'Sir Richard,' she smiled extending a hand.

'Lady Buchanan,' he replied holding her fingers for the briefest moment.

She sat on the closest settee and indicated an adjacent chair. Satisfied she was settled, he sat.

'My dear Lady Buchanan, I have called in person to enquire as to your health and that of your delightful daughters.'

'Most kind, Sir Richard and thank you, we are all well.'

The polite conversation continued with the hostess wondering about the real purpose of the visit. Surely he's not come a-courting.

Bonnie came downstairs and walked quietly to the door to eavesdrop. Straining to hear, she didn't notice Fraser unintentionally hidden behind a large potted plant. He coughed discreetly.

'Oh Fraser, thank goodness you're here,' said the inquisitive daughter, desperate for news.

'Good day, m'Lady.'

'Is my mother unwell?'

Of course it was a pathetic attempt at disguising her curiosity.

'I believe her Ladyship is in good health.'

The butler had served the family since Eve chatted with the garrulous snake and knew the conniving little minx for what she was. Bonnie wanted to slap the man she regarded as a smug old git but instead smiled and headed for the kitchen.

This became a smart move as her hunch paid off. Sir Richard's driver sat at the huge table in the centre of the room beneath a dozen or more hanging pots and pans. The cook, Mrs MacDougal, who had served the Buchanan family longer than Fraser, provided the driver with a steaming cup of tea and a doorstop slice of bread and butter.

Mrs Mac bobbed when Bonnie entered busting for news. 'Good morning, m'Lady. Is there something I can do for thee?'

Bonnie wanted to swear, hating those damn social conventions where the lower classes were to be avoided at all costs and never directly spoken to. She wanted to scream at the driver, who, of course, immediately stood when the lady entered. *Why is your master here?*

Instead, she fell back on her pathetic lies. 'My mother is entertaining, and I wondered if there is something she requires,' said Bonnie eyeing up the young man.

Sneaking furtive glances, and trying hard not to stare, the driver realized the description of one of the Buchanan daughters being beautiful was wildly inaccurate. She was stunning.

'Not that she said, m'Lady.' The following silence whacked Bonnie across her beautiful face. She turned to leave but stopped noticing an enormous bouquet of magnificent blooms.

'Oh, my goodness,' she exclaimed. 'They are breathtaking. Are they from our garden?'

The driver looked to the cook for permission to speak. She nodded.

'Beggin' your pardon, m'Lady,' he spoke with eyes averting the now much excited Bonnie. 'They be from my master, Sir Richard Galbraith. They be a gift for Her Ladyship, Lady Buchanan.'

'How kind,' said Bonnie and wafted away rejoicing in her recently acquired knowledge, her head buzzing with questions.

Why is Sir Richard calling? Flowers for mother could mean an invitation to a cèilidh or wait for it, a marriage proposal for the widow or even her beautiful daughter – Moi. And that driver looked dishy.

Chapter 5

Breakfast was a single malt and a pee.

Staring at his drawing, Hamish addressed the subject of his portrait. 'I believe I have enough of a foundation, Mr Dunbar. Thank you, for sitting so patiently and well.'

'May I see your work?' he asked, his neck aching from sitting so long yet keen as a child on his birthday morning to see the presents.

'Of course, sir. Is your neck sore?' asked Hamish as the minister continued rubbing his body. The pain vanished in an instant.

The sitter gulped as he studied the artwork. 'But it is magnificent.' Hamish copped the equivalent of a punch to his chest. 'You have a rare and brilliant talent, Hamish McKay.'

'Thank you, sir. I'm glad you approve.'

'Approve? I am struggling to express my admiration.' He opened the study door and called to his wife. 'My dear, you must come at once.' He returned to the illustration which occupied a whole page in the large sketchbook. His wife arrived, concerned about being summoned at all let alone in such a manner and voice.

'Is something wrong, my dear?'

The minister indicated the portrait, only a sketch and not yet finished, but with enough detail to display its quality.

'Oh,' said Mrs Dunbar. 'It is an excellent likeness.'

The minister went off on a tangent. 'Hamish, your work with pencil is outstanding. Why have you not tried your hand with watercolours or pigments? Painting portraits could be your forte.'

Confusion reigned. 'I've never tried painting, sir, and I have no brushes or paint.'

'What! That will never do,' said the minister opening the drawer in his desk. He produced a small notebook and scanned the names at the back. 'Here, this is a stationer's shop in Edinburgh I've used before. They stock art materials. We'll go tomorrow.'

It was difficult to decide who was the more astonished—the wife, the artist, or the sketch.

Hamish went home with his two pencils and sketchbook with its newly-created portrait. He wanted to show his family and tell them about his impending visit to the famous old city.

Bonnie returned to her bedroom keeping an eye on the carriage below. She saw her mother's caller leaving and again stared at the young man she met in the kitchen. She imagined meeting him in the estate woods and what they might say and do. Vivid described her imagination.

Reckoning enough time had elapsed since the visitor departed, she went downstairs and knocked on the door of her mother's study.

Surprised and annoyed, Bonnie entered to find her mother talking with sister, Morag. Bonnie's mind caught fire.

What is Morag doing here? She's not a sticky-beak like me.

'Come in, Bonnie,' said Elspeth. 'I was about to send for you.'

The sisters settled.

'I received a gentleman this morning. Sir Richard Galbraith knew your father and called to enquire after our health.'

'I know his niece, Miss Galbraith,' said Morag, and Bonnie's lips pursed automatically.

'He brought flowers from his home. I remember your father spoke of his horticultural prowess and prize-winning roses.'

'Were you pleased to see Sir Richard, Mother?' asked Bonnie probing for an unusual reaction rather than the traditional response.

'He has invited us to a *cèilidh* at his home next month and offered to send a carriage.'

Bonnie struggled to contain her excitement. 'Oh Mother, how wonderful. It's what you need, the opportunity to re-enter society.'

'I'm not thinking of myself but of you, my darling girls.'

Morag interrupted. 'We're fine, Mummy. It's you who needs to be comfortable and happy.'

Bonnie struggled to refrain from slapping her sister.

'I promised your father I would ensure you would meet eligible and appropriate gentlemen and, if you so desire, allow you to marry well and be cared for.'

Bonnie wanted to cheer.

'I've told Sir Richard we will discuss his kind invitation and inform him of our decision in the coming days.'

She studied her daughters and instantly knew their reaction. One was keen with bells on, the other calm and undecided.

If Hamish McKay was over the moon with the reaction to his latest portrait sketch and the possible new genre his art may explore, Rory McGrath did a nice line in teeth grinding.

He hated his life. He hated his wife. His only revenue source, his father-in-law, would be told all manner of tales, most true, of his alleged wickedness. No more easy money. No more money full stop.

Of course, Rory was trying to win favour with his young daughter and subtly portray his wife as the harridan of all nasty mothers. But who would believe the former gambler, adulterer, thief and bully? Certainly not his wife's family.

He could return to his parents, but pride prevented such a move. An old drinking friend would suffice for now. The artist, Fitzroy Arbuthnot, inherited his Scottish grandfather's two-acre estate which included a solid cottage and a tidy sum of cash. Fitzroy worked hard to drink away his pile of money.

Rory came calling in the wee small hours craving succour. Offering a fine single malt, stolen from his father-in-law's supply in his former home, meant Rory was welcomed with open hours, er arms.

Fitzroy couldn't afford a servant, swore a vow to never wash a thing, and took each drunken day as it came on an hourly basis.

'Come away in,' said the painter not the least concerned at the time of day or night as it happened to be.

Rory could stay for as long as his liquor contributions continued.

Fitzroy's alcoholism slowed but never stopped his passion for art. A graduate of the Royal School of Art in 1843 in London, the urge to paint settled in his mind—his heart was too busy hearing complaints from his liver—and the studio, a mess of gigantic proportions, saw him create his unseen, unknown and unloved works of art.

Breakfast in the morning for both the artist and his new lodger was single malt, a pee, and a collapse on the busted sofas.

Chapter 6
She took a shine to sex.

Hamish arrived at the Dunbar manse well before the agreed time. The minister cadged a lift from a farmer en route to Grassmarket in the Old Town part of Edinburgh. From there they walked, and it was mid-morning when they reached their destination.

The bell above the door of the stationery shop tingled.

'Good morning, gentlemen, how may we help?'

Hamish let his minister do the talking but did wonder why the man used the word "we" when he was obviously alone.

'This young man is a brilliant artist and requires art materials to allow his portraits to shine.'

The shopkeeper's heart accelerated. Here was a guaranteed sale. He beamed and displayed a variety of brushes, pigments and an easel.

Mr Dunbar's enthusiasm seemed unstoppable until he enquired about prices. Undeterred, he bought a bare minimum of materials including a plain weave canvas with supports, brushes and pigments.

'These will get you started,' he said leading Hamish outside. The shopkeeper silently cursed.

The minister decided. 'Let us enjoy refreshment before we …'

He stopped mid-sentence and Hamish turned to see why his patron became distracted.

Nearby was an art gallery and Hamish found himself hurrying to keep up as they entered. Various sized portraits lined the walls.

'Look, Hamish. These are outstanding but your work could easily hang in this place.' Hamish observed and tingled. This was his patch; here he felt right at home.

'Good morning, gentlemen,' said the proprietor, a middle-aged overweight popinjay with spectacles settled near the tip of his nose and a handkerchief in his breast pocket the size of a small towel; the handkerchief that is. 'How may we be of assistance?'

Hamish wondered if all the tradespeople in Edinburgh spoke a form of plural pronoun English.

The minister introduced himself and Hamish, singing the praises of his young protégé. Callum Drinkwater listened attentively and encouraged the artist to present his work, when available, to be considered for display and sale in the gallery.

'We are always happy to encourage young and talented artists.'

With appropriate painting materials and an offer of interest from a gallery owner, the two lowlanders left on a cloud. What a day. Their high spirits helped as they set off for home.

Without farmers returning from Edinburgh markets, the entire journey was on foot and the precipitation hardly helped. But with the important safekeeping of the newly purchased materials in hand, a new phase of the young artist's career loomed large. Potential fame and fortune became the light at the end of the tunnel.

Bonnie hated waiting. She needed an answer and the days drifted by with her mother saying nothing. At luncheon only the sound of cutlery, soft of course, disturbed the meal.

'My darlings,' said Elspeth without any forewarning. 'I have written to Sir Richard and accepted his invitation to the *cèilidh*.'

Both daughters showed restraint. 'If that is what you want, Mother,' said Morag feeling apprehensive.

'Yes, Mama,' added Bonnie. 'We are happy to do as you please.' There was a complete lack of apprehension from the younger daughter.

'Go through your wardrobes and tell me if you need anything new to wear. Your father would want you to look your best.'

The young women nodded adding their thanks. The subject was dropped. Bonnie tapped her toes and hoped any sound remained hidden. The kitchen maid cleared away the plates. The Buchanan ladies were back in society.

Hamish set to work with his newly acquired pigments. On the new, his first canvas, Mr Dunbar's portrait came alive. Yes, the young artist was experimenting, but his natural talent shone through. His mother came into the kitchen with her son using the table for his art.

'Oh my, Hamish, what have you done?' she said before her mouth opened and stayed open.

'Do you like it, Ma? It's my first portrait using the new materials on canvas given me by Mr Dunbar.'

'It's as if the minister is here in our cottage. It is so real.'

'What's so real?' asked Moira arriving with potatoes. She saw the portrait, dropped the spuds, and cared not as they bounced around the rock-hard floor. 'Did you draw it, Hamish?' She looked closer. 'Have you painted it? Is it truly your work?'

He beamed more inside than out.

'You must take it to Mr Dunbar now,' said Alma. 'But not before you show it to your father.'

The first reviews were in. George McKay suffered a pride attack upon seeing his son's latest offering. The working-class sheep farmer with a rented smallholding couldn't stop a tear bobbing up in the corner of his right eye.

Half an hour later, with his portrait well-wrapped, he knocked on Mr Dunbar's door. The beaming minister sensed the reason for the visit and carefully drew the young man inside. When Hamish unveiled the portrait, his benefactor's response startled the visitor.

Being hugged was not a frequent activity in the McKay household and certainly not by the adult male in the family.

The minister went overboard with a bear hug which, Hamish reckoned, went on too long.

'It needs to be properly framed,' said Mr Dunbar coming back down to Earth. 'I know a person who can do it. His name is Arbuthnot, Fitzroy Arbuthnot.'

Hamish worried. 'I haven't put my name on the portrait yet, sir, and I would like to add a few more brush marks above your head.'

Dunbar made a face but agreed. 'As you wish,' he said. 'I'll contact Mr Arbuthnot and make arrangements.'

Bonnie spent an age sorting her clothes. She wanted her outfit, makeup, hair, and jewellery to be enticing, ravishing for the world to see. Morag did little. She knew the dress she would wear and the shoes, and returned to her crocheting and later, reading.

The day of the *cèilidh* drew nigh. Bonnie knew her mother would not approve of the risqué nature of the chosen dress. Her figure drew attention whenever she appeared in public, and in the grounds of the family home, if she went for a walk, she knew workers on the estate would cast an eye towards her.

With the wind in a certain direction, she once overheard two farmhands talking about her appearance with their ungentlemanly comments giving her a sliver of pleasure.

Years ago, reaching puberty, a strong discussion with her mother both excited and intrigued her. She took a shine to the idea of sex. Being in the company of young, virile young men quickly became a priority in her life. Roll on the dance.

Mr Dunbar collected the finished now labelled portrait and set off to have the work professionally presented. He knew Fitzroy was not nor ever had been a holy man having met the old artist when visiting a sick neighbour. But knowing how Jesus mixed with and certainly forgave sinners, the minister knocked on the front door of Arbuthnot's hovel.

To his surprise a man he didn't know appeared.

'Yes?' snapped Rory McGrath, still broke, hungry, and angry.

'Good day to you, sir. I am the Reverend Dunbar from the local kirk. I have business to discuss with Mr Arbuthnot.'

Instantly Rory changed character. Whenever the possibility of making money arose, McGrath enjoyed a surge of pleasure.

Knowing the state of the place, Rory hesitated. Would the putrid smells and chaotic interior see this man of the cloth turn tail and flee?

No need for a decision from Rory as his landlord appeared.

'Mr Dunbar, as I live and try to breathe.' The painter thrust out a hand with all its skin in hiding beneath paint, dirt and grease.

'Good day to you, Mr Arbuthnot. I trust I find you in rude health.'

'I could say a few rude words about my health but not to a man of faith.' He indicated Rory. 'Mr Rory McGrath, the Reverend James Dunbar.' The men shook hands and all three moved inside.

'Now what is that I see you are carrying, sir?' asked Fitzroy. 'It's a painting if I'm not mistaken.'

Dunbar unwrapped the portrait. 'Indeed, it is, sir. And I wish to hire you for the important task of framing said piece.'

The portrait appeared, Fitzroy stared at it and gasped.

'It's you but where did you get this? It's magnificent,' he murmured being mightily impressed. 'Who created this masterpiece?'

Rory wondered how he could make money from this meeting.

'There is a young man in my kirk with an untapped and natural talent. This is his first portrait in paint, and we need to have it framed.'

Fitzroy looked at Dunbar and back at the portrait. 'He has captured you in all your glory, Reverend.'

'Please tell me your fee, sir, and I will hire you on the spot.'

'He needs to learn more about pigments. And you say he is young and untrained?'

'In his twenty-first year with never a lesson in his life.'

'Well, he must be encouraged. This young man must be given support to launch his career, and I shall be honoured to frame this portrait sans fee.' Rory didn't know any Latin but sensed money was not to be involved. He growled.

Fitzroy pointed at the visitor. 'Mind you, a wee drop of Scotland's finest wouldn't go astray.'

Dunbar grinned and shook the artist's hand.

'I have an introduction to a gallery in Edinburgh. The owner is a dapper dresser who urged Hamish to bring his work for consideration.'

'You wouldn't be talking about Callum Drinkwater by any chance?'

'I would indeed. You know the gentleman?'

'More's the pity,' said Fitzroy upsetting the minister. 'He'll ask for fifty per cent, but you sign nothing until he drops at least by half.'

Dunbar's excitement faded but he was keen to settle the framing process. 'Shall we say this time tomorrow, Mr Arbuthnot?'

'This time tomorrow, sir. I have the perfect frame in my studio.'

The men shook hands, and the caller left with a spring in his step.

Inside, Rory let fly. 'Are you mad, you useless fool? He has money, make him pay.'

'Not much of an art lover, are we Rory?' said Fitzroy as he searched for a frame.

'And what's this fifty per cent business. Fifty per cent of what?'

The painter found the frame and placed the portrait inside. 'Perfect,' he said.

'Fifty per cent of what?' repeated the lodger.

'Whatever a client is prepared to pay. In this case,' he said admiring Hamish's work, 'I'd guess at twenty pounds.'

Rory's mouth opened and stayed open.

Chapter 7
New clothes are easy to find, not so new teeth.

Finally, Bonnie rejoiced. The day of the *cèilidh* arrived and the three Buchanan women gathered in the main sitting room awaiting Sir Richard's carriage. The horses announced their arrival and Fraser entered to state the obvious.

The women departed with Bonnie keeping a shawl tight around her upper body. The dress she chose displayed an amount of cleavage she knew her mother would not approve and require another outfit.

Morag dressed appropriately wanting to please her mother.

In the carriage, Elspeth spoke. 'I expect you to behave as if your father were present.' Both sisters murmured their assent, and little else was said during the journey.

Music was heard as the carriage arrived. A manservant opened the door, dropped the steps, and helped each guest step down. Sir Richard stood waiting and warmly welcomed the three ladies.

Inside the stately home, their coats were taken, and Bonnie's wrap disappeared. Her mother and sister reacted politely at the sight of Bonnie's décolletage. Elspeth could hardly raise the matter with servants and Sir Richard close by.

He led Lady Buchanan and her daughters to the large room where the music and dancing were in full swing. The three women met Sir Richard's sister, Harriet. Polite conversation ensued while people stared at the younger sister as her figure, beauty, and outfit set fire to conversations. Women used fans to hide their gossiping with other women. With no such item to hand, men muttered to other men or to themselves ogling the new arrival.

Bonnie lapped up the atmosphere and her excitement soared when a young man approached and asked her to dance. She looked at her mother who gave her superbly delivered imperceptible nod. Bonnie was off and running.

Elspeth sat and observed. Bonnie became the star of the dance floor. One gent approached Morag asking her to dance. She preferred the wallflower position, but her mother's tiny smile saw her rise and be led into the dance. Both Buchanan daughters mingled in polite society.

Rory wanted facts. 'So, a kid paints a portrait and makes a small fortune. How does that happen?'

'It's called talent, my ignorant friend.'

'You have talent and a house full of paintings so how come you're dirt poor and living in this dump?'

'Is that your way of thanking me for the free board and lodging?

Rory grunted and Fitzroy worked on Hamish's portrait. The tenant grabbed the landlord's basic fishing gear and left. Trout would be nice for supper. To be truthful, any food would be nice.

The *cèilidh* gathered strength. Love, romance and sex or the possibility of same inspired the social activity. Elspeth tried to relax but kept an eye on her daughters, or rather one of her daughters. Morag was escorted back to her chair beside her mother.

Bonnie, should a stick have been to hand, would have needed same to beat off suitors willy-nilly. Her dance card filled to overflowing. She reckoned her present mood and situation was what heaven would be like. Remembering her mother's advice from days of yore—she was now barely 18—she played hard to get. Mind you playing the tease may backfire and if a couple of earnest lads are given the eye but rejected, things can turn nasty.

As one affronted male passed close to Bonnie on the dance floor, his whispered insult stung her. Her confidence took a hit amidships.

But there were plenty more fish in the sea and soon the smiles of enthusiastic males swept her along. One gentleman, although such a description was debatable, captured her attention.

The dark and brooding type, he outplayed the young lady by beating her at her own game. Having danced with her, he left her for another. And another. Bonnie caught the jealousy bug.

She took a break and returned to her family. 'I'm glad to see you enjoying yourself, my darling,' said her mother, 'but remember the Buchanan ladies maintain their dignity at all times.'

Bonnie wanted to bite back but lacked the heart to hurt the mother who loved her without restraint.

The beauty declined would-be suitors who came forward with an invitation to dance. In deference to her mother, Bonnie smiled and politely declined. But her response was soon to change.

Rory struggled to believe his luck. He fished in this place on the river before and caught a cold. Today he snared two fish. Alas a stunning trout avoided his unattractive bait, but a couple of carp were as desperate as the fisherman.

Back in the cottage, Rory waved his contribution to the night's supper. Fitzroy barely reacted. He was engrossed in the work he performed on Hamish's portrait.

'What do think?' he asked indicating his handiwork. 'Perfect frame, don't you think?'

All Rory could see was the amount, twenty pounds. He grunted as he gutted the fish.

With the liquor cabinet bare, the men retired early. Rory's bed was the tattered couch which made slumber nigh on impossible. He lay awake thinking about money and how he possessed none. Selling his horse would fetch a pretty penny but handicap his ability to go anywhere and more importantly, to escape.

He rose and crept to Fitzroy's studio. The artist snored disturbing spiders and even the rat who lived in the privy. In the studio, Rory lit a candle and surveyed the contents. Miniatures, small paintings, medium sized works akin to Hamish's portrait, and even a couple of large works occupied the room with one enormous canvas without a picture. Rory counted and stopped when he reached forty-four.

He calculated the worth of the works. With little knowledge about the value of art, he guessed the room contained £500 worth of paintings. More. He thought about stealing a few paintings and selling them. How would Fitzroy know? He lacked any knowledge of what he painted. Did he even know what a stock take was?

He retired to his uncomfortable rack and fell asleep trying to remember the name of the owner of the art gallery in Edinburgh.

Bonnie suffered in silence. She knew her popularity was a hit, and this outing broke the ice. There would be more events where she would appear and attract attention. People wanted her. Men wanted her.

Declining each new invitation to dance became boring until a certain person appeared. Mr Dark and Brooding arrived out of nowhere and Bonnie's resistance collapsed. Without deferring to her mother, Bonnie took the hand of the man and joined the activity.

He said nothing but made all sorts of comments and suggestions with his eyes. Bonnie found her legs begin to weaken. Still without a word, the dance partner led Bonnie to the side of the dance floor, paused and spoke. She didn't agree, couldn't agree but did so as he led her through the open double doors and into the hallway.

Her watchful mother saw Bonnie disappear and struggled to breathe. Morag sensed her distress.

'Mother, are you unwell?'

The widow nodded. 'I'm fine. But I think we should leave.'

Morag stood. 'I'll find Sir Richard. Stay seated, Mama.'

Being reluctant to attend this her first social event since the death of her husband, Elspeth Buchanan knew she needed to give her daughters a life outside their home. But her worry was that without their father, her girls, well, one of her girls, might be led astray. Even a whiff of impropriety, let alone a full-blown scandal, could, would bring shame and segregation. Degradation.

Morag appeared with Sir Richard. 'Dear Lady, how can I help? Shall I have your carriage brought round?'

'I do apologize, Sir Richard.'

His response was akin to shock. 'Good heavens, my Lady. Your presence has added class and beauty to the evening, and we are enchanted and most grateful to have you here.' He beckoned to a member of staff and issued a command.

Sir Richard offered his arm to Lady Buchanan. 'Allow me to escort you to your carriage.'

She took his arm, and they moved to the main hallway. Once outside the party room, Elspeth turned her back to Morag and whispered to the host.

'A word, Sir Richard.' He bent to listen. 'I fear my daughter, Bonnie, has been led astray by one of your guests.'

Their eyes met. He saw fear in hers, led her to a seat in the hallway and addressed Morag. 'Please attend to your mother, m'Lady and I shall return in a moment.'

Three of Sir Richard's staff attended the *cèilidh* in disguise meaning they dressed "up" and were available at any time should Sir Richard require their services. Now was such a time.

The landowner looked at his ghillie who joined his boss for instructions. The host returned to the distressed guest.

McAdams, the ghillie, recruited Alice the chambermaid.

Into the garden went the staff attending to a situation not for the first time. The ghillie stopped in the darkness and listened. He crept to another position and waited. The sound he heard pinpointed his prey. He made the sound of a nocturnal animal. Alice appeared and they communicated by gesture. She remained still.

'Come on,' whispered a male. 'You know you want to.'

A female squealed.

'Quiet,' hissed the male before he screamed.

From behind, McAdams, slapped the male's ear with force and the pain was as bad as the shock. With lover boy holding his face, McAdams easily grabbed his quarry.

Bonnie fell back in shock to be gathered by Alice who spoke calmly, leading the guest from the garden to a powder room where Alice indicated a mirror. Bonnie gasped. Her hair and dress were unacceptable for polite society and running repairs commenced.

Back in the boxing ring, the cad managed to break free and shaped up to fight. Another member of the estate staff, having been tipped off by Sir Richard, arrived shifting the odds.

'Look,' blurted the sex fiend, 'the bitch was up for it.'

'Liar,' snarled McAdam then nodded at his fellow worker who heaved the contents of a bucket over the unwelcome guest.

He spat, spluttered, and swore. The bucket contained dung with an abrasive sautéed mixture of equine urine. Lover boy's clothes were ruined, he would stink for days and be forced to walk home.

'Count yourself lucky, son,' snapped the ghillie. 'New clothes are easy to find, not so new teeth. Now begone before we give you a proper thrashing.'

Bonnie's seducer played it smart and ran.

Chapter 8

It is the way of the world; men gloat while women grovel.

Almost respectable, Bonnie entered the hallway, and her mother and sister enjoyed enormous relief. Elspeth made no mention of her disappointment or anger but politely fussed over the equivalent of her prodigal son.

Sir Richard treated the matter with consummate good manners and the women entered their carriage and waved to the waving host.

The silence grew louder until Bonnie spoke.

'Mummy, I'm so sorry …'

'Be quiet,' said her mother in a voice her daughters seldom heard, and silence resumed. At home, Fraser stood ready to assist. The girls went inside while their mother spoke briefly to the driver.

'Please convey my thanks to Sir Richard.'

He touched his cap with the crop of his whip and set off on the return journey.

Elspeth met her daughters in the hallway. 'We will discuss the matter in the morning. Good night,' she said and floated upstairs.

The sisters stared at one another. Bonnie turned defensive. 'It's not my fault. How can I help it if my beauty attracts so many men?'

Morag took her time in replying. 'Will that be your defence in the morning?' Her question took the wind out of Bonnie's sails. 'Good night,' said Morag and set off after her mother.

Rolf fell out of bed at an ungodly hour. The hint of a plan took shape. He would pinch Fitzroy's paintings and sell them. No-one would know, certainly not the artist. With the money, he would gamble half and use the rest to flee to a big city—Glasgow, Manchester or even London. Or why not somewhere like Australia?

He needed a plan to carry out the heist then transport the stolen paintings to Edinburgh.

Bonnie was the last to come down to breakfast. After Morag scoffed at her sister's excuse, Bonnie knew she was cooked. But what could happen to her? She could survive a stern reprimand but being ordered to remain on the estate would be a death sentence.

She entered the room where her mother and sister ate breakfast.

'Good morning, Mother. Good morning, Morag,' she said taking toast from the sideboard.

The others replied after which all three ate in silence.

Elspeth stood. 'We will meet in your father's study in ten minutes. Please don't be late.'

She left and the sisters made eye contact.

'What has she said?' asked Bonnie.

'About you, nothing,' said Morag who left the room.

The day before, James asked his wife to bake. He went to the orchard to pick apples. With his bag full, he kissed his wife and set off to collect the framed portrait of himself as painted by Hamish McKay.

The walk was pleasant. He knocked on the cottage door and a dishevelled Fitzroy appeared. He was always dishevelled.

'Ah, Mr Dunbar, sir, the man in the painting. Come away in.'

Rory stayed out of view.

'What think you, sir?' asked Fitzroy indicating the framed portrait.

Mr Dunbar dropped his bag and moved closer. 'Oh Mr Arbuthnot, you have given it the perfect presentation. Many congratulations, sir, my gratitude overflows.'

Rory spoke from the kitchen, now a war zone. 'So, where's the payment, priest? Is the man of the cloth not a man of his word?'

Fitzroy glared at Rory.

'It is right here, gentlemen,' said the minister taking items from his bag. 'First there are at least two dozen apples picked this day.' Rory growled, as did his stomach.

'Most kind, Mr Dunbar,' said Fitzroy knowing the fruit would need to be boiled and mushed owing to the state of his teeth, all four of them.

'And my wife has baked you fine, fresh shortbread.' The visitor looked sheepish. 'But I regret I have no single malt, gentlemen, although can offer you a fine half bottle of cooking sherry.'

Rory went to explode only to be overruled by the cottage owner.

James covered the portrait and packed it in his now empty bag. 'I can't wait to show it to the young man. Thank you again, gentlemen and God bless you both.'

When Fitzroy turned back from waving to the minister, Rory was swigging the contents of the bottle. 'Hey!' shouted the artist and grabbed the sherry before it was all gone.

The sisters entered the study. Their mother stopped writing. 'Sit.' She turned to face her daughters. Bonnie wanted to be sick.

'I have explained this before. A woman, and especially one of our class, must behave to a much higher standard of acceptable behaviour than a man. Should a woman behave, even to a slight degree, below these lofty standards, the price she must pay is far greater than the consequences for a man. In fact, a woman can destroy her reputation behaving in an unladylike manner whereas a man will often be praised, even rewarded for his outrageous conduct. It is the way of the world; men gloat while women grovel.' Elspeth paused. 'But you know all this.' Her daughters did but not know if the speech was over.

Morag spoke first. 'Yes, Mother.'

Bonnie echoed her sister. 'Yes, Mother.'

'What I do not understand, Bonnie,'—now it was personal—'is why you should disrespect the memory of your dear father. Were he still alive, your behaviour would have driven a stake through his heart.'

What could Bonnie say? She wept in silence.

'We will say no more about it. You may leave.' The sisters stood. 'Oh, and a consequence of your conduct, Bonnie, apart from attending the kirk, means you are confined to the estate until further notice.'

Elspeth returned to her correspondence and the sisters departed. In the corridor, Morag tried to comfort her sister.

'Chin up, Bonnie, it could have been much worse.'

Bonnie flared; her tears long gone. 'What could be worse than being stuck in this boring, God-forsaken place?'

She stormed off leaving Morag aghast.

Chapter 9
Callum could pick a liar a mile away.

James Dunbar grinned and whistled. His body and soul copped a surge of happiness. The portrait by Hamish McKay took pride of place in his humble manse. His wife and children admired it whereas he loved it.

It hung on a wall in his study, and it was unknown how many times, day and night, he looked up from his sermon preparation and matters of the kirk to examine the picture. Dozens perhaps, even more.

The fact he, Dunbar, promoted the young artist, gave him pride and pleasure. The fact he was the subject of the portrait became the icing on the cake. How many other ministers in Scotland boasted a stunning portrait of themselves in their study?

His wife gave him the idea.

'You should show your parishioners the portrait,' she said.

'Do you really think so? Is it not an act of self-aggrandisement?'

She didn't know the word but continued. 'It is the work of a member of the kirk, and he should be commended.'

Dunbar nodded. He didn't need encouraging.

On Sunday morning, the minister finished his sermon before a packed congregation which included the Buchanan women. Remarkably, Bonnie appeared pleased to go; she supported any reason or event which allowed her to escape the estate.

The final hymn finished and instead of the minister walking through the kirk to greet worshippers as they left, he surprised them by walking to the side of the building and stopping next to an easel with a red velvet cloth covering the shape of a painting.

'I have a special announcement. You will know Hamish McKay and his wonderful talent for art. I've loved the privilege of encouraging the young man and was persuaded to sit for him. This is the result.'

The faithful stared at their minister who carefully took hold of the cloth and, in a theatrical gesture, lifted same to reveal the framed portrait of James Dunbar.

Audible gasps and murmured comments buzzed inside the kirk.

'I hope you agree we have a superbly talented artist in our midst.'

Hamish was forewarned of the event when he called to the manse for a first viewing. His parents rejoiced in the portrait. His sister reaffirmed her opinion that Hamish was the smartest brother, ever.

'I shall retire to the porch to greet you as usual. But before you leave, you may wish to examine this marvellous portrait.'

He set off and Elspeth became uncomfortable. With others in the congregation respecting her status, she would leave first. But should she do so via the painting? To not do so might be seen as disrespect for the minister and the artist.

She looked at her daughters who stood and stepped into the aisle. They waited for their mother. The congregation watched. Elspeth gave a slight nod; her daughters stepped back then followed their mother as she headed to the portrait.

It was the talk of the village. Locals who chose not to worship were miffed they missed the only public exhibition. One non-believer called at the manse on the pretext of having the minister visit his ailing mother and found himself staring at the portrait. He would tell all in the local public house and, amazingly, his ailing mother enjoyed a rapid return to good health.

Elspeth received a letter from Sir Richard Galbraith. The contents bothered her as did the thought the gentleman was beginning a slow and barely seen courtship of her good self. She knew being a wealthy widow would attract interest from various men. The fact she happened to be beautiful only compounded the issue.

But the offer from Sir Richard left her thinking. Ever so subtly he suggested trying to repair any damage to Bonnie's reputation. This involved having a dinner party where only the most respectable—are there degrees of respectability?—of eligible gentlemen would be invited giving Bonnie a chance to make a match suitable for all parties.

Elspeth pondered the idea. Having a striking daughter who posed a risk to herself, and her family was a grave concern. How to manage the situation proved tricky. Here was a suggestion with merit.

She replied immediately thanking Sir Richard for his letter and asked for time before giving her response.

But she suffered. *It might work,* she thought, *but is he trying to impress me, is he using my daughter to woo and propose marriage to her mother? Oh why did my darling husband have to die?*

Rory needed funds. At night, when Fitzroy's snoring found its rhythm, he collected the four small paintings he chose days before, wrapped them well and hid them in the woodshed. Tomorrow his plan would take flight.

In the morning, he told the artist he would be visiting friends.

'You haven't got any friends,' scoffed Fitzroy. 'You wouldn't be here if you had even *one* friend.'

Rory laughed knowing his landlord's quips were spot on. He led his horse around the back, collected the paintings and rode off.

In Edinburgh he found a place to leave his steed before locating the gallery Fitzroy described. Callum Drinkwater, suspicious of any fellow human, was about to meet a man who wanted to rob him blind. No problem for the gallery owner with such behaviour being his raison d'etre. Two lovely chaps.

Callum heard the bell tinkle and bounced out of his office.

'Good morning, sir. How can we help this fine day?'

'I have a few paintings.'

'And?'

'Do you want to see them or not?'

'With a view to do what, sir?'

'Well, if you're not interested.' He turned to leave.

'Now, now, not so fast, sir. I am always keen to study fine art.'

Rory unwrapped the paintings, placed them on a table, and Callum was all over them.

'Interesting.' He turned them over to study the back. 'May one ask your position regarding these works?'

'My position?'

Callum maintained his cool. 'Did you paint them, are you the painter's representative, and how are they in your possession?'

'I own them and am looking to pass them on. Clear enough? Comprendi?' he snapped with an Italian accent.

'Perfectly. I require 55% commission on every sale. Clear enough? Avez-vous compris?' he snapped back with an exaggerated French accent. Touché.

The sarcasm grew lumpy.

'How about 100%,' said Rory, and Callum, for once, could not respond until he understood.

'Ah, you want shot of them They are for sale, here and now.'

'At last, said Rory. 'Fair price to me; you cop 100% of future sales.'

Callum was certain they were stolen but with unintelligible or no initials or identification on the paintings, he knew he could make a quid with buyers ready to roll. No names, no investigation.

'Two pounds,' he said.

Rory fired back. 'Two guineas.'

Callum hesitated before offering his hand. 'Deal,' he said.

'Each,' said Rory and Callum exploded.

'Each!'

Rory gathered his goods. 'Okay, I'll try down the street.'

'No, wait.' The silence took over. 'Four quid is my best offer.'

'Guineas and they're yours.'

Callum knew he could make money even paying £4 and four shillings but hated losing, having to accept the customer's demand.

'Done,' he said and left to collect the cash.

Rory studied the layout of the premises.

Callum returned with the money. 'So, who is the artist?'

'Does it matter?'

'Yes, the origin can influence the price, often dramatically.'

'Look, squire, he's old, dying and I'm helping the future widow.'

Callum could pick a liar a mile away but kept probing.

'It looks like the work of an old artist. If you ever find paintings by a young and undiscovered creator, I'll make it worth your while.'

Rory flashed his filthy teeth, grabbed his bag, and left. In his pocket, he fondled the cash.

Chapter 10

The Church of Scotland minister grinned like a Cheshire cat.

Morag addressed Elspeth during supper. 'Mother, Bonnie and I have been talking.' This was news for both the listeners. Morag gave her sister a look which said, "agree with me".

'Oh,' said Elspeth, 'about what may I ask?'

'You know the wonderful portrait we saw of Mr Dunbar?' Elspeth and Bonnie wondered where this was going. 'Both your daughters believe you should have your beautiful face portrayed in a portrait and displayed in your home.'

'*Our* home,' corrected Elspeth.

'Yes, Mother,' added Bonnie keen on the idea despite never having considered it before. 'It's a wonderful idea.'

'I don't think so,' replied Elspeth.

'But you are the perfect person to have such a painting created,' said Morag.

'Indeed you are, Mother,' added Bonnie now firing. 'In the future when you have grandchildren and great-grandchildren, they will look up and hear stories about the wonderful Countess Elspeth Buchanan.'

Morag worried Bonnie would go too far. Elspeth struggled to believe Bonnie would state the possibility of her becoming a mother. With procrastination being one of the matriarch's key characteristics, she moved to shut it down. 'It's a lovely thought, my darlings. Please let me think about it.'

Morag persisted. 'I could ask Mr Dunbar for his advice. After all he has experience sitting for a portrait, and the young man, McKay, has exceptional talent and his family are well-known in the village.'

Elspeth was not keen but yielded to end the conversation.

Morag smiled at her sister and mimed the word "thanks."

Mrs Dunbar answered the door of the manse. Morag stood there smiling.

'Good morning, Mrs Dunbar.' She was about to give her name but saw how silly such an introduction would be especially when the minister's wife bobbed.

'Good morning, your Ladyship.'

'May I have a word with Mr Dunbar, please?'

'Of course. Please come in.' She ushered Morag into the front room. 'I'll fetch my husband.'

'Who?' asked James when told of Morag's presence. A visit from a member of the wealthiest and most influential family in the county was unusual, unexpected and intriguing.

The minister greeted Morag and after small talk about the health of Lady Buchanan, he waited for an explanation.

'I'll come straight to the point, sir. My sister and I believe our mother should have her portrait painted and we wondered if you might ask Mr McKay if he is willing to perform such a task. Naturally, he would be paid the appropriate fee.'

James squeezed his hands, grinned and politely celebrated. Here was the perfect opportunity for Hamish, his protégé, to be discovered. Painting not an unknown, balding and humble Scottish parson but a beautiful woman, a titled lady from one of the most important families in the land. Her portrait would reveal the undoubted yet, at present, unknown talent of the young artist.

'I cannot wait to tell Hamish the good news,' he purred.

Morag's face and body language put a dampener on proceedings.

'To be honest, sir, my mother may need persuading to agree to the idea. As you know she is a humble person, prefers the background, and even more so since becoming a widow.'

James turned serious. 'I completely understand. You may rely on my discretion.' He paused. 'So, how would you like to proceed?'

'You could visit my mother and discuss the situation.'

'What a splendid suggestion. Would this afternoon be suitable?'

'It would, Mr Dunbar, and thank you for your kindness and support.'

Rory purchased basic food supplies and cheap whisky using a small fraction of his ill-gotten gains, returned to the cottage and greeted Fitzroy by holding aloft the goodies. The artist scoffed.

'Oh yes, and how can you afford such luxuries?'

'A little bit of business, my friend. And there's more where this came from.'

For luncheon, they ate and drank well, and Rory suffered a personality change by feigning an interest in Fitzroy's latest creation.

'What's going on?' sniffed the old chap. 'You ain't never been keen on my art before, never.'

'First time for everything, Fitzy. I might even give this painting lark a whirl m'self.'

Fitzroy laughed so hard, he choked and much of his luncheon ended up on the floor although you could hardly pinpoint the vomit among the detritus.

James Dunbar called on Hamish en route to Buchanan Hall. It meant a trip out to the paddock where the artist helped his father repair a fence on their smallholding.

'I bring wonderful news, young man,' said the minister. Both father and son paid rapt attention. 'I am off to Buchanan Hall to discuss the painting of a portrait of the lady of the house. I've recommended you, Hamish McKay, and this could well be your first commission.'

Hamish gasped and George whistled.

'I'm told she is not enthusiastic about the idea, but her daughters have asked if you will agree to be the artist,' said James.

Hamish nodded, his tongue struggling to speak. 'That would be wonderful, sir. Are you sure you mean Lady Buchanan?'

'Indeed, and as soon as I have confirmation and more news, I will return. Find your Sunday best, young man. You'll need it to visit Buchanan Hall.'

The minister knew the magnificent house well. His previous visits were to pray for His Lordship who lay dying. This time, happiness ruled.

Fraser welcomed the visitor. Dunbar was led along the hallway, big enough for its own *cèilidh*, and stopped outside the main sitting room. The door opened and Morag appeared.

'Good afternoon, Mr Dunbar. Thank you so much for coming to see my mother.'

James nodded and murmured, 'Thank you, m'Lady.'

She entered the room, Dunbar followed, Fraser closed the door and vanished.

Elspeth sat tall on a single chair and smiled. Her ballet training as a child ensured her perfect posture. 'Good afternoon, Mr Dunbar. Thank you for coming to see me. Do please sit.'

'Lady Buchanan,' he said trying to avoid being obsequious and waited for Morag to sit. He sat and turned to Elspeth who spoke.

'I trust your family are well.'

'Thank you, my Lady, they are indeed.'

He wondered how long the small talk would continue but was certain he should not raise the portrait issue. Morag saved the day.

'As we discussed, Mr Dunbar, my mother is still considering the portrait issue, and I hope you will be able to help in her decision-making.'

'Of course,' said the minister re-evaluating the younger woman's intelligence and common sense. 'As you have seen, my Lady, I am a proud supporter of young Mr McKay. His God-given talent must be encouraged.'

'I think it is a noble thing you are doing, sir,' said Elspeth. 'My late husband enjoyed the arts and would be pleased to see young talent on display.'

'Do you think my father would want to see you have your portrait painted, Mother?' asked Morag. Dunbar admired the way she cut to the chase and gently but firmly put pressure on her mother.

She paused. Dunbar saw an opportunity and seized it.

'A portrait of the matriarch of our county's most prestigious family is an important historical record, my Lady. If I may say so, the preservation of our history is vitally important.'

The ball was back in Elspeth's court. The minister and daughter looked longingly at her, holding their breath.

'Very well, I agree,' she said, and the tension evaporated. Smiles and a return to normal breathing resumed.

'Oh Mother, I'm so pleased,' said Morag.

Dunbar joined the praise. 'Thank you, my Lady. You have done a wonderful service to your family and to a young and talented artist.'

'What are the next steps?' asked Elspeth feeling better now the decision was made.

Morag quietly took control. 'Perhaps Mr Dunbar, you could return with Mr McKay and have him explain the process to my mother.'

'I would be happy to do so,' replied the Cheshire cat disguised as a minister of the Church of Scotland.

A time was set for two days hence and the tea and shortbread which followed proved useful as the family beauty, Bonnie, arrived and wanted to know the news.

'Do you think your daughters might follow your lead, my Lady,' said James, now on a roll, 'and have their portraits painted?'

Bonnie was up for it, up for anything, while her sister showed modest enthusiasm.

The artist, one Hamish McKay, faced a promising future.

Chapter 11
'Are you deaf? I said Kiss me!'

That evening, chatter around the kitchen table, which doubled as the dining table in the dining room and sitting room combined, situated in the kitchen of the McKay cottage, settled on a single topic.

Son and brother Hamish won the best-person-to-paint award.

Sister Moira provided a vast array of questions. 'Will you be painting Her Ladyship inside the big house?'

'No, I'll be at the front gate, at the start of their mile-long drive, and she'll be indoors.'

'How much will you be paid?' asked his father.

'I have no idea,' said Hamish. 'Mr Dunbar will arrange the fee.'

His mother replaced the questions with an order.

'Remember there are two young ladies in the house, and you make sure you only speak when you're spoken to.'

'Yes, Mother.'

'She's a beautiful lady, Hamish,' said his sister. 'You make sure you paint her lifelike and lovely.'

Hamish copped even more attention and grew weary. 'With all this fuss, I'm beginning to wish I never knew how to paint.'

'What will you do if she doesn't like your portrait?' asked Alma.

Hamish thought about that question the moment his benefactor first told him of the proposed commission.

The young man sighed. 'It's my recurring nightmare,' he said shocking his family. 'I have no idea.' That night he struggled to sleep.

Fitzroy and his thieving lodger drank the night away. Whether it was the whisky or a promise of easy money, Rory decided to push his luck.

'How many paintings are in your studio?' he asked.

'No idea.'

'You must have some idea, ten, twenty, how many? And why don't you sell them? Here they're gathering dust. Put 'em in a gallery and collect your share.'

'I'm finished, McGrath. Me liver's pickled, I have the talent of a minor poet, zero ambition and the only thing keeping me going is art.'

'And single malt.' Fitzroy grunted. Silly comment.

Rory thought before asking his next question. 'Why don't you let me sell your paintings? When I go to Edinburgh on business, I could visit a gallery. You never know what might happen.'

Fitzroy was drifting to sleep. He stirred, unhappy. 'Shut up. I'm trying to get to …' His speech faded as snoring took over.

The minister headed to the McKay cottage early. These folk worked the land. There were eggs to collect before breakfast and a cow to milk. He caught the McKays in their kitchen.

'This time tomorrow, Hamish,' he announced, 'we have an appointment with Lady Buchanan at 10. This will be the meeting before the first sitting. Please bring your biggest smile and cleanest boots. Her Ladyship has offered a generous fee.' He saw smiling faces. 'Well, till the morrow, good day to you all.'

He left and again the breakfast table chatter featured Hamish and his paintbrush, with a minor mention of the important sitter.

Bonnie Buchanan hated being stuck at home. Certain would-be beaus wrote to her with Fraser instructed to deliver all mail to the matriarch and say nothing to her daughters about missing letters.

Elspeth disliked such deception but knew the consequences for any young woman, and especially one of noble birth, should they become enmeshed in scandal. She would be better off dead. The scandal need only be talked about to become ruinous.

Her older daughter, Morag, behaved in a sensible fashion, respecting her mother's wishes, and carrying herself as a polite and chaste young woman.

But Bonnie gave her mother nightmares. Despite warnings and heart to heart chats, the younger daughter, the one whose stunning beauty turned heads, hated restrictions. Her hormones let down their hair telling Bonnie life was meant to be lived or loved or both.

Hamish rose early, scrubbed his torso and face in the trough in the yard where the icy water ensured he was wide awake.

Sunday best dress code meant his mother and Mr Dunbar would approve his appearance.

Off they went. The minister and the artist stood before the massive front door of Buchanan Hall. Hamish knew he was shaking and, to hide his fear, stood a little behind his mentor.

Fraser did the usual, and once inside, the visitors were met by Morag. 'Gentlemen, good morning and welcome. We have been so looking forward to your visit.'

'Good morning, m'Lady,' said James as Hamish nodded and remained silent.

The well-behaved daughter led them to the main sitting room where Hamish found it hard to speak being in awe ever since he entered the house, this being his first visit. Lady Buchanan smiled as she greeted the visitors.

After the small talk, Morag took the lead. 'Could you please explain, Mr McKay, how you go about creating a portrait?'

No hiding in the corner now, Hamish. It's over to you.

'Certainly, my Lady. I first make sketches in my book and from these I develop the portrait.'

'And where would you require Lady Buchanan to sit?'

James wanted to help but only the artist could answer these questions. Hamish studied the room.

'I suggest beside that large window,' he said indicating a floor to ceiling piece of glass letting in much light and allowing an uninterrupted view of the glorious garden.

Elspeth became involved. 'Is there a specific time of day you require for your work?'

'The morning light, my Lady, is always good, especially by that window. From the north, you have an even and constant light.'

James Dunbar didn't realize his mouth had opened.

'Excellent,' said Elspeth. 'Is there anything else you need from us?'

Hamish paused. 'Thank you, no, my Lady.'

'Well, there are matters I need to discuss with Mr Dunbar so if you would be kind enough to wait outside, I look forward to having you start your work.'

Hamish stood, nodded, and set off for the door. What a journey. Morag followed him from the room. He opened the door, looked into the young woman's smiling eyes, and left.

He wandered a little way down the hallway. His shaking stopped but would soon return.

'Psst,' or similar sound came from an unseen source. He looked around. 'Psst.' There it was again. 'Over here,' the whispered voice said.

He couldn't see anyone, but a door opened a smidgen.

'Over here,' came the whispered voice, louder and more insistent.

He looked up and down the hallway, saw no-one so moved hesitatingly to the door. It moved again.

He stopped close to it and spoke, 'Hello?'

Without warning, the door opened wider, a hand reached out, grabbed then dragged him in. He floundered but entered a small room, a vestibule or, in this case a rich person's broom cupboard, and stood facing the second daughter of the Buchanan family, the one who attracted looks, glances, and stares because of her widely acknowledged beauty.

She moved past him and closed the door.

'I don't think I should be here, my Lady' he said trying to escape.

'Listen to me,' she said standing on tippy toes to be close to his face. 'You know who I am. I'm the woman every male in the county wants to meet and, more importantly, wants to kiss. It's your lucky day, Mr Artist. Now kiss me.'

She grabbed his jacket and pulled him to her. He resisted.

'I'm sorry, m'Lady, I need to leave.'

Now angry, she hissed. 'Are you deaf? I said, "Kiss me!"'

'No,' he spoke firmly and tried to break free.

'No!' She threatened. 'If you don't kiss me on the lips right now, I'll scream and that'll be the end of your painting career, and your life!'

From deep in his chest, a foreign place, he returned the threat.

'Scream and I'll flatten your nose and turn you into Lady Ugly!'

She froze and genuinely couldn't believe this low-class person, this nobody, in *her* home, would dare even consider such action.

She gasped. 'You would strike a lady?'

'A lady, never, but a woman who behaved outrageously, yes.'

Their eyes, locked on the other's, blazed. His blazed brighter and she believed her perfect nose was in imminent danger of changing shape. Forget the pain and shame, think of her lost beauty. Her grip weakened, he broke free, opened the door, and fled.

Fraser appeared and Hamish froze.

'Good morning, sir. May I be of assistance?'

What could the young artist say? Tell the truth? But surely that way danger lies. Who would believe a working-class man, living in a rented cottage, the son of a tenant farmer on a smallholding, against the word of a titled lady, living in the largest house in the county? He couldn't think. From behind came a familiar voice.

'Mr McKay.' Morag walked towards the men. 'It's all right, Fraser. I can show the gentleman the way.'

The butler vanished as if by magic.

'Thank you, m'Lady,' said Hamish never having felt so grateful.

'No, thank *you*, sir. My mother is now looking forward to sitting for you. She and Mr Dunbar are discussing your fee, the canvas and other matters. He will be along shortly.'

Hamish looked at her. Her smile both settled and stirred him. She was nothing like her sister but certainly feminine and appealing. His mind raced. *Could there be a greater contrast between the sisters?*

In her hideaway, Bonnie brooded. She was in a permanent state of frustration having been "imprisoned" by her mother for what the young woman regarded as a frivolous incident.

I slipped into the garden to admire the plants in the moonlight.

But now, this exact moment, an oik from the village turned her down. Lady Bonnie Buchanan, the most gorgeous female in the county. She swore and determined to escape her current ridiculous life.

She was about to enter the hallway when she heard voices. Her mother and the minister were saying their goodbyes. Bonnie waited. She heard other voices, further away, as the two male visitors spoke with Morag. Those voices faded and Bonnie made her move.

She didn't know her sister was still in the hallway.

'Bonnie! What on Earth are you doing in there?'

The sisters had been close until Bonnie chose her new hobby of men. Morag considered the same interest but from afar. Bonnie flared.

'Mind your own damn business,' she snapped and flounced away.

Chapter 12
If I get this wrong I'll ruin my reputation.

Rory was at it again. It was mid-morning, but Fitzroy slept at any hour. He waited till the old painter's snoring rattled one of the several loose windows in the cottage before creeping into the studio. The thief reckoned size equals wealth so chose three medium to large-sized works. He wrapped and hid them in the shed behind his horse.

'Off to Edinburgh tomorrow, my lass,' he said patting the animal.

At home, Hamish was bombarded with questions about the Hall, the furnishings, the garden, the people and, of course, the painting of her Ladyship's portrait.

'I start next week with sketches before painting as I did with Mr Dunbar. Lady Buchanan will sit beside a huge window in a huge sitting room which overlooks a huge garden.'

'How big will the painting be?' asked young Moira.

Hamish hesitated. 'I'm not sure,' he said genuinely uncertain.

'It will have to be big, son,' said George. 'An important lady, a member of the nobility can't possibly be pictured in a small frame hanging on the wall with all them other fancy folk.'

'You mean she will have to be full-size and not only her head like Mr Dunbar?' This was a new and worrying thought.

His family stared at him and saw the distress on his face. He possibly faced a much bigger challenge. Her hands and clothes would all need to be captured. He thought. *If I get this wrong, I'll embarrass the whole Buchanan family and ruin my reputation, such as it is.*

At the same time, a family discussion was taking place in the dining room with Lady Buchanan and her two daughters.

'If we are happy with the portrait, I will ask the young man to create one for both of you,' said Elspeth.

Bonnie struggled to control her pleasure. 'I would need to have my hair done perfectly,' she said, not caring at all about her recent run-in with the artist.

'It's a kind idea, Mother,' said Morag. 'Why don't we wait until Mr McKay finishes his first Buchanan portrait?'

It was easy to read between the lines. Bonnie was desperate for her beauty to be shown to the world whereas Morag would rather read a book.

'There is another matter I need to raise,' said Elspeth and her daughters paid rapt attention. Their mother rarely made announcements but when she did, they carried weight.

'Sir Richard Galbraith has invited us to dine with him.' Again, the sisters held widely contrasting reactions. Bonnie couldn't believe her luck as Morag groaned inside.

'There will be a small group of respectable young gentlemen present from families both Sir Richard and I have chosen, and I am happy for you both to meet such possible suitors. Your father would heartily approve of this occasion.' She paused, looking hard at her daughters. 'Do you agree?'

They did and Elspeth enjoyed relief hoping and praying her girls would make a suitable match. God alone knows what Elspeth would have thought if she discovered Bonnie's recent behaviour with the artist in the broom cupboard.

Rory repeated his latest Edinburgh journey this time complete with three stolen paintings from Fitzroy's collection.

'Ah, we meet again,' said Callum Drinkwater smiling behind his silk handkerchief and specs.

Rory lost his bluster. Trying the same bluff may not work and he knew no other art gallery owners in Edinburgh or anywhere.

'Good morning, sir,' he said even frightening himself by sounding polite and reasonable.

'You have more works of art, I see.'

'Three paintings all of a larger size.' Never mind the quality, measure the frames.'

The stolen art was unwrapped and examined. 'By the same artist, I see.' This threw Rory. He wanted to spread misinformation about his ill-gotten gains but knew his ignorance about art would soon be exposed. Too late.

'Who is this artist friend of yours?' asked Callum.

'You wouldn't know him. Painting was his hobby, and as the old boy's getting on, I'm helping him make a bit before he dies.'

'And by "a bit", I assume you mean modest or small.'

Rory tensed. He cursed himself for using such an expression.

'Come now, sir, the larger works are surely more valuable than the smaller ones I offered last time.'

Rory faced two problems. His previous gambit of bluff was exposed and Callum dealt with thieves and desperate relatives on a regular basis.

He was prepared to go to £5 for all three so offered £3. Rory wanted £10 so scoffed at the offer and turned into a ham actor explaining how the elderly painter's grandchildren were poorly.

'It breaks my heart to see them go for a penny less than eight,' said Rory.

Callum cut to the chase. 'A fiver or you try your luck elsewhere.'

'Done,' said Rory dropping his guineas claim and craving a handshake before the offer was withdrawn.

Callum handed him the money and walked with him to the door.

'Remember what I said last time. New blood is what the investors crave. Bring me paintings by a talented, unknown artist and you will be well rewarded.'

Rory bought the cheapest whisky available. His mind spun as he trotted back to the man he robbed blind.

Where can I find art by a young and talented painter?

Chapter 13
His mother told him to nibble, never chew sandwiches.

Hamish wasn't a bag of nerves but a hundred bags of nerves. What was sleep? He washed and dressed, and triple checked his modest supply of sketchbook and pencils. He travelled alone. James reckoned the young man needed to make his own way in the world. There was no doubting his talent. The test centred not on his artistic expertise but on his ability to deal with people.

Fraser opened the door, well primed as to the visitor and his role. Was Hamish a tradesman? No. Fraser received specific instructions. This visitor held a special status and should be treated as such.

Morag stood inside the hallway and greeted the young man with a warm smile. He relaxed a miniscule amount.

'Good morning, Mr McKay,' she said. 'I trust you are well.'

'Thank you, my Lady, I am.'

'Please come this way.' They walked along the hallway and approached the infamous broom cupboard. Hamish couldn't believe there would be another, 'Psst.'

There wasn't and Morag led him into the main sitting room, bigger than the entire McKay cottage twice over, three times more like. Elspeth sat in the chair by the window ready for the "art" to begin.

'Good morning, Mr McKay. I am pleased you are punctual. It is one of a person's better qualities.'

'Good morning, my Lady.'

'Am I in the correct position? Please say if you require me to move.'

'Your position is perfect, my Lady.'

She indicated a chair. 'Please sit.' He did. Morag remained a little distant from the couple.

His heart beat faster. 'I have a question, my Lady.' Both women fixated on the artist. 'Would you prefer a larger portrait featuring yourself seated or the portrait of your face similar in size to the one I painted of Mr Dunbar?'

Elspeth seemed taken aback. 'I have never thought of such an alternative, Mr McKay. Do you have a preference?'

'I would be happy with either, my Lady but I wondered if a person of your importance deserves a full-length portrait. I have seen several in a gallery where even a family pet was included.'

'Oh, how wonderful,' gasped Morag. 'You could have Kelso seated beside you, Mother, and in the garden beneath your favourite tree.'

The young woman's enthusiasm ran wild. Hamish didn't have a clue how to respond and wondered where this would lead.

Elspeth raised a dainty hand. Morag settled. 'It sounds wonderful, Mr McKay but do I understand your plan is to make a sketch first before painting the portrait in a size and style to the one you made of the minister.'

'You are correct, my Lady.'

'Then please let us have the original plan and see what happens.'

'As you wish. And thank you again for the opportunity.'

She smiled at him. 'It is we who should be thanking you. Please begin.'

Morag watched, fascinated, looking more at the artist than his subject.

Bonnie enjoyed both beauty *and* brains. She was sure her mother intercepted her mail and hated being controlled in this manner. The so-called gentleman with whom she enjoyed a romantic flurry in Sir Richard Galbraith's garden was top of her list of potential lovers.

She wrote a brief letter to the scoundrel, Temple Kensington, an Englishman, and the proud holder of being sent down from more institutions than anyone else in his illustrious family. Anyone else full stop. He would have been awarded a First in Womanizing had not the Oxford dons united in their desire to send him packing. Seducing the Master's wife was hardly cricket, old chap. The maid, certainly, but not the Master's Missus.

Temple resided in Scotland having been banished to said part of the United Kingdom to keep him as far away as possible from the bad name he developed in England. Old money can afford such a luxury. His father wanted him shanghaied into the army but not before the blighter copped a jolly good thrashing. He fled to the Lowlands and a wayward uncle.

For Bonnie, sending her letter was the first hurdle. She needed an ally. Mary the maid was holding the parcel when the music stopped. She was to meet the postman away from the house, say nothing to anybody, and hand over Bonnie's missive.

It was addressed to the Honourable Temple Kensington, (Honourable? Seriously?) Esquire, c/o Sir Richard Galbraith, Lauriston Estate, The City of Edinburgh.

Bonnie knew her secret activity might be exposed but what could be worse? Remain on the Buchanan estate and only be allowed out for visits to the kirk with its boring minister and even more boring congregation, and even then on a short lead. Forget that. Nothing ventured, nothing gained.

Miracle or luck, Temple received the letter and thought his life was soon to become wonderful. The woman possessed money and a stunning body with the best bit, she fancied him.

But Bonnie's second hurdle was her return address. The younger sister would have made a first-class spy having decided to create a dead letter drop.

Sketching away, Hamish eventually relaxed. His current portfolio consisted of a sketch of his father on the back of a letter, a painted portrait of the local minister and some doodling.

Today's sitter never spoke. Morag wanted to but knew it might upset her mother and possibly the artist.

After thirty minutes, with all the detail he wanted, he closed the sketchbook. 'I have finished, my Lady,' he said and stood.

'Already?' she replied. 'I'm afraid, Mr McKay, I do not know the procedure. What should I do? And may I ask to see your handiwork?'

'Of course,' he said, moved to her and opened his sketchbook. Elspeth's eyes widened and Morag hurried to see.

The women looked at one another, and Hamish panicked inside wondering. *Have I failed spectacularly?*

'You are very clever, Mr McKay,' said Elspeth not given to exaggeration, 'decidedly clever indeed.'

'It's wonderful,' whispered Morag overcome with admiration.

'I'm so glad,' said the artist struggling to hide his relief.

'Mother, it is a perfect image of you and when it is painted it will be something we all will cherish.'

Morag looked at him and smiled and Hamish wondered if anyone would notice as he started to slightly shake.

'So, what is the next step, Mr McKay?' asked Lady Buchanan. 'Do you require me to sit for you again?'

'I don't, your Ladyship. I will take the sketch home and produce the painted portrait.'

'But not before you partake of refreshments.'

Oh no. This became the hardest part of the visit. Sketching, as challenging as it was, became simple alongside sitting on an expensive chair while nibbling—his mother told him to nibble, never chew sandwiches or cakes—and handling cup, saucer, plate, spoon, fork, sugar tongs, and a napkin, let alone cake, presented Hamish with a nightmare.

He tried to remember half the topics of conversation knowing his family would demand intimate details of the entire event.

He survived sipping and nibbling, and Morag escorted him to the front door. None of this tradesman's exit for our artist.

'I can't thank you enough, Mr McKay. You are a brilliant artist, and my mother and I will have high expectations of your finished work. If there is any way I can assist you, do please send word.'

She held out a hand and Hamish struggled, juggling his sketchbook and pencils before taking it. Thank you, my Lady. I look forward to seeing you when I return.'

He didn't realize how sincere his words sounded. Fraser appeared as if a ghost passing through walls. 'For you, sir,' he said handing Hamish the blank canvas with supports purchased by the sitter.

He set off for home clutching his possessions. The pride in his work was matched by his thoughts about Lady Buchanan's older daughter.

'What are sugar tongs?' asked Moira when the artist arrived home and came under attack.

What a day!

Chapter 14
Money, land, widow, spinster daughters, sex and more.

Temple Kensington received Bonnie's letter by chance. Sir Richard was away on business and his overseer, who knew nothing of the bounder's behaviour, found his address and forwarded the envelope to the cad who rejoiced reckoning his charm remained on song.

He followed Bonnie's instructions and replied leaving his letter in the designated dead letter drop. There was a slim gap, a foot above the ground where two walls on the estate's Western boundary were joined. Bonnie successfully claimed the letter on one of her pretend constitutionals and rejoiced reckoning her charm remained on song.

She told her would-be lover about Sir Richard's proposed dinner party. Alas, having blotted his copy book, Temple became persona non grata. Bonnie fumed. An alternative rendezvous was required.

Hamish took his sketch to James Dunbar who slipped into raptures at the first viewing. 'It's brilliant as is, Hamish, but when painted will be astonishing.'

'Thank you, sir. I was given great support by Lady Buchanan and her daughter, Lady Morag.'

'But not Lady Bonnie?'

Hamish flinched at the mention of her name. 'She did not appear.'

James dismissed the comment being clueless as to the incident with the younger sister. What would he have said if that story got out?

'Now I have a surprise, young man. I know how difficult it is for you to paint in your tiny cottage. How your mother can cook and clean with you mixing pigments and applying brush strokes is beyond me.'

'We manage, sir.'

'I have cleaned out the shed at the bottom of my garden and would like you to use it as your studio.'

Hamish couldn't speak. He knew some artists found a patron, usually a wealthy person giving support to an impoverished creator. Mr Dunbar earned a stipend barely enough to feed and clothe his family, and this latest gift was worth its weight in gold.

'You are more than generous, sir,' he said.

'Come, let us have an opening ceremony for your new studio.'

Through the garden they went and stood outside the basic shed. Gardening equipment was moved to under the house and the now renovated shed contained a small table and easel.

Hamish puffed his cheeks and shook his head as emotion swept through his body. The minister studied his protégé and took delight in the smile on the artist's face. It was a natural reaction for the men to embrace.

Elspeth announced the date for the dinner party. Bonnie barely responded and felt even angrier when her mother and sister spoke about the portrait due soon. She knew next to nothing about it.

'I wonder if Mr McKay will use the same colours he used with Mr Dunbar's portrait,' said Morag.

More pain for Bonnie. The artist was the same man who not only refused to kiss her—what type of man would refuse her beauty?—but was the brute who threatened to strike her. Her desire for revenge, to seriously harm even destroy this man could not be stronger.

'Need I remind you, my darlings,' said Elspeth, 'Sir Richard is behaving in so kind and gentlemanly a fashion for your benefit.'

'Thank you, Mother,' said Morag.

'Do we have to accept the attentions of all these gentlemen?' asked Bonnie turning the atmosphere frosty.

Elspeth paused. 'Before you speak or act, Bonnie, I would ask you to imagine what your father would have you do.'

Knowing she was in a checkmate position, Bonnie fell silent.

James Dunbar never overdid his visits to the garden shed, now an artist's studio. When he did approach, he would give a polite knock and wait for Hamish to open the door and invite the minister inside.

The Lady Buchanan painting brought the sketch to life. The praise the minister lavished on the young man veered towards hyperbole.

'Do you think Her Ladyship will find it appealing?' asked Hamish.

'No,' said James, and Hamish gulped.

'No?'

'Not appealing, I think she will be overjoyed.' Hamish smiled with pleasure and relief. 'Now, I will ask Fitzroy Arbuthnot to provide a frame before we deliver the finished portrait to Lady Buchanan.'

The two men smiled at one another. It was a serendipitous coming together of a talented and unknown artist, and a poor but caring patron.

The dinner party at Sir Richard's was rehearsed to the nth degree. Food and wine selections were debated at length and place settings took as long. Having the Buchanan sisters sit between perfect gentlemen was of paramount importance. Of course, the choice of said males needed approval from Sir Richard who in turn sought Lady Buchanan's final say. Nothing was left to chance.

Morag behaved in her usual ladylike fashion supporting her mother at every turn. Not so younger sister Bonnie whose anger bubbled away beneath the surface.

On the night, the weather turned nasty and stepping from the carriage to the shelter of the grand entrance might have ruined the event. It proved an omen. Morag sat between two young men who were kind and polite. One may have been related to Mrs Dunbar suffering as he did from alogia. The other, Finlay McLeish, came from a background of wealth. Both his parents were from old money and the oldest grandson, Finlay, was in line to inherit a vast estate in Aberdeenshire.

'I believe, Lady Morag, your mother has recently been widowed,' he said after they were introduced and before the soup arrived.

She appreciated both his knowledge and the sincerity with which he spoke.

'She is, sir, and continues to be a wonderful mother in caring for me and my sister.'

'Do you enjoy outdoor pursuits, my Lady?'

'I ride but fishing and shooting are not to my liking. Reading and playing the piano are my favourite activities.'

'Ah,' he said, seizing on her hobbies, 'Pray tell who are your favourite authors and composers?'

Without realizing it, Morag revealed herself to a stranger. The thing which impressed her being his sincerity. So many gentlemen she met wanted to talk about themselves while regarding women as being required primarily for breeding and running a household.

Bonnie found herself surrounded by two of the "safest" selections possible. One chap, a studious type in love with numbers, wanted to engage Bonnie in matters mathematical and sought her opinion on Newton's Binomial theorem. On *what*? She did well not to scream.

On her other side sat an attractive fellow, well-spoken with perfect manners and who secretly adored men. One could be tempted to feel sorry for the randy daughter, the unfortunate young lady now being on a hiding to nothing, although a hiding, as in bottom spanking, was something she would seriously consider.

When the sisters returned home, Elspeth awaited their news. Bonnie wanted her bed with preferably a dashing male, or *any* male, with whom to keep company. She retired to nothing and nobody.

Morag told her mother about Finlay McLeish. Elspeth asked sensible questions and Morag gave detailed answers. Who better to know a daughter than her mother? Not fully convinced but leaning towards the positive, Elspeth enjoyed the possibility of Morag making a solid match.

James Dunbar arrived at the cottage owned by the failed artist. Rory McGrath stood in the yard attending to his horse.

'Good day to you, sir,' said Dunbar.

'He's asleep or hungover or both,' said Rory continuing grooming.

'I need his help again to frame a new portrait. It's a wonderful painting of a titled and wealthy lady.'

The word *wealthy* twanged inside Rory's head. Not his heart, he didn't have one of those.

'Does this noblewoman have a name?'

'Countess Elspeth Buchanan, widow of the late Earl of Buchanan and mother of two beautiful young ladies, Morag and Bonnie.'

Rory came alive. Money, land, widow, spinster daughters, sex and more. He stopped grooming the horse and tried working on the priest.

'So, who is this famous artist?'

'Ah, not yet famous but soon will be. This latest portrait will have young Hamish McKay's name on everyone's lips. He will not be the talk of the town but of the county.'

'Is he young?'

'In his twenty-first year.'

'Sounds interesting,' mused Rory with the words of Callum Drinkwater ringing in his head.

New blood is what the investors want. Bring me paintings by a talented, unknown artist and you will be well rewarded.'

'I'll see if the reprobate is awake. Keep an eye on the horse.'

Rory departed before returning and waving the minister inside. Fitzroy could correctly be described as death warmed up.

Dunbar did the usual caring routine of a man of God before pitching his request for another frame.

'All right,' croaked the old artist, 'but this time I'll prefer silver instead of shortbread.'

James was prepared to reluctantly agree when Rory crashed in with his pathetic over-acting.

'Now come along, Fitzy, you need to consider the youth of the artist.' The others stared at him. Who on Earth is speaking? 'We must encourage the young, give genuine talent a leg up. You have always believed in helping others, ever since you first picked up a paintbrush. Right?' Fitzroy grunted. Rory spoke the truth.

James wanted to leave. 'I'm sure we can come to an agreement. I'll bring the painting in the next few days. Good day, gentlemen.'

Confused, he left wondering why and how the lodger experienced such a Damascene conversion.

Fitzroy was too drunk to care.

Chapter 15
Bonnie drooled.

Bonnie went for a walk in the grounds of her family's estate. Fraser was under instructions to inform Her Ladyship of any unusual peripatetic activity when it came to her younger daughter.

Nothing dramatic was seen. She was clever. Walking within sight of the house while drifting ever indirectly to the "post box," she reached the dead letter drop.

Bliss oh joy whenever a new missive was found. Once her would-be lover replied, she wrote to Temple Kensington at an address other than Sir Richard Galbraith's estate and their correspondence became an ongoing activity.

She opened his latest, her heart on fire. Thank God her mother never saw the contents. Temple possessed the ability to suggest intimate activities using polite language. Bonnie drooled.

Alone in her room with her correspondence hidden in such a way and place, even the mice remained clueless, she made plans.

In her last letter she described the dinner party and the moronic males who bored her to tears. She wanted fun, life, adventure, and any activity which could be described correctly using adjectives such as wild and dangerous.

His final sentence in this latest letter was read a dozen times, more. The sentence, "Let's run away and live the best life ever," caused Bonnie to cry. What a fabulous idea, what a fantastic offer. There was no argument, no thought of "this is still up for discussion." She wanted out, to be with the dangerous man who set her juices flowing.

Okay but when and how?

She gave no thought for her mother's reaction or if her lover could support her and keep her in a lifestyle to which she was accustomed. Bugger all that. Let's flee.

Elspeth wanted her daughters to further report on what they thought of the gentlemen they met at Sir Richard's dinner party. Morag hated to disappoint her mother and gave what a coroner would call an open finding. However, Bonnie described her experiences with an air of excitement. Each word she spoke about Gent A and Gent B was in fact a description of her one true love, Temple, the cad, the blackguard.

Both mother and sister struggled to believe Bonnie's report with no understanding of her incredible and potentially scandalous plan.

Accompanied by his patron, Hamish carried the well wrapped finished portrait to Fitzroy's cottage. Both residents were at home.

'Ah,' declared Fitzroy, 'I get to meet the man himself, the child genius and his beloved patron. Come in, gentlemen, come away in.'

Fitzroy shook the hand of a fellow artist. 'I'm honoured to make your acquaintance, sir.' Hamish became awestruck whereas Rory's shifty eyes followed the action being desperate to see the latest work.

James took control, moved to a small table and displayed the painting.

'Jesus,' whispered Fitzroy not considering the religious in front of him. He moved for a closer inspection. 'Look at those brushstrokes,' he murmured, his face an inch from the painting.

'Do we take it, Mr Arbuthnot, you approve of the portrait?' asked the minister.

'I do, I do,' he said continuing a detailed inspection.

James turned to the equestrian. 'And what say you, sir?'

'You're asking the wrong fellah,' said Rory. 'I know nothing about art.' True but he knew a possible money-making scheme when he saw one.

Fitzroy held the portrait in front of him. 'A work of this quality needs the best frame I can find. Give me twenty-four hours.'

James hesitated but asked. 'And your price, sir?'

'No charge.' The room stood still.

'I beg your pardon?' replied James.

'I'd be proud, honoured to frame such a perfect portrait.'

The minister and the artist walked home struggling to believe Fitzroy's reaction. Conversation bubbled. Both hoped the woman in the portrait would think the same. In the cottage, Rory exploded.

James called at Buchanan Hall anxious to deliver the latest news.

'The portrait is complete my Lady and all who have seen it are full of praise. We so hope you too will be pleased.'

'It sounds exciting, Mr Dunbar. When may I see it?'

'Whenever it suits, my Lady.'

'Would tomorrow afternoon be convenient?'

'Indeed, it would. I shall arrive with both portrait and artist.'

Hamish was helping his father with lambing when James arrived.

'It's tomorrow afternoon, Hamish. Lady Buchanan will receive both you and your portrait.' Father and son shared the excitement.

'You'll need a good wash, son,' said George and the two older men laughed. He looked a sight wearing working clothes decorated with straw and mud.

Rory laid out a plan. He needed to know where the portrait would reside, how he could steal said object and what he should ask Callum Drinkwater to pay.

Questions piled up. This portrait was obviously by a different artist. Rory's excuse about an old man wanting to sell off his ancient creations wouldn't work with the youthful Hamish McKay.

The criminal reckoned his luck was due to run out. This sale would be his last. Pinch portrait, grab cash, leave town.

Chapter 16
One he took a shine to; one he almost gave a shiner to.

Morag shared her mother's excitement at the prospect of the portrait's arrival. They discussed it at length over luncheon. Bonnie, like Rory, had other fish to fry and worked on her secret plan.

Morag's excitement grew with the chance to meet the artist again. They could hardly ignore one another in Morag's home and, unknown to the wealthy daughter, the artist too looked forward to the portrait presentation with the additional benefit of seeing Lady Morag.

Sir Richard had purchased an easel, an expensive model, presenting it to Elspeth for her much-awaited portrait.

There was no command from their mother but both Morag and Bonnie were expected in the sitting room for the unveiling. Bonnie knew to be absent would cause a stink and with her plan to run away taking shape, the less fuss she created the better.

Surely the artist, the young man several classes below her, would never say or do anything to disclose their recent contretemps.

Fraser tapped gently, entered, and announced. 'My Lady, the Reverend Dunbar and Mr McKay.'

The visitors entered as the butler performed his regular disappearing trick hiding his disappointment at missing the first viewing. The visitors nodded to the assembled women. Hamish found such a move tricky as he it was holding the cloth-covered portrait.

'Good afternoon, gentlemen. Thank you for coming and we are all looking forward with much anticipation to the unveiling.' She indicated. 'The easel is available.'

James led Hamish to the fine-looking object. The Buchanan women sat facing it with both daughters a little behind their mother. A hush settled. Bonnie eyed off Hamish remembering their interaction. Morag eyed off Hamish thinking about an interaction.

For Hamish, regarding the sisters, one he took a shine to; one he almost gave a shiner to.

The minister held the easel steady as Hamish placed the portrait in position, still wearing its cloth covering.

Nerves took over. The cloth didn't co-operate. As Hamish tried to lift it, the cloth snagged on a top corner of the frame. The two men shared a nervous glance. As Hamish tried again, his tug caused the easel to wobble. Females gasped.

'Higher,' whispered James. Hamish obliged and the cloth rose and fell to the floor.

This time the gasps from the females sounded much louder.

The men stepped back revealing the portrait in all its glory. Morning sunshine landed in the ideal spot highlighting the painting. Without prompting, the Buchanan women applauded. Bonnie was less enthusiastic than her mother and sister but even she was touched by the beauty of the artist's work.

She wanted *her* portrait painted.

Elspeth moved to the portrait, her daughters following.

'Mr McKay you have produced a wonderful, wonderful painting.'

Hamish instinctively nodded. 'Thank you, my Lady.'

'I congratulate you, sir, and thank you both for all you have done. I am amazed, young man, at your skill and ability.'

'We are so glad you like it, my Lady,' added James.

Refreshments were served. Sir Richard and his sister arrived having accepted Elspeth's invitation. They inspected the portrait, and their praise was the most fulsome yet.

Bonnie was able to hide in the crowd with two domestics on hand to help with food and drink.

Hamish stood near the portrait and Morag joined him.

'I can tell you a family secret, Mr McKay.' He waited wondering what she was about to say. His mind failed to concentrate as his eyes strayed to her creamy white neck and the dancing curls hanging beside her delicate ears.

'My mother has not fully recovered from the loss of my father, and this wonderful portrait has lifted her spirits and taken her out of herself. So, thank you, sir, twice over.'

Hamish smiled. 'I'm glad to be of service, my Lady.'

'Will you now become a professional artist?'

Her question threw him. 'I haven't thought about it, and my father does need me on our small holding, especially now the lambing season is upon us.'

'Well, all I can say is the sheep's gain is the art world's loss.' She smiled and he knew his knees wanted to wobble.

Their conversation ended when Sir Richard made a speech. He congratulated Hamish, and Mr Dunbar for his support of the young man, and announced the date of an occasion when the portrait would receive a special, an official unveiling.

'Lady Buchanan has honoured me with the task of welcoming her friends and family as she unveils this magnificent portrait. Invitations will be sent for the second Saturday next month at 2 o'clock.'

Smiles spread and Elspeth spoke. 'Thank you, Sir Richard. I am most grateful for all the help you have given me and my family.' The smiling spread as refreshments were served.

James Dunbar was at home mingling with this class of person but not so Hamish McKay. Give him a straw-strewn shed with ewes giving birth and life was all right.

He stood to one side and was approached by Sir Richard's sister, a spinster, Harriet Galbraith.

'Good day to you, sir.'

'My Lady,' said Hamish thinking all the people in the room, bar himself, his patron and the domestics, were titled.

'I have no title, young man, I'm plain old Miss Galbraith.'

'I beg your pardon, ma'am.'

'Now to business,' she said in a most business-like way. 'My titled brother has a milestone birthday later this year and I reckon the perfect present would be a portrait of his good self so, two matters. What's your fee?' She held up a hand to stop him replying. 'Whatever it is I'll double it. And two, can you do the job without him sitting for you? I'd like it to be a surprise.' She paused. 'Well? Wotcha reckon?'

The questions were tricky enough, but her common way of speaking threw him. She sounded like a Scottish cockney.

'Oh, I get it,' she said. 'The minister is your agent. All deals go through the Church of Scotland chappie.' She tapped her nose. 'Mum's the word, laddie. I look forward to collaborating with you.' She turned to leave, stopped, and indicated the portrait. 'Bloody good job.'

Hamish stood pole-axed. The offer and vocabulary left him speechless. He fancied leaving, his spirits high, soaring at times, and struggled to imagine how he could explain this incident to his mentor and family. If being dragged into a broom cupboard by a sex-mad titled young woman was one thing, some of today's other events gave that episode a run for its money.

The walk home was easier with no portrait to carry. James bubbled away at the wonderful reception given to the painting. Hamish agreed but said nothing about Miss Galbraith's offer and coarse language. One important event at a time. They stopped at the manse garden gate.

'Is there any item you need from your studio?' asked the minister.

Hamish thought this was a trick question and hesitated.

James continued. 'Do you need your sketch book to start your next portrait?'

Hamish thought the minister had been told about Harriet's offer. 'Do you mean the request from Miss Galbraith?'

'Miss Galbraith!' exclaimed the stunned minister. Hamish explained. The mentor pumped the artist's hand. 'Congratulations, my dear friend. You are about to start a glorious artistic career. You can give your father part of your earnings allowing him to employ a farmhand and you and your family will both be winners.'

'Thank you, sir. And whatever happens, it's all because of your kind and tireless support.'

'I'll see you in the kirk on Sunday,' said the minister, squeezed the young man's arms and set off up his garden path.

Hamish pondered how much of today's news he would share with his family.

Chapter 17
It was a terrible night and about to get worse.

Calling unannounced worked differently for different classes. People visiting the McKays in their cottage would go around the back and knock on the never-locked kitchen door. People of an appropriate class visiting Buchanan Hall would approach the front door and wait for the staff to grant them admission.

Their calling card would be given to the butler and thus to the lady of the house who would decide if she was or wasn't at home.

The McKays could hardly behave like so. You could see the family through the kitchen window, and they were always home.

Finlay McLeish took a shine to Morag Buchanan and when he discussed the young woman and her situation with his parents, they gave him strong encouragement to woo the woman with a view to plighting his troth. Financially, this was a marriage made in heaven.

Elspeth studied his card and sent for her older daughter. They discussed the presence of the young man who was granted admission.

'Please forgive this intrusion, my Lady,' he said to Elspeth once all three were seated. 'I was in the area and as I found your delightful daughter's company to be enchanting at Sir Richard's dinner party, I thought I should take this opportunity to meet you.'

Finlay played a blinder. Win the parent to win the daughter.

'You're most welcome, sir. Sir Richard has been a loyal friend to my family. Will you stay for luncheon?'

'Too kind, my Lady.'

'In the meantime, perhaps Morag could show you the grounds.' She looked at her daughter who stood and smiled. Finlay shot up like a startled grouse.

'Of course. This way Mr McLeish,' she said, and they went outside. Elspeth enjoyed a warm inner glow.

Bonnie bounced in. 'Who's that?' she asked full of curiosity.

'Good morning, my dear' said her mother trying in vain to teach her daughter a snippet of good manners. 'You met Mr Finlay McLeish at Sir Richard's dinner party. He has called to see Morag.'

Bonnie loathed the gentlemen she met at the dinner party but how dare her sister have a caller and she not. She glared at her mother before leaving the room in a frump. Elspeth despaired.

In the garden, Finlay made all the right noises about the magnificent house and grounds before switching to the real purpose of his visit.

'I believe I should be honest with you, Morag. May I call you Morag? I feel as if I know you already.'

'Of course,' she said realizing his interest in roses was superficial, and she was being courted.

'I told my parents I met a beautiful young lady, and they were happy to see me so ... so happy.' He looked at her without flinching. 'I do apologize for being so forward.'

'No apology is needed, sir.'

'Please, call me Finlay.'

She returned his steady gaze. 'No apology is needed, Finlay.'

At luncheon where Bonnie ground her teeth more than her food, Morag made her big announcement.

'Mother, Finlay has invited us all to his family estate to celebrate Hogmanay this year.'

'How kind,' said Elspeth who stared at Bonnie.

'Most kind,' said the lying sister.

'My father will provide transport, and we have a marvellous cottage by the loch to accommodate you and your staff.'

For Elspeth and Morag, the future looked promising, rosy, and potentially wonderful. For Bonnie, it became vomit-inducing.

Hamish couldn't help himself. He looked at the cheap calendar on the wall and counted the days. The official unveiling of his portrait of Lady Buchanan drew ever nearer.

'Staring at the calendar won't help, son,' said his mother. 'Wanting something to happen doesn't make time fly.'

He grinned at her. 'You always was the wise one, Ma.'

'Were,' she corrected him. 'Get your speech right now you're mixing with the rich folk.'

The groom awoke. He slept in the stables at Buchanan Hall to be close to his charges. The smell whacked him, the smoke choked him, and the flash of flames scared the life out of him.

'Fire!' he screamed. 'Fire!' he yelled repeatedly as he ran to rouse the others, save the horses and himself. Horses panicked and whinnied. Kicking the stable in fear reeked of danger to animals' legs.

From the staff quarters, domestics, gardeners, and the ghillie and his wife rushed outside in their night attire. Loud voices filled the air. Buckets of water were grabbed by young and old and carried to the fire burning fiercely at the far end of the stables.

Inside the big house, sleeping residents woke. Looking out first-floor bedroom windows, the Buchanan women saw flames, people rushing, and heard shouting. The Buchanan women grabbed expensive dressing gowns and ran downstairs. Morag and Bonnie joined forces.

'Where's Mother?' asked Morag.

'In her room, I don't know,' said Bonnie.

'I'm here,' called their mother coming down the stairs.

Mother and daughters hurried through the house, into the kitchen and into the yard. Pandemonium.

All they saw were people running, shouting, carrying buckets, working a pump, and leading frightened horses to safety.

The ghillie came towards the women and ushered them inside.

'Please, my Ladies, wait inside. The fire won't spread to the house.'

The women did as directed and sat there as Mrs MacDougal made tea. It was a terrible night and about to get worse.

The fire died. Moving bales of hay was dangerous but it saved the stables from destruction. The flames ran out of fuel.

The women waited in silence in the candlelit kitchen. They turned as one as the ghillie entered.

'It's over, my Lady. The fire's out, the horses are safe, and the damage is limited.'

'Thank God,' said Elspeth. 'And no-one's hurt?'

'A few cuts and bruises, but all will be back to work in the morn.'

'Do we know what started it?'

The ghillie shrugged. 'As you know, my Lady, we are extremely strict with smoking and candles. My guess is we'll never know.'

'Thank you, Jackson and please thank all the staff. I'll speak to them after breakfast.'

He touched his cap, nodded to the others, and left.

'Bed,' my darlings,' said Elspeth but froze when Fraser burst in, panting. This shocked the women as the butler was renowned for his lack of exertion and would never enter a room without knocking.

'My Lady, it's gone.'

The women stood rooted to the spot.

'What's gone?'

'Your portrait, my Lady. I think it's been stolen!'

Chapter 18
Rory's hand stopped an inch from Callum's face.

The empty easel looked lonely in the moonlight. Next morning in daylight it looked worse. The beautiful, much celebrated painting of Lady Buchanan was nowhere to be seen.

The house was searched with nothing found. It was obvious the portrait had been stolen. Elspeth, like others, saw a direct link between the fire and the theft.

'It was a distraction, my Lady,' said Fraser. 'With you and the staff concentrating on the fire and saving the horses, the thief crept inside, grabbed the painting and fled.'

'But why?' she mused aloud. 'Who would want such a thing? It's not as if I'm famous and besides, the painter is young and unknown.'

No-one spoke. What could they say? Morag broke the silence.

'Mother, we must tell Sir Richard. The unveiling will have to be cancelled.' It would have sounded better if she said postponed.

Elspeth stifled a sob. Sir Richard's work on her behalf was pushed aside. The wonderful portrait was stolen. And the worst aspect being not having a clue as to why and by whom.

James Dunbar received a note delivered by one of the gardeners at Buchanan Hall. He read Elspeth's words and thought he might swear. He yelled to his wife about going to see Hamish and left.

In the small barn on the McKay farm, the young artist looked up in surprise. When told the news, his heart copped a sharp pain, and his face screamed sorrow.

'Stolen?' he whispered.

The minister explained the fire. 'This was planned, Hamish. The thief lit the fire and, in the confusion, stole the painting.'

Without thinking, Hamish spoke. 'I could paint another. She wouldn't need to sit for me.'

James studied the young man. 'Or we could find it,' he said. 'Tell your parents we have a special job today.'

Their first destination was Buchanan Hall. Fraser greeted them and led them to the library. Elspeth couldn't bear to be in the room with the empty easel. Morag sat with her mother.

'Good morning, gentlemen. Thank you so much for calling and I can't begin to say how sorry I am the beautiful portrait has gone.'

James looked more desolate than the others. 'Hamish and I are willing to do all we can to retrieve your portrait, my Lady.'

'How kind but we have no idea why the theft happened.'

'I could paint another portrait my Lady,' said Hamish and his offer flattened the conversation.

Elspeth looked shocked and Morag reckoned the gesture told her so much about the character of the painter.

'I hope that won't be necessary,' said Lady Buchanan.

'There are some ways to try and track down the portrait,' said James. 'It might be better to discuss them in private, my Lady.'

Elspeth wasn't sure why such a request was made but nodded and Hamish set off with Morag following. They stood in the massive hallway.

'Are you serious about offering to paint another portrait?' she asked.

'Of course, and an even better one. I've already discovered an artist can learn from their mistakes. Experience is a great teacher.'

'Mistakes? I thought your painting was perfect.'

He produced a wispy smile. 'Thank you, my Lady.' Neither knew what to say. 'Have you decided where your mother's portrait is to be hung?'

'We think in the family gallery. Come and I'll show you.'

They walked along the hall and stopped at the flight of broad stairs leading to the floor above. As they mounted the stairs, Morag stopped and described the portraits. At the break in the stairs which turned left, she stopped.

'Each time I climb these stairs; I stop here and look at my father.'

The man in the portrait stood tall and proudly wore a kilt of the Clan Buchanan tartan. Hamish was impressed by the appearance of Morag's father and the artist's work in producing so fine a portrait.

'Please forgive me, my Lady, but I was sure your father passed away not so long ago. I attended his funeral in the kirk.'

'You are correct, of course you are, and this portrait is of my great-grandfather, and I'm told my father was an exact image of his grandfather. From this portrait, my mother feels my late father is here in the house keeping watch over us.'

Hamish nodded. 'I think that's a lovely story.'

'Now I should not keep you from your work.'

'Indeed,' said the Reverend Dunbar from the foot of the stairs.

Morag accompanied the two visitors to the front door and watched them depart along the tree-lined driveway.

At the same time, in Edinburgh, Callum Drinkwater's bell tinkled bringing the snazzy-dresser from his office.

'Oh, it's you,' he said as Rory McGrath entered carrying a portrait covered in rough hessian.

'You won't be so cocky when you see this.'

Rory revealed the painting, and Callum clamped his lips shut so as not to reveal his true feelings. To him, this was gold.

'Look at the quality of the brush strokes,' said Rory mimicking his former landlord's comment.

Callum moved in and studied the work. Rory, who knew less than nothing about art, was spot on. Callum loved the portrait but found suspicious thoughts romping around inside his brain.

'Right, what's its provenance?'

'Provence? Who said it came from France?'

'Provenance, you idiot. What's its history? Who's the lady? Who painted her and, most importantly, where did you get it?'

Rory turned angry and desperate. It's yours for a tenner.' Callum scoffed. 'And I want 50% of the purchase price when you sell it for fifty quid.'

This time Callum laughed. Rory stepped forward and grabbed the portrait preparing to leave. For this painting, he held all the aces.

'All right, all right,' snapped the frustrated dealer. 'A fiver now and 40% when it sells.'

Rory's hand stopped an inch from Callum's face. It was a request for the money now and a threat if the deal was not honoured, a sort of "cheat me and you're dead, pal" gesture.

A Bank of Scotland five-pound note appeared, was snatched and the ne'er-do-well stormed out. At the door, he turned and yelled.

'I'll be back.'

James and Hamish arrived at Fitzroy's crumbling cottage. He was alone. When told the stolen portrait tale, he swore. 'I can understand why it was stolen. There is class in the brushstrokes, the eyes, face, neck, quality beyond your years, laddie.'

'Thank you, sir,' said Hamish, 'but can you help us find it?'

'Where is your lodger, Mr Arbuthnot?' asked James.

'Don't know and don't care.' He scratched his pepper 'n salt whiskers. 'Stolen paintings, hey? Did you ever met that flashy art dealer in Edinburgh, Callum Drinkwater?'

'We did, when shopping for art materials,' said the minister.

'If anyone knows about stolen paintings, it's Callum. But tread careful. "Snake in the grass" is the nicest thing you can say about him.'

The visitors thanked the elderly artist and left.

'It's too late to go into town today,' said James. 'We'll go first thing in the morning.'

Hamish looked uncomfortable. 'Not tomorrow, Mr Dunbar. We are flat out with lambing and my father needs me more than ever.'

'Of course you must help your father. I can go alone.'

'No sir,' snapped Hamish. 'If Mr Arbuthnot is correct and that art dealer is a crook, there is strength in numbers. If you can leave it a few days, no more than three, I will come too.'

'Good man,' said the minister and slapped the artist's arm. Hamish thought about finding the missing portrait but, at the same time, was planning at least two new works of art.

Chapter 19
The weapon plunged into the portrait, and the madman slashed.

Three days later, the mentor and his protégé made their way to Edinburgh. All Dunbar's enquiries about the missing portrait came to nothing. This art gallery visit was their last hope.

Callum heard his bell and bowled out using his hail fellow well met fake bonhomie. He wasn't sure why, but his stomach played tricks.

'Good morning, gentlemen.'

'Good morning, sir,' said James. 'We came here some time ago.'

'I remember, and how can we help you today?'

'We are looking for a portrait, painted by this young man, a portrait which has recently been stolen.'

Callum's tummy stirred.

'Oh dear, how unfortunate. But why come to my respectable gallery?'

'We thought you might have heard of this portrait being offered for sale.'

Callum shook his head. 'Sadly no, gentlemen. But if I do hear of the painting, if you leave your details, I will certainly let you know.'

Hamish lost control. 'But you don't know what it looks like.'

Callum bit back. 'And I will know as soon as you tell me.'

Hamish described his work—the size, frame, colours, person, and the subject's position, even the brushstrokes—and Callum knew exactly the portrait, who stole it and where it now resided.

He puffed and bluffed. 'If I have any news, how can I contact you?'

James produced his card. 'Can you suggest any other contacts?'

'There are more galleries in the High Street, but all honest dealers would report any art they thought stolen so I'm afraid, the black market is probably involved and, of course, I know nothing of such people and their wicked ways.' He produced an unctuous smile. 'I wish you success in your search, gentlemen.'

Miserable, they left and headed off to find other galleries. They were gone twenty minutes when Callum's bell rang, and the customer was someone he knew.

Rory had sailed through his five quid and wanted his 40% of the sale price of Lady Buchanan's portrait.

'It's not sold. Come back next week,' he said heading to his office.

It takes a liar to spot a liar. Rory raced at Callum who threw on his "how dare you" routine. 'Stop!' screamed the gallery owner. 'Get out!'

Rory barged past Callum and started searching the office. Paintings, stacked against one another on the floor, were pulled back.

'If I can't find that bloody painting, you're dead.'

'Careful,' screamed Callum as the barbarian cum burglar treated the art as if it was rubbish. They squabbled, yelling and swearing.

In the High Street, James stopped. 'We need a notice.' Hamish looked confused. 'A Lost Painting notice. We'll describe the painting and offer a reward. Art galleries will put the sign in their window. Let's go,' he said and headed back the way they came.

'But what sort of reward?' asked Hamish struggling to keep up.

'I'm sure Lady Buchanan will gladly pay a small sum if it means we find her portrait.'

They reached the gallery and entered. The bell sound was drowned out by raised voices, threats and the clatter of paintings being re-arranged.

'Ah!' hissed Rory. 'It *is* here.' He placed the portrait on the desk.

The two visitors looked at one another and headed to the office. They filled the doorway, and the minister found he could project, if not his sermons, then certainly his demands for justice.

'What the bloody hell is going on here?'

The tone of voice and choice of words stopped the world spinning causing a minor earthquake.

The fighters froze. Hamish looked at the desk and saw his portrait.

'There it is!' he cried as he pushed into the office.

Rory turned his aggression towards Hamish. 'Oh no you don't.'

Hamish was adamant and pointed past Rory. 'That's my portrait!'

'*Was* your portrait, laddie. Now back off.'

Hamish didn't think of fighting; he wanted his creation. He took a step towards the desk but froze when Rory produced a dagger from inside his belt.

James screamed. 'No! Hamish, come here!'

'Get back, all of you!' snarled Rory. The others were in no doubt he could and would use the weapon.

'For God's sake, Rory,' begged Callum. 'You'll get a few years for burglary but if you kill him, you'll hang.'

'He's right,' said the minister. 'Put it away, Rory, please.'

The wild man looked and sounded desperate. 'Back off,' he snarled. 'I'm walking out, and no-one is going to stop me.'

'We can't let you go,' said James in a quiet but determined voice. 'Arson and theft are serious crimes, not to mention threats to kill.'

This was the climax of the scene. Would someone get wounded or killed? Would Rory flee or be captured? He glared at them hating the situation and himself. He knew he was cooked.

He snarled. 'Well, if I can't have it, no-one can.' He turned to face the painting and raised the dagger.

'No!' screamed Hamish as the weapon plunged into the portrait and the madman slashed. James leapt at Rory and tackled him to the floor. The dagger was ripped from his grasp and kicked aside.

The Reverend James Dunbar used his unarmed combat skills to leave the attacker groaning and cursing but helpless.

Hamish wanted to cry. Callum took over and ordered him out. 'Turn right at the front door and right at the first crossroad. The police station is across the road. Now go!' Hamish fled.

Callum felt much relief at Rory's capture but knew he needed to produce a tall tale. 'I bet you didn't learn that routine in the seminary,' he said to the heavy-breathing minister.

'Former chaplain with the Royal Highland Regiment,' said James increasing pressure on the prisoner who kept complaining, swearing and threatening. The trio waited. The wrecked portrait joined them.

The shop bell tingled as Hamish arrived with two policemen. They struggled with Rory who left as a beaten man resigned to his fate.

Nearby, he had beaten down the price he paid to have his horse tethered, and when he failed to collect the beast, it was sold and Rory lost again.

Hamish, now heartbroken to have come so far and lost his precious painting, stood over the work, fondling the slashed canvas.

'It's ruined,' he said, 'ruined.' Tears ran down his cheeks.

James didn't know how to comfort his friend.

'No it's not,' said Callum and the others stared at him. He nodded to a corner. 'Look over there behind the cabinet.'

Hamish knelt, peered, then stretched a hand into the narrow gap. He gripped a frame and gently removed it. James saw it first.

'It's the portrait!' he shouted. 'Hamish, it's your portrait!'

The young man stood and held his painting. A different tear appeared and ran down his cheek. He moved to the desk and looked at the destroyed painting.

Callum explained. 'It's a copy. I have an artist here in town who does the odd job for me. Your original is so good I knew I could sell it abroad so used the copy to fool McGrath.'

Hamish grew angry. 'You helped the man who stole my art. You're as bad as he is. The police should have arrested you as well.'

'Yes, but I'm wealthy, can afford the best lawyers and know important people. Getting me convicted will be nigh on impossible and look, you've found what you wanted. Why not take your beautiful painting and forget you were ever here?'

Hamish didn't want to let the matter drop. James moved to him, touched his arm and whispered.

'You've enjoyed a massive win here, Mr McKay.' Hamish looked at his mentor surprised at being called, Mr McKay. 'Your art is so good, Hamish, this man who makes his living from art has ordered it copied.' A pause before a gentle tug. 'Come on. A certain titled lady is waiting.'

Chapter 20
Morag and I are walking out.

Callum spoke the truth when he mentioned his wealth and circle of important friends but still feared being dragged into Rory's crime spree. He gave the visitors his best carrying case for Hamish's portrait. Bring on Scotland's worst weather because nothing could damage the portrait housed within its new container.

The two men were exhausted when they reached Buchanan Hall. Bonnie spotted them from her upstairs bedroom window. Normally she would have skipped downstairs wanting to be the bearer of good news. However, as the chap carrying what was obviously a painting, and who happened to be a dirt-poor farmer's son, the one who refused to kiss her desirable red lips, and who threatened to strike her, she chose to remain in her room and brood, Fury her new middle name.

Fraser changed his usual welcome to, 'Have you found it?'

'Yes, Mr Fraser,' said James whose grin matched the one by the artist. The visitors removed their coats and caps then followed Fraser.

He moved along the hallway at a rate which even startled the furniture. The longcase clock near the library sounded two minutes before the quarter hour. The butler knocked on the library door and opened it without Her Ladyship speaking. He bubbled with joy beaming at the surprised gathering.

'It's been found, my Lady. Your portrait has come home.'

Lady Buchanan gasped as James and Hamish entered, the young man with portrait case in hand.

Elspeth stood. 'Oh, how wonderful. Is it really the portrait?'

'It is, indeed, my Lady,' said James who followed Hamish to a table and helped to extract the painting. Gasps were heard. To make the matter even more memorable, Fraser abandoned his vanishing act and remained in the room.

The portrait appeared looking exactly as it did before the theft.

'But how did you find it? And where?' she asked.

'If I may, my Lady,' said James, 'I believe your portrait should return to its rightful place in the sitting room.'

'Of course,' she said and led the others along the hall with Hamish wearing a big smile which grew bigger when he looked at Morag. Fraser brought up the rear, his happiness on show.

In the large room with its empty easel, the portrait settled back in its original setting.

'And now, my Lady,' said James, 'I believe the unveiling event should be returned to its rightful place on your calendar.'

'Of course you're right, Mr Dunbar. I shall inform Sir Richard to set a new date. Oh, please do forgive me.' She turned to the young man standing beside Morag. 'May I introduce Mr. Finlay McLeish.' She indicated James and Hamish, and the three men shook hands.

'And I must apologize for next Sunday, Mr Dunbar. Finlay's family has kindly invited my family to spend a week on their estate at Musselburgh.'

'We shall miss you,' said James. 'And of course, wish you a safe and enjoyable trip.'

'Now you must stay for refreshments,' she insisted.

'Lady Buchanan, if I may be so bold, we have come directly from Edinburgh, are tired and wet, and our families have need of us.'

'How inconsiderate of me. But gentlemen, please, you must return soon and tell us all your detective news.'

'This way, gentlemen,' said Fraser and led them to the door.

Trailing behind, Hamish was stopped by the man he just met. 'I say, old chap, Morag has told me about your brilliant artistic skill, and she is absolutely right.'

'Thank you, sir, most kind.'

'I hope we can see more of you now Morag and I are walking out.' Finlay extended his hand and Hamish shook it. As he turned to leave, he saw Morag watching. He nodded to her, and she tried to smile but it fizzled.

Walking along the hallway, certain words bounced around Hamish's brain. *Morag and I are walking out.*

Chapter 21
This type of scandal can never be forgiven or forgotten.

Lambing for Hamish and visiting sick members of his human flock for James, became their new lot in life. The ewes gave birth, and the elderly remained poorly. As far as painting portraits went, Hamish received a commission from Sir Richard Galbraith's sister and pondered a couple of private projects he kept to himself.

Harriet Galbraith wanted a portrait of her brother done in secret as a surprise for his 60th birthday. No sitting. The sketching was well underway, and he showed this initial work to James.

'What think you, sir?' he asked when James joined Hamish in the minister's garden shed, now a studio.

'Well it's certainly Sir Richard. You've pictured him perfectly. I feel honoured in having my portrait painted by someone so talented.'

'Thank you, sir, but please remember it's a secret with the subject to receive a surprise on his 60th birthday.'

The days went by with no-one surprised when Lady Buchanan and her daughters were absent from the kirk for the Sunday morning service. They were staying with Morag's young man on his family's large estate near the shores of the Firth of Forth.

Hamish surprised himself noting how often he thought about Morag and her beau. Why? Probably because she was the first woman who caused his heart to beat faster, and now she had found a beau, he realized he was hurting.

Of course he knew his status, possessions and minimal income would prevent any likelihood of a romantic association with a woman whose family owned a vast estate and enjoyed titles and prestige.

He found himself looking forward to the following Sunday when the Buchanan ladies would return and be seen worshipping in the kirk.

Sunday morning always meant extra activity for the male members of the McKay family. George and Hamish were under strict instructions to clean their fingernails. Stripping to the waist for a good wash on Saturday night plus shaving on Sunday morn was not enough. Even clean shirt and trousers didn't complete the job. No, commanded wife and mother, 'You be sure to clean all the muck and mud from under your fingernails.'

The family walked together to the kirk. Hamish tried to control his excitement. The only guaranteed opportunity where he might see and hopefully speak to Morag was on the Sabbath. And the date of the re-scheduled official unveiling of the portrait was still a fortnight away. Hamish looked at the calendar daily counting down the days.

It was usual for the congregation to wait for the Buchanan ladies to arrive before entering the kirk but today they were late, and as rain fell, the ordinary folk, the worshippers took to their pew.

Hamish didn't fancy turning around to see if any latecomers appeared. The rustle of dresses would give his heart a start but of rustles came there none.

The Reverend Dunbar entered from his poky robing room and Hamish could see from his expression he too noticed the absent ladies.

During the service, the minister referred to the newly-completed portrait of Lady Buchanan but kept his remarks short and low-key. The subject of the portrait and her daughters failed to appear.

After the service, greeting the minister, Hamish and James were at a loss. Without the lady of the hour, what could they say?

'I do hope her Ladyship is not unwell,' said James.

'Or one of her daughters,' added Hamish.

There was nothing more to say. The McKay family returned to their cottage to enjoy a substantial meal of rabbit stew with each ingredient home grown.

On Tuesday next a letter arrived for Mr Dunbar. Reading it shocked him so much he accidentally bit his lip. The contents, written by Lady Buchanan, told him everything and nothing. The intriguing part read as follows.

> *Unfortunately, due to a serious incident, I must cancel the social event where Sir Richard was due to unveil the portrait. I do apologize for the cancellation and would ask you to convey my apology to Mr McKay.*

James re-read the letter. All manner of thoughts came to mind. What is the serious incident? She refers to *the* portrait and not *my* portrait. A postponement means the event will happen later. A cancellation means it will not occur at all.

Unwilling to tell anyone the news, not even his wife, for fear of gossip within the village, he set off to speak to Hamish and found him caring for the family flock.

'Greetings, my friend,' said James and immediately Hamish saw a worried face and sensed bad news. The minister explained the letter stressing the importance of telling nobody the news.

'Of course,' said the artist. 'But what do you think has happened?'

'Like you, I have no idea. But it must surely be serious for her to act the way she has.'

'If someone has died, would you not have been told?'

'You would think so. And I believe it is the Christian thing to visit Lady Buchanan.'

'Would it not be better first to write, to respond to her letter?'

James saw wisdom in Hamish's reply.

'You're right. It's clearly a delicate matter and if she wants my counsel or help, she can ask, and of course I will respond.'

'What do I tell my family and friends, and the people I've told about the unveiling?'

His question stumped the minister. Avoiding even the whiff of scandal was his top priority. 'I think you should say nothing until we discover the nature of the issue.'

'But what if Lady Buchanan wants to keep the matter private?'

The situation became trickier by the minute. 'Say nothing to anyone and I'll follow your advice and write to the dear lady.'

A letter was the key to Elspeth's problem. Shortly after the women returned from their brief holiday with Finlay's family, Bonnie was late for breakfast, not an unusual event.

Mary, the maid, knocked and entered the dining room. 'Excuse me, my Lady. I found this envelope on the pillow in Lady Bonnie's room.'

Elspeth took the envelope addressed simply to *Mother*.

As she read, a spear plunged into Lady Buchanan's heart. Morag studied her mother, both their pulses accelerating. Neither spoke. It would have been easier to cut the atmosphere than the toast.

Morag held her breath and when her mother gasped and clutched her throat allowing the letter to fall onto the butter, the daughter leapt up and to her mother's side.

Elspeth broke down, weeping silently. Morag picked up the letter and read.

Dear Mother,
I have run away.
I cannot live the sheltered life you require.
The man I love has a friend who has given us his holiday cottage.
We will be safe and happy.
Please do not follow or try to find me.
I will write when things are settled.
Your loving daughter,
Bonnie

Morag sat beside her mother holding her hand, the child comforting the parent. 'She'll be all right, Mummy. She's a clever and determined girl.' Elspeth's despair grew deeper. Silence set in and their breakfast went cold.

At last, the distraught mother spoke. 'She has ruined her life. This type of scandal can never be forgiven or forgotten.'

Morag struggled. Distress came from different directions. Her mother's heart was broken, her sister's life destroyed. *Thank God*, she thought, *my dear father is not alive to see this.*

The word spread about the star quality of the rescued portrait Hamish created of and for Lady Buchanan. The staff on the estate heard from a talkative domestic in the Big House and soon the news leaked into the local public house and, well, from there it travelled extensively except New Zealand and Tierra del Fuego. Fortunately, the painting and its return was the sole topic of conversation. Thus far, news about the daughter fleeing remained a secret.

The following day, Lady Buchanan received a letter from the local minister. He expressed concern at Her Ladyship and her daughters' absence and hoped all were well. He finished with an offer of support should it be needed.

Far from being helpful, Dunbar's letter drove Elspeth deeper into misery. Worry about her daughter was bad enough but to have the scandalous action made known would crush the spirit of the now wretched mother.

Invitations to the portrait unveiling were posted and acceptances began arriving. How could the event go ahead? People would ask about the absent Bonnie and wonder why the lady of the house looked so pale and drawn.

Of Bonnie, the excuse or explanation could be, 'Oh, she's come down with a terrible cold and is confined to her bed.'

It was all too much. Elspeth needed help and the only person she believed she could trust was the Reverend James Dunbar. She knew him to be discreet and better still, he enjoyed a close relationship with the brilliant young artist, Hamish McKay. She invited the minister to call.

Chapter 22
I don't suppose you have a bottle of fine English gin in your trouser pocket.

Hamish's latest idea kept him awake at night. Unwilling to discuss it with James Dunbar weighed on the young artist's mind and heart. As his mentor left to visit Lady Buchanan, Hamish left to visit Fitzroy Arbuthnot.

Hamish didn't knock on the cottage door. It looked like a good knock would cause it to die. Instead, he called.

'Hello, Mr Arbuthnot, it's me, Hamish.'

The sound of crockery—unwashed of course—hitting the floor accompanied by groans and the odd belch or fart was heard.

'Wait!' cried the old man and Hamish was pleased the homeowner was in. The thought occurred he'd never known Fitzroy to be out.

Under protest, the door creaked opened, and Hamish was given a warm welcome.

'I don't suppose you have a bottle of fine English gin in your trouser pocket,' he said.

'I'm afraid not, sir.'

'Even cheap English gin would do.' Hamish shook his head genuinely disappointed to leave the man befuddled. 'Never mind. I'm delighted to see you, laddie. Been on my own since that mongrel tenant rode off on his high horse in high dudgeon.'

'I don't think he'll be back any time soon, sir.'

'Oh yes, meaning?'

Hamish told Fitzroy the whole story from the fire, theft, fight in the gallery, fake portrait, recovery of the real item and arrest with the former tenant being marched away to a cold and miserable cell.

The old painter's mouth opened and kept opening. In-between the tale, Fitzroy muttered, 'No!' and 'Never!' several times.

'Let me put the kettle on, sir,' said Hamish and entered the battlefield erroneously described as the kitchen.

When they settled and sipped a brew, Fitzroy became interested. 'So, what is your latest project, young man. Tell me about your choice of colours, subject, your sketches and how you plan each brushstroke.'

Hamish loved talking art with someone who knew so much. He told him about the commission to paint Sir Richard.

'And you say he's not sitting for you?'

'The portrait is meant to be a surprise.'

'I'd give the wife a preview.'

'It's his sister, sir.'

'Her too. You must satisfy the one paying. Damn the recipient. They can like it or lump it. The patron's your god.'

Hamish lapped up the advice before changing the subject. 'I need your help, sir.' Fitzroy purred. He was old, dying, couldn't find the energy to paint but to be sought out, to be recognized as a man of wisdom on matters artistic, that plucked at his heart strings.

'Ask away, me lad.'

'I have an idea for a large portrait.'

'How large?'

Hamish needed to think so stood and used his body. 'About this high,' he said indicating a foot or so above his head, 'and about this wide.' He spread his arms.

'That's big.'

'I need to paint in secret and cannot do so in my current studio. I was wondering if I could paint in your woodshed.'

'Nah,' said Fitzroy struggling to stand and leave the room. 'You can paint in my studio. Come on.' Hamish followed bubbling with excitement. In the paint-splattered studio, Fitzroy pointed. 'You can have that big, old canvas. I'll never need it.'

Hamish stood dumbfounded. 'Sir, I do not know what to say.'

'Start stacking all those old paintings and set your big masterpiece against yonder wall. Better light if you're stood facing there.'

Hamish was gifted the perfect place to paint and looked at the large canvas covered with various attempts at creating he knew not what. Talk about landing on his feet. Now a hurtful thought struck.

Am I going behind the back of the Reverend Dunbar, the man who gave me my start and has helped and promoted me? How will he feel if he discovers I have a second patron?

He decided. *I will tell him when next we meet.*

That first patron arrived at Buchanan Hall and greeted her Ladyship in the library. They were alone.

'Thank you for coming, Mr Dunbar. I have a delicate problem and would ask for your absolute discretion with the details I divulge.'

The minister could not have paid greater attention. 'That goes without saying, my Lady.'

She trusted him, needed advice, and jumped in at the deep end.

'My daughter, Bonnie, has run away with a man she barely knows.'

He paused before speaking with a soft and sympathetic voice. 'I'm sorry to hear that, my Lady.'

Elspeth needed to talk knowing Dunbar to be an excellent sounding board. Off she went into detail she hated but needed to get off her chest.

He promised to pray for the safe return of Bonnie and would call again soon with any news he may have heard. His suggestion about not inventing an excuse for the Buchanan ladies attending the kirk one short, so to speak, appealed to Elspeth. Amid her turmoil, she enjoyed a sliver of peace.

'I recommend you continue to live your life as you have always done. Worship on Sundays as you have done, and if anyone asks after your wee girl, simply tell them the truth.'

Elizabeth gasped. 'Tell them she's run away and living with a man to whom she is not wed?'

'No, my Lady, say only she's gone away. It's the truth and it's nobody's business but thine. Be brave and I'll do all I can to discreetly find Bonnie and will certainly keep you informed of any news.'

Elspeth enjoyed a warm feeling of relief. Sound advice is often hard to find and here it came from a wise and generous man.

They relaxed as he spoke of Hamish's latest portrait where it was Elspeth's turn to promise to say nothing.

'Oh, Sir Richard will be delighted,' she said. 'Of course, another problem I have is the unveiling of my portrait. I am in such a state, to go-ahead would-be counter-productive. What can I say in asking Sir Richard to cancel the event?'

James pondered the issue. 'You might care to wait until the last moment in case your daughter makes a miraculous return.'

Both were unsure and she again expressed her gratitude. After he left, she decided to cancel her portrait's unveiling. Once was bad enough, twice depressing. Bonnie's departure was all too much. She wrote to Sir Richard requesting the cancellation advising it was due to a family crisis.

Next Sunday, Elspeth and Morag arrived at the kirk looking as normal as possible. Internally they were a mess. Worshippers wondered where the bonny daughter might be. Nasty gossipers guessed she might have run off with a dashing young cad. If only they knew.

After the service, the minister greeted the two Buchanan women in his polite fashion. The missing daughter was never discussed.

In the afternoon, James made his way to the shed in his garden. Inside the painter could be seen busy with a paintbrush.

'Ah, the artist at work,' said James stepping inside.

'Good afternoon, sir. I hope you won't object to my painting on the Sabbath, but Sir Richard's special day draws nigh, and I need to get a wriggle on to finish the portrait.'

'Perfectly understandable and I think the subject, his sister and all who see the portrait will be delighted with your work.'

'Thank you, sir.' He hesitated. 'I need to tell you something, sir. A hesitation as this sounded serious. 'I have decided to paint another portrait, a rather large painting, too big for your shed, and have asked Mr Arbuthnot if I may do so in his woodshed, the outbuilding.'

James was aghast. 'No! You can't. You mustn't. It's full of rats and spiders and the weather's worse inside than out.'

'He kindly offered his studio and even provided me with the appropriate large canvas.'

James changed in an instant. 'Oh, how wonderful. May I ask about the subject of your portrait?'

'Of course, sir, but I'm still trying to work out a few issues. Once I do so, I'll be happy to fully explain the situation.'

'Good fellow. Well, I'll leave you to get on.'

Chapter 23
Mother, I must tell you something.

No moon tonight, darkness flooding the land, and the belting rain shifted towards the horizontal. The carriage moved along the Buchanan estate driveway. The driver wore good protective clothing, the horse wore a bridle. It whinnied when pulled to a halt at the front door. Mind you the front door was a cricket pitch from the driveway.

Wearing a long cloak and hood, a passenger stepped out and dashed through the rain to bang on the door. The bell press joined the ruckus.

Fraser appeared in his night attire complete with cap. Alone in his bedroom, the only person to impress was himself.

The front door opened, and the traveller pushed inside. Fraser thought he recognized the visitor and was about to close the door.

'Oi!' cried the driver. 'I ain't leavin' till I gets me fee.'

The butler's greatest attribute was his ability to never become flustered, until now. Finding a coin for the driver proved the simple part. Stepping into the Scottish weather in his silk pyjamas and dressing gown was a bridge way too far.

He returned with the money; held it aloft, placed it on the slate step and scampered. A roof is useless when the rain turns horizontal. Fraser disappeared.

The household was asleep, but door banging, doorbell ringing, and a shouting voice stirred folk from their slumber. Fraser looked around for the visitor and saw no-one. He heard noises and entered the kitchen. Bonnie Buchanan, looking a lot worse for wear, was stuffing cake and grapes into her mouth.

'My Lady,' said the butler hiding his surprise and shock.

'Where's the sherry?' she demanded.

Mrs MacDougal entered complete with hair in a myriad of bows. Fraser passed a glass of sherry to the new arrival and ushered the housekeeper from her domain. His face spoke louder than his words.

He whispered. 'All under control, dear lady.' She disappeared.

He panicked when he heard her Ladyship.

'Fraser? What's happening?'

Bonnie and the butler stared at one another. Now we're for it.

Elspeth entered, saw her daughter, and screamed. The mother acted like a mother, rushed to Bonnie, and embraced her, kissing her repeatedly. Morag entered and copied her mother.

'Fraser, please see Lady Bonnie's room is prepared.' He left. She called. 'Mrs MacDougal.' The housekeeper re-appeared. 'A hot meal please, soup and toast.'

Elspeth and Morag helped Bonnie from the kitchen. Elspeth called again. 'Have Mary light the fire in the snug and place a warming pan in Lady Bonnie's bed.'

Late at night, Buchanan Hall buzzed with food, fires, and feelings. As the fire crackled, Elspeth and Morag sat either side of Bonnie wanting to ask a multitude of questions but were frustrated as servants kept popping in and out. When alone in this the smallest of sitting rooms, Elspeth asked the most important of questions.

'My darling girl, are you all right?'

Bonnie nodded and found it difficult to speak being plied with food and beverages. She preferred not to answer as a shred of a conscience appeared, a feeling of guilt. First time for everything.

Conversation continued with Elspeth and Morag trying to explain their news not thinking their happiness only made Bonnie feel worse. Once food and drink were consumed and with heat from the fire filling the room, Bonnie came clean.

'Mother, I must tell you something.' The clock stopped ticking. 'I'm with child.'

She would have said, 'I'm pregnant,' but people of her class didn't use such flamboyant and unladylike language.

Elspeth found herself in unfamiliar territory. Becoming a grandmother was all new to her and when the grandchild might be illegitimate, well, what does one say?

With pauses and silences filling the conversation, Bonnie came clean. 'The father is dead.'

Elspeth exhaled and Morag swallowed. More questions begged to be put to the new arrival.

'And before you ask,' said Bonnie, 'we were not married.'

Elspeth showed her true colours. 'Well, my darling, the most important thing is you are back in the bosom of your family, you are safe, and we will care for you and your baby.'

'Hear, hear,' said Morag and squeezed her sister's arm—again.

Soon the pressure, travel, conscience and overwhelming love from her mother and sister became too much. Bonnie wept.

Morag escorted her baby sister, with unborn baby, into the long-abandoned bedroom helping her by pulling back the bedclothes, hanging up her clothes and adding more fuel to the fire.

With Bonnie in bed, Morag sat looking at her sister.

'When is the baby due?'

'Not sure.'

'There's something you can do to reduce the gossip and help Mummy who's been worried sick about you.'

Those last words hit Bonnie hard. She knew from birth her mother stood as a rock for both her daughters. Morag looked at her.

'When you go out, dress in black to show you are a widow carrying her child.'

'I won't be going out.' She turned her back on her sister who was going to tell Bonnie about a certain Finlay McLeish. Instead, Morag leant in, kissed her sister's head, whispered, 'Welcome home,' and slipped away. Bonnie's pillow was moist before she fell asleep.

When all the household retired, Elspeth lay in her bed unable to sleep. Her thoughts kept multiplying. One involved the father of the baby being dead. *Was he dead? According to Bonnie, he fell from a frightened horse and struck his head on a tree. Was Bonnie's explanation true? Did she discover his wicked ways and kill him herself? What is the state of her mind? If the father is dead, does this mean Bonnie can be passed off as a widow?*

Elspeth didn't so much care for herself but rather her daughter's reputation. If she was married, the scandal would fade.

Chapter 24
You haven't answered my question.

Sir Richard's birthday drew close. James Dunbar received a note from Sir Richard's sister enquiring about the surprise present, Hamish's portrait. A visit to his garden shed allowed the minister to assure her.

Naturally, Lady Buchanan and her daughters were invited to the soiree. Bonnie wasn't interested and Elspeth didn't push the matter.

From Elspeth, Sir Richard learnt about Finlay McLeish keeping company with Morag Buchanan. The McLeish family were acquaintances and so invited to Sir Richard's party. The guest list kept swelling.

James entered his garden shed for a final viewing. Hamish became a fusspot wanting to repair or improve what, to James, appeared minor, even minutely small imperfections.

'It's brilliant my friend,' said the minister staring in wonder. 'The birthday boy will be speechless. And now you can even frame your own paintings.'

'With help from dear old Fitzroy. Now, what's the procedure?'

'Miss Harriet has arranged a carriage to collect us and the gift, and we are to arrive at the tradesman's entrance no later than 12 noon with the portrait wrapped as if it were the Crown jewels.'

'That sounds hush-hush.'

'Indeed, now tell me, how is your huge project at Fitzroy's place? Have you made a start yet?'

'Not yet, only a brief outline. I have serious doubts and think I may have overestimated my ability.'

'Never, and my curiosity runneth over.'

Bonnie's bump showed. The servants rarely saw her. Elspeth and Morag were in and out of her new bedroom on the ground floor always trying in a low-key way to boost the expectant mother's spirits.

Elspeth worried about Bonnie's state of mind and shared her concern with Morag. Bonhomie inside Buchanan Hall at this time didn't appear or, if it did, it was contrived.

The day of Sir Richard's birthday celebration dawned. Elspeth and Morag were glad to have a reason to leave the house. A midwife from Edinburgh arrived and was put up in one of the servants' bedrooms. She was an elderly woman who had delivered countless babies with mothers from various classes of Scottish society.

Elspeth would not leave the estate unless the midwife was in residence.

The Buchanans arrived at Sir Richard's stately home to be greeted by the host and his sister. She gushed even more than usual leaving the Buchanans to wonder if she may have imbibed before the luncheon.

Finlay and his parents were there and after greetings, the young man led Morag into the garden.

'I've missed you,' he said and kissed Morag gently on the lips.

'Finlay, I have some news you should hear.' He sensed something important was brewing.

'Does it concern your sister returning home?'

Morag reacted. 'I was unaware you knew.'

'News travels fast in the countryside. I hope you and your mother are delighted. Is your sister well?'

'She is and with child.'

He looked startled as if his beau had slapped his face. 'Oh, and is she married?'

'Sadly, the father is dead.'

'You haven't answered my question.'

In an instant, the mood changed. Before she could reply, a gong sounded signalling luncheon and in they went, neither speaking.

Twenty-six guests sat around the magnificent dining table with Sir Richard at one end and his sister, Harriet, at the other.

As food and wine was consumed by the guests, a small carriage with two male passengers and one unique birthday present stopped near the stables at the rear of the house.

Harriet was nothing if not a perfectionist. She would have made a fine military officer with her planning and issuing of orders.

The ghillie followed her instructions to a T. Dunbar and Hamish were fed like noblemen albeit outside the kitchen. Once the meal inside ended, it was time for speeches.

The covered portrait finished its final journey being collected by two chosen members of the estate staff dressed as if going to a wedding.

The artist and his patron entered the main house and were required to wait in the hallway. Harriet's timetable worked a treat.

She stood and tapped her glass. The guests knew she was the power behind the throne and Sir Richard relied on his sister not only for the running of the house but for all his career and social activities.

'My Lords, Ladies and Gentlemen,' she addressed the attentive guests. 'And of course I should add Friends as you are all here to help celebrate my dear brother's birthday.'

Outside, James and Hamish could hear smatterings of laughter and the odd words from speeches.

Harriet knew the importance of brevity and concluded by wishing Sir Richard a happy birthday and announcing the cue.

'For you, dear brother, a special gift.'

She gave two rapid hand claps, the dining room double doors opened and two staff entered with the covered portrait which was placed on a small empty table. She spoke to her astonished brother.

'Feel free to unwrap your gift, Dickie.'

Her nickname for him spoken aloud only added to the intrigue and expectant atmosphere. The birthday boy looked uncertain as he walked to the present. He lifted the cloth and stepped back in shock. He raised the portrait showing it to the guests and a loud gasp raced around the room before spontaneous applause erupted.

In the hallway, James and Hamish looked at one another and each made a face.

Another member of staff entered carrying an easel and Harriet took the portrait and placed it there.

'Now to another important person, may I introduce the artist who painted this marvellous portrait.' She raised her voice and spoke to the hallway. 'Mr Hamish McKay.'

Outside, Hamish wasn't sure what to do. James was a part of Harriet's grand scheme. He led the artist to the door and ushered him inside. A loud and long burst of applause filled the room. Hamish was stunned. People smiled at him, and called, 'Bravo' as the applause continued. Harriet beckoned to James.

He stepped forward on her announcement. 'And here is the artist's mentor, the Reverend James Dunbar.'

More applause and people mingled. Many wanted a closer inspection of the portrait and to shake the painter's hand. Elspeth joined Sir Richard.

'Welcome to the club, Sir Richard.'

His smile revealed his happiness. He was thrilled with his surprise. She wanted to reveal her family situation but knew now was not the time.

The party was a tremendous success, but the star was the portrait. Guests wanted to speak to the young man. Others went outside to the garden.

Finlay wanted to speak with Morag and took her aside.

'My parents have a cottage by the coast. Your sister could live there and raise the child away from prying eyes. And there are baby farms where people are paid to raise illegitimate children.'

'Thank you but no,' said Morag, repelled by even the mention of a baby farm. 'We have decided the baby will be raised at Buchanan Hall by its mother, grandmother and aunt.'

Puzzled, Finlay pressed ahead. 'But the risk of a scandal, of your family's name being ruined is too great. You must remove the child and its unmarried mother from public view. It's what people of our class do.'

'But how is that helpful to my sister and her baby?'

Finlay twigged. The penny dropped. He'd made a huge mistake courting this woman. He realized he'd escaped a dreadful match by a whisker. What a relief. His blank face said it all. He turned and walked inside.

Morag found her mother talking to Sir Richard and the daughter's eyes told her mother they should leave. Elspeth made her excuses and led Morag outside.

'I need a moment, my darling,' she said, and Morag waited in the hallway. From out of the crowd, Hamish approached.

She smiled and nerves prevented him from doing the same. 'Mr McKay, congratulations,' she said. 'Not one outstanding portrait, not two but three. Your brilliant reputation is rightfully spreading.'

'Thank you, my Lady.' He paused. 'I hope you'll not think me presumptuous, but I would like you to accept a small gift in appreciation of the kindness you and your family have shown me.'

From his pocket he produced a small package, beautifully wrapped. She hesitated before accepting.

'Thank you, sir. You are most kind.'

This time he did manage to produce a smile before turning to leave as Lady Buchanan approached.

'Mr McKay is leaving?'

Morag slipped the package in her handbag. 'Yes, Mother.'

'I couldn't find Finlay or his parents.'

'Don't worry, I said goodbye for you.'

Elspeth studied her daughter and knew two things. Morag wanted to leave and something important or serious had recently happened.

Chapter 25
A terrifying scream echoed through the house.

In their carriage, Elspeth knew not asking questions was the wisest approach. She talked about the portrait, Harriet's speech and Sir Richard's reaction to his present. Morag kept her troubles to herself.

Once home, mother and daughter made their way to Bonnie's current bedroom. They knocked and entered and found the midwife examining the would-be mother.

'What's happened?' asked Elspeth hurrying to the bedside.

'Nothing, my Lady,' announced the elderly woman having done what she had now done more times than she could remember. 'All the signs are pointing to a perfectly normal birth.'

Mother and sister waited until the midwife finished her examination and departed before moving to either side of Bonnie.

'You missed a remarkable party, my darling,' said Elspeth. 'That young artist from the village has produced another outstanding portrait. Mr Dunbar, Sir Richard and I are all incredibly lucky.'

Bonnie showed no interest in social matters or art, and mention of that damn artist sent her blood pressure soaring. Morag tried to get her sister talking.

'So, what will you call the little one? What if it's a boy?

'Rumpelstiltskin,' said Bonnie without a trace of irony. Mother and sister could see any further discussion would do more harm than good so chose to leave. As they walked away, Bonnie called.

'And if it's a girl, Elspeth.'

Her response stopped the visitors. They looked at one another. Elspeth used her head to indicate they should keep walking. At the door, Elspeth called. 'Get some sleep, my darling,' before both left.

In her room, Morag placed her handbag on the dressing table and stopped. She'd forgotten the gift from Hamish McKay. She removed and unwrapped the item covered in paper and tied with a ribbon.

Did the artist wrap this item? He is a shepherd and an artist; what a combination. What is it and why give it to me?

She discovered a small, flat box. Lifting the lid, her heart jumped. The contents were enclosed in a cloth bag. More intrigue. She loosened the bag and reached in for the contents.

It was an oval-shaped ornament, a large brooch. She turned it over and gasped. It was a miniature, a tiny portrait. Morag stared at herself.

The likeness was uncanny. She could not take her eyes off the face, *her* face. Beautifully painted. She asked herself a question. *Is it me?*

She searched the bag, box and wrapping paper. Nothing. No card or letter. She tried to remember what Hamish said when giving her the item. At the time, her mind was a mess. Her beau, former beau, the man she once enjoyed walking out with, gave her family an offer she found offensive. The not-so-subtle message being, do not wash your dirty linen in public. Bury your unmarried sister and her illegitimate offspring far, far away.

Morag rebelled. No, no, such action was unacceptable. Her response shocked and repulsed Finlay. He walked away from her.

Now, something needed to be done about this miniature. It's beautiful. One thought was to show it to her mother but not her sister. Another thought was to put it away and only make it public when the time was right. For now, she would thank the artist. Sitting at her dressing table, she wrote.

Dear Mr McKay
I find it hard to describe my beautiful miniature. Your portraits of Mr Dunbar, my mother and Sir Richard have rightly been acclaimed by all who have seen them. But to me, your lovely gift has filled me with gratitude and will always hold a special place in my heart.
With every good wish for your painting career,
Yours sincerely
Lady Morag Buchanan

She did not know his address and didn't want to create a storm of gossip by handing an envelope to Hamish after a service in the kirk. She addressed the envelope to:

The Artist, Mr Hamish McKay
c/o The Reverend James Dunbar
The Manse
Church of Scotland
Crain

She sealed the envelope and went downstairs to hand it to Fraser who would arrange the postage. Halfway down the massive staircase, a terrifying scream echoed through the house.

Morag froze. It must be Bonnie. It happened again even louder. She took off not realizing she dropped the envelope.

More screams led her to Bonnie's bedroom. It could mean only one thing. Even with the bedroom door closed, Bonnie's screams were clearly heard. When Morag opened the door, the volume doubled. She ran to her sister who lay on the bed screaming. The midwife behaved in a calm and relaxed manner.

'Push, madam,' she said her face nowhere near Bonnie's. Morag clasped her sister's hand. 'I'm here, Bonnie, I'm here.'

Elspeth appeared and, on the other side of the bed, copied Morag offering words to try and help. The screaming got busier.

Morag decided she would never marry and thus never give birth. The relentless pain and suffering was … relentless. Who would choose to suffer such pain?

Mother and sister became assistant midwives mopping Bonnie's brow and constantly switching their attention from Bonnie to midwife and back to the mother to be.

'What can I do?' asked Elspeth desperate to help.

The midwife spoke without looking at Elspeth. 'Tell her she's not the first woman to have a baby.'

Bonnie switched from screaming to grunting, for her a new experience. She wondered if this was what she expected when she fled the family home with a man who smothered her with kisses and promises of eternal love which faded once he became bored.

The maid, Mary, entered performing a juggling act. She carried a bowl of hot water while balancing towels on her shoulder. Morag helped her.

Remaining calm, the midwife kept urging Bonnie to push. Fraser waited outside awaiting instructions. He would rather shoot himself than enter the room.

The longer the birth took, the more worried the Buchanan women became, although not the midwife who remembered an all-night and through to luncheon the next day session as her longest delivery.

It did happen and when it did, the birth was quick and simple if ever the word *simple* can be applied to childbirth.

'Well done, Missus,' called the midwife, 'well done.'

The baby cried aloud, the grandmother kissed the new mother, Morag cried soft tears, Mary clasped her hands and smiled, and, in the hallway, Fraser clenched his fists and performed some Highland dance steps remembered from his childhood. Bonnie swore.

'Congratulations, Madam,' said the midwife. 'It's a girl.'

The newborn was wrapped well and handed to Bonnie. For the first time in an age, she behaved like a human with a heart. She sat, propped up against the most expensive pillows in Scotland, cradling her baby.

Grandmother and aunt peered in to study the little one's face. 'She looks exactly like you, Mummy,' said Morag, meaning her mother. 'Bonnie, you chose the perfect name.'

No response from the new Mum. Bonnie saw her family staring at her. They wondered if she would revert to her cruel and self-destructive persona and give her daughter a different, even a silly name.

'You're right,' she said. 'Elspeth meet Grannie Elspeth and Auntie Morag.'

Chapter 26
Misery flooded his body.

Hamish attacked his large painting in earnest. For the first time, his sketch book filled with multiple ideas of the layout. Painting the face of one person on a small canvas presented challenges. A painting which was many times bigger, and with challenges galore, needed planning the likes of which he'd never performed. Had he bitten off more than he could chew?

He knew the way to his second studio blindfolded.

When he arrived, Fitzroy was usually asleep or in a stupor. Door knocking became unnecessary. Alma, Hamish's mother, always gave her son food for the elderly artist. When the old cottage owner "came alive," he would enter the studio and watch the young man in action.

'There's a rabbit stew in the kitchen, Mr Arbuthnot,' said Hamish.

'Aye but there's a mistake in your proportion there, lad,' he said pointing at the canvas. 'Come back here.' Hamish moved beside Fitzroy. 'Towards top left.'

Hamish saw exactly what was wrong.

'Thank you, sir. Is there anything else I might repair.'

'Nothing. It's looking interesting, full of mystery and intrigue, and I can't wait to see the finished picture.'

Hamish loved the challenge and even more so, the advice from a man who practised his art for decades. The only issue causing anguish for Hamish, apart from failing this painting task, was when to invite his original mentor to see the project. Nagging Hamish was his wish for secrecy. Telling no-one about the painting, other than Fitzroy, dominated his thinking.

Elspeth (the senior) knocked on Morag's bedroom door and entered. The mother sat on the bed and Morag knew she was in for a serious chat.

'How is Bonnie's feeding routine going?' asked Morag.

'She's still struggling,' said the grandmother. 'Every new mother meets challenges but with our love and support, I'm sure she'll become a wonderful mother.'

Morag knew this topic was the preliminary. To what, she wasn't sure.

'There's something I wanted to give you,' said Elspeth who produced an envelope. Morag moved to her mother and took it. Her mother patted the bed, and the daughter sat. She recognized the envelope. It contained the note she penned to the artist who gave her the gorgeous miniature portrait.

'I wondered what happened to this.'

'I found it on the stairs when I came down for the baby. As you know, we've been preoccupied with another certain matter.'

Morag's mother would never intrude on her daughters' privacy, but curiosity got the better of her. Why was her daughter writing to the artist?

Morag went to her dresser, took out a small box and handed it to her mother.

'This will explain the letter inside the envelope, Mummy.'

Elspeth opened the box and discovered the miniature. Her eyes widened as did her mouth.

'It's beautiful.'

'Mr McKay gave it to me at Sir Richard's party. I didn't open the present until we arrived home and, like you, because of Bonnie and the baby, I put it aside.'

'It's exquisite. It must be difficult to create something so lifelike in such a tiny space,' said Elspeth who became serious. 'If this is a token of his affection, my darling, you need to be careful when being courted by two suitors.'

The women looked at one another. Morag decided to tell all. 'Mr McLeish and I are no longer courting.'

Elspeth wondered why Morag took so long to tell her. No woman is keen to reveal she's been rejected, told she is no longer desirable, and when an unmarried sister gives birth, the relevance of the former topic loses its importance.

'Why do you think Hamish gave me the miniature?'

'I should have thought it was obvious.' Elspeth kissed her daughter's hand and gave her back the miniature. 'Like you, it's beautiful.'

The huge painting took shape. Hamish's confidence crept higher. Fitzroy gave praise in a low-key way. He loved the talent of the young man and reckoned he could die happy by giving him the space and the encouragement the lad deserved.

James Dunbar stopped asking about the project. In time, the minister heard about Bonnie's baby and offered his services to baptise the infant in the kirk or at home.

'It need not be a public event, Lady Buchanan,' he said when paying a visit.

'Thank you, sir. My daughters and I will let you know what suits everyone the best including yourself.' He nodded understanding the delicacy of the matter.

'Tell me, sir,' continued Elspeth, 'what news do you have of Mr McKay? As you know, his three portraits have caused a minor sensation in the county. Is he at present painting someone you know?'

James paused. If he said yes and couldn't explain a thing, not even the smallest hint, he would look foolish. If he said no, he would be lying. He took the middle ground.

'I'm not sure, my Lady, but will make enquiries and let you know.'

He realized he copied her by using the phrase, "I will let you know."

On the walk home, he determined to press his protégé about the work being created in Fitzroy's cottage.

That protégé walked with a spring in his step en route to Fitzroy. The massive painting took shape and the praise from his second mentor fired his heart. A positive reaction to this work from those in his orbit would mean the world to him.

He'd long stopped knocking on the Arbuthnot cottage front door instead using the unlocked kitchen door around the back. He would call out when he entered.

'Hello, Mr Arbuthnot, it's Hamish.'

Sometimes the old man would call back, and other times Hamish could hear the snoring and would navigate the rubbish tip, previously known as the kitchen, and make his way to the studio. Today it was snoring sounds, so Hamish got busy painting.

After about half an hour, he stood back to get a proper view of the entire work. His heart kept telling him it was good, but he desperately wanted the old man's honest opinion, and blessing.

Fitzroy lay on the sofa in the next room, the sofa being older than its occupant. Hamish approached and called. He needed to be loud to wake the old bugger.

'Mr Arbuthnot, I may have finished.'

No response so Hamish did what he'd done before and gently shook him. 'Sir, it's Hamish, sir.'

Fitzroy lay still, as still as a corpse can be. Hamish fell on his knees and put his face close to the artist whose pickled liver refused to die even when his heart stopped beating.

The old man's eyes were open and facing the studio. Hamish moved to one side allowing Fitzroy's vacant stare to see the painting.

'This is your work as much as mine,' said Hamish in a normal voice. 'You gave me the studio, the canvas, and the advice to create this work. Your name deserves to be on the painting as much as mine.'

Fitzroy didn't reply and Hamish found it tricky to see the former painter's expression as liquid blurred the young man's vision. He remained on his knees, weeping and saying nothing. He discovered life could be cruel. He wanted his friend to see the final creation. He needed the old man to help him frame the painting.

Hamish lost track of time and when he pulled himself together, he tried to close Fitzroy's glassy eyes. He struggled and failed. He found an old sheet, last washed when Queen Victoria was crowned, and draped the material over the body.

In the studio, he stood on the small stool he used when painting the top part of his canvas, and, using his Mahl stick, hoisted the soft cloth, another gift from Fitzroy, to the top corners thus covering his latest work. He liked to think his greatest work.

Misery flooded his body. Forget the painting, he needed help for Fitzroy. He wrapped up well and the Scottish rain showed no mercy as he left, heading for the Reverend Dunbar and his advice.

The soaked artist knocked on the front door of the manse. Mrs Dunbar stepped back in shock and Hamish apologized.

'I beg your pardon, Mrs Dunbar. Is Mr Dunbar at home?'

She nodded and used her slim book of phrases. 'Please come in.'

Dripping all over the corridor carpet would never be approved by Hamish's mother, not that their rented cottage boasted any such floor coverings.

'Thank you, no, I'll remain here.'

She disappeared and her husband came from his study.

'Hamish, how good to see you even looking like a drowned rat.'

The young man's expression spoke volumes. James asked. 'What's happened?'

'Mr Arbuthnot's dead.'

'Oh dear. Where is he?'

'In his cottage.'

'Wait there, I'll fetch my things.'

He appeared dressed for a Polar expedition. Hamish could not get any wetter and off they went. Mrs Dunbar took the pot of soup off the fire. This was one of these expect-me-when-you-see-me situations.

Talking while walking could happen naturally but not when your uncovered mouth kept being filled with rainwater. They trudged to the cottage of the late Fitzroy Arbuthnot.

Inside, they removed their coats and Hamish stood beside the draped body. He worried the resident rat may have found an alternative food source.

James lifted the sheet showing respect and checked the old man was dead. Dealing with locals who died, often in their bed or armchair, was a regular event for the minister.

'I'll contact the authorities and have the undertaker collect the body. Fitzroy's been a good friend to you, Hamish.'

The young artist knew what was coming. Standing a few feet from his latest work, a massive work, he could hardly ignore the painting from the man who supported him from the beginning. To do so would be churlish, cruel, and pointless.

James looked at Hamish who nodded and spoke. 'This way, sir.'

They stood in the studio now dominated by the cloth-covered shape against the wall.

'Mr Dunbar, I apologize for keeping this work a secret.'

'There is no need for an apology.'

'Well, allow me to offer an explanation, sir. As you can see it's big, much bigger than any other work I have created. I was worried I would not be able to make it work and if it didn't work, the fewer people who knew, the less embarrassing it would be for me and those in the painting.'

'If you are trying to make me curious, you have succeeded.'

'Because it needs a special time and place to be made public, I would ask, sir, you say nothing until such a time occurs.'

'Of course.'

Hamish stood on the small stool and unhooked one corner of the cloth. It dropped but what was visible gave no clue to what lay beneath. The other corner was lifted and the cloth collapsed.

Dunbar struggled to speak.

Chapter 27
Behind closed doors, misery reigned.

Bonnie suffered. The sight of her baby became a constant reminder of how she believed, no *knew* her life was ruined. The stigma of an illegitimate child now rammed home her predicament. Her body lost its previous perfect shape. She was no longer an object of attraction. Going to parties and dances was now not unlikely but impossible. Who would invite a woman who ran off with a cad and ended up pregnant?

Her motherly task of feeding her baby became a challenge. It wasn't so much she couldn't but more she wouldn't. She didn't dislike the infant or wish it harm but wanted to be left alone with no responsibility for the babe. Depression swamped her body and mind.

Her mother and sister despaired. They would comfort and cajole the new mother. She would try feeding but misery struck her down.

The midwife was summoned and asked for advice. 'She needs a wet nurse, madam. I know two or three in the district. You'll have to pay of course but it's the only way the little one will survive.'

Elspeth agreed, of course she did, and a woman was hired who provided for her own children by feeding the babies of wealthy families. It was a long-standing practice going back centuries.

Bonnie wandered in the garden when her mother approached. 'Bonnie, darling, I know you fret about feeding little Elspeth, but I have great news. We've found a wet nurse who will help.'

The news created the opposite effect. Instead of it being a relief, Bonnie took it as a further insult.

'So, not only have I ruined my life by producing a bastard child, I'm now incompetent and thus unable to keep it alive.'

Elspeth wept internally, the physical pain from her despair now raw and soul-destroying. The grandmother kept the wet nurse away from Bonnie and only brought the infant to her daughter when a member of the family was present. The new mother was not to be trusted.

Buchanan Hall filled with sorrow. The impact meant visitors to the estate and trips from Buchanan Hall stopped. Morag no longer welcomed an admirer. Elspeth reckoned attending the kirk became an ordeal with all their pretending to be calm and happy. Worship stopped.

The minister knew enough of the situation to reckon if he tried to help, he might do more harm than good. It turned into a terrible time. At least his work kept him busy. Hamish's massive painting occupied his thinking as did the funeral of Fitzroy Arbuthnot.

Only a few locals attended. After all, the old painter was a hermit, a heretic and worse, English. Two elders approached the minister and questioned why the man was granted a funeral in the kirk to which he never came. And furthermore, why was he to be buried in our churchyard? No-one will ever visit his grave; no-one will pay for the headstone, and the space should be reserved for a faithful member of our congregation. Well? Please explain, Reverend.

Dunbar didn't see a distinction between various denominations and, using such logic, between theist and atheist; we are all God's creatures. Besides, he saw firsthand how much support the old painter gave to the young painter and wanted to farewell the aged codger in style. The minister wondered why he needed to explain compassion and charity to so-called fellow Christians.

Before the funeral, a small working party tackled Fitzroy's cottage. The undertaker removed the body, but a major cleanup and lockup was needed to stop thieves and rats running amok.

Hamish and a couple of locals, one with a horse and cart, joined James and all tackled the heavy workload. Two outdoor fires blazed as most of the furniture demanded destruction. Hamish removed Fitzroy's paintings and stored them on the cart. His large painting was the last to go with its cover now secured.

James prised open an old desk and collected Fitzroy's personal effects. Surprisingly, he found two ancient sketches among the papers, probably Fitzroy's parents, and bundled the lot into a hessian bag for a later inspection.

'Where shall we store the paintings, Mr Dunbar?' asked Hamish as they prepared to leave. 'Your garden shed is too small.'

'I've been thinking about that and may have the answer.'

Baby Elspeth thrived. Good fortune smiled upon the little one despite the history of wet nurses and infant mortality making terrible reading. Of the four Buchanan females, one was thriving, two were struggling and the fourth teetering.

Grandmother Elspeth made her regular visit to daughter Bonnie's room. This was not so much her duty but rather a fervent desire to help her daughter escape her mental and physical quagmire.

The usual light taps sounded, and Elspeth opened the door.

'Good morning, my darling,' she said but stopped when Bonnie was not in bed. She was rarely out of it. Elspeth panicked. The bed was perfectly made. In Buchanan Hall, bed making was an art form.

The large room provided a couple of possible hiding places and Elspeth looked around. Her heart stopped when she spied a white envelope against the white pillows. She cried as the envelope was opened.

Dear Mummy
I'm sorry to do this again but I can't bear the pain I have caused you and Morag.
I know you will care for the baby.
I have a friend in Edinburgh, and she will welcome me.
I will write once I am settled.
Your loving daughter
Bonnie

Elspeth collapsed on the bed and slid to the floor. Her weeping made no sound. Shocking thoughts filled her brain. She only snapped out of the trough of despair when Morag popped in on one of her regular visits.

She helped her mother to sit then read the letter.

'What I cannot understand is how she travelled,' said Elspeth. 'I mean she packs a bag and creeps away in the dead of night. How does she travel and where does she find the courage to do so?'

'You underestimate your younger daughter, Mummy. Your girl has determination to burn. She also loves her baby.'

Elspeth continued to struggle. 'Then why abandon her? How is that love?'

'She knows her family will always care for little Elspeth. She chose a name to please and honour you, her mother. We will care for the baby and raise it, and we will always hope for the day when Bonnie and her daughter are reunited.'

Morag moved to her mother and the women hugged and remained hugging until Mary knocked wondering if she could make the bed.

All the paintings by Fitzroy, plus the large one by Hamish, found a new home. They were slid underneath the kirk. The foundations left a space of about eighteen inches between the ground and the joists supporting the floor of the building.

'But sir, the damp will set in and ruin the materials,' protested Hamish as the minister used a hammer to remove the boards.

'Covers, young man. There are old curtains in my robing room, and I saved these covers from the fire at Fitzroy's. And it won't be forever. We'll sell Fitzroy's collection and use the funds to pay for his headstone. And your masterpiece will soon find a special place to be hung. Come on, let's get cracking.'

In his study, James removed the materials he collected from Fitzroy's ancient desk. He spread the papers and read. There were letters and receipts from dealers where the sums involved would never keep anyone in comfort. A few personal letters in which he was advised of a death in the family. Two deaths, his parents. The one important one was advising him of his paternal grandfather's bequest leaving the then middle-aged painter the cottage and a hefty wedge of cash.

A final envelope, buried under frayed receipts, caught his eye. This was a recent item without fading, whisky stains or mouse droppings. It was sealed and had never been opened.

A letter-opener slid the top and Dunbar withdrew the contents. The document was from a firm of solicitors in Upper Berkeley Street, Marylebone, London.

To say the minister was hooked would be an understatement.

He waded through the covering letter with the *Dear Sir*, and the *I remain your obedient servant* bits and studied the matter in hand—the last will and testament of one Fitzroy Benedict Arbuthnot.

It was short, straightforward and shocking. Briefly, Fitzroy's estate, the lot, the cottage, furniture, (what furniture?), paintings, paint, pigments, brushes, canvas and frames were left to Hamish McKay, painter, near the village of Crain, Edinburgh, Scotland.

Bloody hell!

To the outside world, life in Buchanan Hall was plain sailing. Behind closed doors, secrecy reigned. The wet nurse moved into the main house and the baby thrived.

Elsewhere, in the kitchen of the rented cottage occupied by George McKay, his wife and family, their shock was about to take wings.

James Dunbar arrived and asked Hamish if he might speak to all the family. They sat in the kitchen wondering why. No-one they knew had died. Hamish remained tight-lipped about his large painting and only three knew of its existence, and one of them was dead.

'I have something to tell you, Hamish, which will be of interest to all your family.'

'He's not in trouble, is he sir?' asked Alma, giving a typical mother's reaction.

'No trouble, Mrs McKay, quite the opposite.' Tension filled the room. James looked at Hamish. 'You have an estate, young man.'

The family gasped and Hamish invented a fresh look of confusion.

'I don't understand,' he said.

'Fitzroy Arbuthnot has made a new will and left his cottage, the land and all his possessions solely to you.'

The family buzzed. Hamish trembled.

'To me?' he gasped. 'All his paintings to me?'

'And the cottage and the land, enough for a smallholding.'

The buzz in the kitchen bounced off the walls with everyone talking before being stuck for something to say.

'I've made scones, Mr Dunbar,' said Alma. 'Would you like one?'

'I would indeed, Mrs McKay. In fact, I could go two,' said the minister and the cottage erupted with laughter and happiness.

Chapter 28
You don't own a suit!

The McKay family travelled together to Fitzroy's, now Hamish's cottage. The paperwork was incomplete, and a London solicitor explained in language no-one north of the border could understand, how probate was yet to be granted and challenges, if any, to the will were yet to be received. James Dunbar reckoned visiting the cottage would be all right although his knowledge of the law was shaky at best.

Off they went, soon to be no longer tenants under the control of some wealthy landowner, but free to live and work, hopefully, on their own piece of real estate.

George wandered the land checking on fences, water troughs and soil quality. He counted rabbits. Inside the cottage, the women checked the rooms with Hamish being told his studio was now a bedroom. These were fun and exciting times. The family McKay landed on its feet.

In terms of wealth, the family Buchanan long ago landed on their feet but now were impoverished with sadness. Bonnie abandoned her baby with the mother's whereabouts or health unknown.

Lady Buchanan took to her room. Her granddaughter thrived and appeared content even happy. She brought a sliver of joy to the household.

A letter from Mr Dunbar offering to baptize the infant in a private service, if required, occupied Elspeth's mind.

'I think you should agree, Mummy,' said Morag.

'Yes but who will we ask to be godparents? We have the minister and the infant but where are the parents let alone the godparents? It will be the talk of the county with us a laughingstock.'

'Do we have to have godparents?'

Elspeth looked at Morag and despaired. Even non-church-going folk knew a baptized baby required both a godmother and godfather.

Morag's mind kept spinning. 'Could I be the godmother?'

This time Elspeth stared at her daughter and saw light at the end of the tunnel. 'Of course you can, but who could be the godfather?'

'Sir Richard?'

'He's forty years your senior, my darling.'

'Would you consider Mr McKay? He is much younger and a highly respected member of our community, and his art can be found in our home.'

Elspeth paused. She craved recognition and respectability for her granddaughter. Could Morag's suggestion be the answer? The child was much loved and needed the best start in life.

'I'll write to Mr Dunbar and ask his advice.'

James replied agreeing to visit. He went to the original McKay cottage and found Hamish still living with his family on their rented smallholding.

'Lady Buchanan has asked me for advice on some family matters. Do you want me to see if she's willing to unveil your wonderful painting?'

'But won't she want to know the subject?'

'She may but if she learns it is an important historical record of the area, she might be persuaded.'

Hamish so wanted this painting to be successful. He couldn't bear to fail after his success to date. 'But what if it doesn't appeal?'

'You can't leave it under the kirk forever, young man.'

The painter nodded and settled in for a nervous wait.

Lady Buchanan welcomed the minister and explained the latest situation with Bonnie. 'I'm afraid my daughter has found the whole business of raising a child to be overwhelming. She has gone to a friend in Edinburgh and the family has taken over the care of little Elspeth who, I'm delighted to say, is thriving.'

'She couldn't be in better hands,' said James. 'Would you like me to conduct an infant baptism service here at Buchanan Hall?'

'Oh, would you, Mr Dunbar? That would be the perfect solution.'

'Consider it done.' He looked for an opening as to how he could persuade Lady Buchanan to unveil Hamish's largest painting. She gave the minister the cue.

'My daughter, Morag, has volunteered to be the godmother and I was wondering if your friend, the wonderful young painter, Mr McKay, would consider taking the role of godfather.'

James purred. He thought the suggestion splendid and said so before following on from Lady Buchanan's mention of Hamish.

'As it happens, my Lady, Hamish has recently completed a new painting and is seeking a venue and suitable person to unveil it.'

This threw her. 'Oh, well, surely the person in the portrait would be better suited.'

'It's a much larger painting than Hamish has ever produced, and your magnificent home would be the perfect setting for the unveiling, my Lady.'

'But the subject of the painting?'

'It's not a portrait like his previous work and I'm told it has some important historical record of the area.'

What could Elspeth say? She agreed and after consulting her diary, the one which currently was devoid of any engagements, they chose a date and time for both the baptism and painting unveiling.

'I can give Hamish a run down on his role as a godfather and you will have your granddaughter formally welcomed into the church.'

Elspeth smiled for the first time in an age.

The biggest shock came when Hamish was told details of the launch of his major work of art only to have a second piece of news top it. He was requested to become godfather to a child he'd never seen.

He told his family who offered a mixed reaction. His father reckoned the whole idea suspicious. 'What's the son of a penniless smallholder doing mixing with nobility?'

'You don't own a suit!' worried his mother.

His growing sister reckoned she knew what was what. She spoke with a cheeky grin. 'It's because you're now a wealthy landowner, Hamish, that's why they picked you.'

The potential godfather role worried him but not as much as his new painting. What would people think?

The weather smiled on the big day which helped the carriers with the massive painting being transported to Buchanan Hall. The baptism and unveiling were set for two o'clock. Instructions were clear. The work of art must remain fully and safely covered until after the religious service. Hamish woke that morning to discover he was sweating. The pressure increased daily, hourly. *Me, a godfather, and how will the painting be received?* No wonder he perspired.

He came in for breakfast to be greeted by his mother commenting on his fingernails. 'There is no way on God's Earth you will be holding a wee baby with the dirt I can see from here, my boy.'

'Yes Mother,' he said starting on his porridge.

'And there's a letter come for you,' she said handing it over.

He stopped eating and struggled to open his mail. He looked up and saw the other three members of the McKay family frozen, staring at the artist.

'Any chance it'll be a cheque?' asked George.

'Do you want help reading it?' cheekily asked his sister, busting to know the news.

He studied the contents giving away nothing. He shook his head. 'Nah, it's a notice about this year's sheep and dog trials.'

The others knew he was teasing and complained as one. His whole body changed as he slapped the table giving his porridge a bit of exercise. He stood and announced. 'The probate thing's been granted, and the will's been approved.' He roared, 'We own the cottage!'

Let the celebrations begin. Moira danced, George and Alma hugged one another and drew Hamish into their embrace. The documents from London were studied over and over with the McKay family realizing it was true; they indeed had landed on their feet.

When the minister arrived to check on Hamish and give him final instructions on how a godfather behaves at a baptism, he soon learnt why the family were celebrating.

In the cart with the covered painting, now framed, the artist and the mentor were having words.

'Remember, young man,' said James, 'the baptism comes first and takes preference over the unveiling.'

'Yes, but the element of surprise is vital. I need to be sure the painting is in position, and nobody can touch it or the cloth covering.'

'It'll be fine. And when are you going to tell Lady Buchanan you've risen in the ranks?' Hamish looked confused. 'You're a fellow landowner, my friend, a member of the landed gentry.'

The young man grinned and liked the thought. Would he dare mention his new status to Lady Buchanan and her daughter?

They arrived, drove the cart to the rear of Buchanan Hall and waited on help from the staff. 'Gentlemen, please give Mr McKay a hand with this rather large painting and when finished, please send him to the library.' The covered portrait moved inside.

James set off with his clerical robes and implements for the service. He walked to the front of the house where Fraser welcomed and led him to the library.

The faithful servant tapped and opened the door. Lady Buchanan smiled and drew the minister inside. 'Thank you again, Mr Dunbar. You are so kind to come all this way and help my young granddaughter.'

'It's both a privilege and a pleasure, my Lady.'

'Morag is much looking forward to becoming the godmother to her niece.'

'Good afternoon, my Lady.'

'Good afternoon, Mr Dunbar.'

Elspeth struggled with her next question. 'I do hope you brought the baby's godfather, sir?'

'I have indeed, my Lady. He is supervising the delivery of his latest painting which we are delighted to have unveiled by you.' There was a tap on the door and Fraser entered.

'Mr Hamish McKay, my Lady.'

Hamish entered and moved to the others. Elspeth was all smiles. Not only did this young man offer to help her family but he produced outstanding works of art which were much loved by the recipients.

'Now you haven't meet my granddaughter, sir. Morag, if you'd be so kind.'

Hamish copped a mixture of emotions. Being a godfather and having his latest painting unveiled produced one type of excitement but being close to the young woman who set his pulse racing produced a completely different type of emotion.

Little Elspeth behaved impeccably.

'This is your goddaughter, Mr McKay,' said Morag. 'I'm sure the wee lass is thrilled to have you as her spiritual advisor.'

James had explained the role of the godparents and Hamish smiled and nodded. He found himself looking more at the baby's aunt than the baby.

'Well, if we are all here, let us begin,' said Dunbar.

He placed his materials on a small table and began the service.

Being in a private home and without a congregation, the service became intimate and moving. The minister spoke calmly and looked at both godparents when asking each a question. Lady Buchanan kept thinking of Bonnie, wondering where she was and how she would feel knowing her child was about to be baptized.

The minister held the infant and spoke, 'In the name of the Lord Jesus Christ, and in representation of Him, I now lay my hand upon you and commend you to the gracious care and protection of God through all your days and may His richest blessing rest and abide with you always.'

The service ended. Elspeth held little Elspeth with Morag on one side and Hamish on the other. There were smiles all round.

Lady Buchanan thanked the minister again and handed the infant to Mary the maid who put the newly baptised infant in her bassinet.

'And now Mr McKay,' said the grandmother, 'we all await your latest work. What an industrious young man you are.'

'Thank you, my Lady,' he replied not sure about the word industrious.

They headed to the hallway and walked to the main sitting room. Hamish spied the broom cupboard wondering if the child's mother was hiding therein.

He was the last to enter the large room and immediately looked to see if his painting remained in place with its cover.

James and Hamish had rehearsed the routine. 'If you would be seated here, ladies,' said the minister indicating two chairs placed in front of but back from the covered painting. They sat and waited. 'I have asked the artist to say a few words.'

Hamish moved in front of the cloth. 'My Ladies, I have much enjoyed the great pleasure of visiting your wonderful home and garden and being able to paint both of your images. A few months ago, I received help from Lady Morag and her words inspired me to create this latest painting. It is something new for me being of such a size. I do hope it meets with your approval, and I will be honoured, Lady Buchanan if you will now unveil the painting.'

Hamish had rigged the cloth so a tug of a cord attached to one side would cause the cloth to fall.

Both women were fascinated. Morag couldn't think how she may have inspired this painting. And what or who was the subject? It must be an enormous head to take up such a space.

Elspeth took guidance from Hamish as she reached for the cord. James and Hamish stood back holding their breath; not concerned about the quality of the painting but rather if the simple knots would unravel and see the cloth collapse.

The cord was gripped, she paused and gave it a gentle tug.

Chapter 29
The lady of the house embraced and kissed him.

Morag gasped. Lady Buchanan was too close to the painting and to one side. She stepped back and stared. She stared at a painting of two people. A full-length portrait of Lady Buchanan was standing wearing a gorgeous dress with flowers in her hair. Seated beside her was her late husband wearing a Buchanan tartan kilt, and full Scottish regalia.

The men thought Lady Buchanan was about to faint. Dunbar moved towards her to offer support, but she stood strong and turned to Hamish. 'What have you done? *How* have you done that?'

'Do you approve, my Lady?' he asked with trepidation.

'Approve? It is the most wonderful portrait I have ever seen. It is simply perfect.'

Hamish came alive but nearly died when the lady of the house embraced and kissed him in a delicate and refined manner.

Morag followed her mother although her approach involved a longer and more enthusiastic move. Hamish was twice kissed.

'Oh, we must celebrate,' said Elspeth. 'Where's the bell. Fraser!' she called in a most unladylike way.

The Johnny-on-the-spot butler appeared. 'Tea, my Lady?'

'Later, come and look at this.'

Fraser stood before the painting with a shocked expression on his face. 'But that is His Lordship, my Lady.'

'Tell Mary and Mrs MacDougal to come and see.'

'My Lady,' said the disappearing butler.

'And bring *all* the staff!' she yelled.

Elspeth needed to sit and fan herself. It wasn't a fit of the vapours but seeing her late husband in such a clean and clear image, you could swear the people in the portrait were both alive.

'Tell me, Mr McKay, did you ever meet my husband?'

'No, my Lady, I saw him from a distance but never up close.'

'But how did you know his likeness? What you have created is as if he sat for you.'

'Well, in a way he did, my Lady. I was shown a portrait of Lady Morag's great-grandfather. She told me the gentleman was a striking image of your husband. I copied that portrait for this one.'

'How clever,' sighed Elspeth unable to take her eyes from the painting.

'Lady Morag was the key. She inspired me to create it.'

There was a lull in the room. No matter where you stood to study the painting, the characters remained relaxed but strong and beautiful. Yes, beautiful accurately described the couple, the Earl, Lord and Lady Buchanan of Buchanan Hall, Crain, Scotland.

It wasn't long before confused and curious members of staff—gardeners, stable hands, the ghillie of course, and domestics quietly entered the main sitting room.

What is happening? Are we really allowed into the main house?

Yes, they were encouraged to enter by the lady of the house. 'Stand over there,' she said like someone directing traffic. 'Now tell me what you see.'

'It's His Lordship, my Lady,' said one after another. Their praise flowed freely with the artist moving out of the limelight.

Refreshments arrived and Elspeth insisted on the entire estate workers staying to celebrate the arrival of the marvellous painting. Staff relaxed and a party atmosphere developed. Lady Buchanan came alive and revelled in the comments about her and her late husband.

Morag noticed the baby becoming restless so leaned into the bassinet to comfort the infant. James approached Hamish and nodded towards the recently baptized child.

'Go on, godfather,' he said, and Hamish hesitated. 'Do your duty.'

The painter pursed his lips and set off.

'Is the godfather required to assist?' he asked.

Morag looked up and smiled. Are you experienced in feeding and changing a baby?' Hamish gulped. She laughed. 'Your goddaughter needs fresh air. Would you pick her up, please?'

Talk about pressure. After months of work in secret, Hamish faced the possibility of his painting being rejected, and that was the stuff of nightmares. But this. This was a dozen nightmares worth of pressure.

He ever so carefully picked up the baby ensuring he supported her head, his mother's words bouncing around his brain. 'Always support the wee one's head, Hamish.'

'You're a natural, Mr McKay. This way to the garden.'

She opened a French window and led him outside. With the gardening staff living the grand life indoors, the trio stopped in the shade of an ancient oak tree, the illegitimate child and her godparents.

Morag continued. 'I'm not sure why but you have painted three members of my family, and we will forever be in your debt. You have helped my mother in so many ways.'

He gently swayed little Elspeth.

'I don't wish to embarrass you, Mr McKay, but in case you haven't been told, my sister has left Buchanan Hall, and her baby will be adopted by me and raised as my daughter.'

Hamish was in unfamiliar territory. 'You will make an excellent mother, my Lady.'

Morag reacted but it didn't show. 'I only mention this because, as wee Elspeth's godfather, you have a right to be aware of the situation.'

'Thank you,' he said and hesitated. 'If I can help in any way in raising the baby, I would be honoured to do so.'

She looked at him with a strong, fixed gaze. She was about to speak when interrupted.

Mary approached. 'My Lady, your mother is looking for Mr McKay.'

'He's coming, Mary. Please tell Lady Buchanan.'

Mary bobbed and left. Morag leant in and the baby passed from one godparent to the other. With the baby exchange in action, the godparents were as close as could be. They both looked at what they were doing and then, as one, looked at one another.

Their eyes spoke. They weren't listening but speaking.

'Hamish,' called a voice, it was the ghillie, and the painter gave his apologies and left.

Inside, a speech from Lady Buchanan about the artist finished with a rousing round of applause. It was time for his speech. He thanked her Ladyship and Mr Dunbar and mentioned Fitzroy

Arbuthnot. Not many knew who he was and fewer knew he was dead, but all now knew how much help he gave to the young man and his art.

Gradually the unveiling party wound down and staff, who could have slipped out through the French windows to the garden, chose the longer route getting to walk on carpet and stare at furniture, knick-knacks, and paintings en route to the back of the house and beyond.

Mary took the baby to Morag's room. Elspeth took James to the library to ask for advice regarding the baby being seen in public. Hamish wandered into the garden and saw Morag sitting on a bench.

He approached but stopped. 'May I join you, my Lady?' he asked.

She smiled, stood, and moved to him.

'My sister was always what you might call a forward woman. I am not so although right now, I am inclined to copy her.'

'May I say something, first?' She hesitated so he continued. 'I have always admired you, my Lady.'

'Please, not my Lady. You must call me, Morag. After all, we are fellow godparents and, I hope, friends, are we not?'

He tried to produce a smile as his heart became excited. It was his turn to hesitate. 'I would like to help you raise your daughter.'

'Of course you would, you're a kind and caring man.'

'I know I am from a poor, working-class family and cannot offer anything other than painting but …'

'I agree,' she said her eyes glowing.

He knew this speech backwards, had rehearsed it over and over, and didn't understand her interruption. He returned to the rehearsed script. 'Although I have little to offer …'

Again she interrupted. 'I will say "yes," Hamish.'

Now he was seriously confused. 'I'm sorry, Morag, I don't …'

'At the end of your speech, the one I keep interrupting, are you going to ask me to marry you?'

His jaw dropped but her smile told him everything. Forget the speech. She moved closer. He nodded. She spoke softly but with power.

'I accept your proposal and would love to marry you.'

It was his turn for eyes to shine. The speech remained unspoken as they embraced, their lips joining hesitatingly at first and soon becoming a fierce and prolonged kiss. They separated and stared at each other both excited and surprised.

'Is this really happening?' he asked trying not to look silly.

'I have loved you in secret ever since we met.'

'I don't know what to say,' he gasped wanting to shout his happiness.

Despite her joy, her feet remained firmly grounded. 'I think we need to ask the Reverend Dunbar to perform another ceremony.'

He turned pale. 'I think I must first ask your mother for permission to marry you.'

Morag threw back her head and laughed and he found a new way to love her.

Holding hands, they hurried inside and to the library. Morag tapped and opened the door. Lady Buchanan had recently unburdened her soul telling the minister about Bonnie abandoning the baby. The lady of the house was never so low. Her spirits hit rock bottom. The new painting with her late husband gave her soul a huge boost but the runaway mother continued to haunt her.

She and James looked up when the couple appeared. Elspeth politely asked them to come back later.

'We can't Mummy. Hamish has asked me to marry him.' Stunned silence. 'We are engaged.'

The wedding in the kirk could correctly be described as perfect. A marriage between the nobility and a commoner caused excitement. Gossip dominated conversations. With his bequest from Fitzroy, Hamish moved his parents and sister to the old cottage, and under his mother's decision-making, acquired a new suit. He scrubbed up well.

The bride and her mother looked exquisite. The Reverend Dunbar couldn't stop smiling. Sir Richard gave away the bride. Even Mrs Dunbar found herself chatting as never before. The wedding breakfast took place in the orangery at Buchanan Hall.

Departing on their honeymoon, the number of tears shed would have filled a small loch. During the despair over Bonnie came the joyous delight over Morag and her artistic husband.

Chapter 30

His wife, their children, and the glorious garden were all captured on canvas.

15 months later

Lady Buchanan stood by the window in her library. She admired the garden on a glorious summer's afternoon. Behind her on the wall above the fireplace hung the large portrait of Lord Buchanan wearing the tartan of his clan with his wife beside him. The painting was a constant source of comfort to the widow.

Outside she watched as Morag nursed Lady Buchanan's grandson, Michael George McKay, named after his grandfathers. Her granddaughter, also Elspeth, played with flowers and her doll at the feet of her aunt who adopted her niece.

A short distance away, Hamish McKay, stood beside an easel painting the scene. His wife, their children and the glorious garden were all captured on canvas.

Often, and especially at Christmas and on Bonnie's birthday, the family thought of the missing woman. Apart from a letter sometime after she left, the younger daughter and sister remained lost to her loved ones. Hope lived on awaiting her return.

Hamish would regularly visit his family in the cottage once owned by Fitzroy Arbuthnot. The elderly artist wouldn't recognize the place since the McKay family moved in and scrubbed and painted it anew.

Moira had an admirer and loved taking him to visit her big brother and his family in the cottage in the grounds of the Buchanan estate. The family line was now well established with Elspeth's grandchildren primed to occupy Buchanan Hall well into the next century.

Life continued and the once impoverished son of a farmer on a rented smallholding became an established artist. Commissioned portrait requests arrived causing an ever-lengthening waiting list.

The Reverend James Dunbar soldiered on. He continued ministering to his congregation. His children grew into young people capable of talking without hindrance.

One of the minister's happiest memories was of the local lad who enjoyed a talent for drawing and painting. Whenever a visitor called and sat in the minister's study, the portrait of the reverend gentleman stood out like a beacon.

'Oh, that was painted by a young man, a member of my congregation,' he would say never losing the pride he enjoyed in nurturing the extraordinary natural talents of one, Hamish McKay, the young man who found love from afar.

All Their Christmases

Chapter 1
No, it's the Loch Ness Monster.

In winter, Enrico Salvatore's wonky left hip gave him gyp and he cried. But the likeable codger refused to succumb to old bones. He hated carrying a walking stick but needed it. To show off, he popped it on his right shoulder and pretended to be the man who broke the bank at Monte Carlo.

Only his older widowed sister, Sofia, and a few lifelong pals called him Enrico, with his great nephews and former customers calling him Ric. His niece, Maria, called him Uncle.

The gent with Italian heritage, cut the hair of men and boys for half a century. His sister told everyone he was a hairdresser but Ric, who fussed exclusively over male heads, remained proud to be called a barber.

When Sofia and Enrico's elderly widowed mother died, Sofia took over the matriarch role and cared for her now 71-year-old "baby" brother. He was a rock-solid bachelor and Sofia decided he needed someone to keep an eye on him, supervise his medications, and check he hadn't died in the night.

'Is that you, Enrico?' she would ask when ringing every morning as soon as the 9am pips sounded on her radio. She used his land line not having a mobile herself.

'No,' he would reply, 'it's the Phantom of the Opera.' (Sometimes it was the Prime Minister, the Holy Father or even the Loch Ness Monster). 'How are you, Sis?'

'Did you take your tablets this morning?'

'Same question every morning and the same bloody answer,' he replied with more love than anger or impatience.

Sofia prattled on about her divorced daughter, Maria—divorce was a major no-no in Sofia's life. She sensed shame the event took place in *her* family. Enrico forever tried to persuade his sister she was living in the Dark Ages.

'Look at the Royal Family in England,' he would say. 'They have more failed marriages than you've made carbonara dishes.'

Maria's two sons, Enrico's great nephews, were strapping young men and their grandmother couldn't stop talking about them as well. Enrico loved his great nephews but reckoned they needed bringing down a peg or two.

He didn't like the way they treated their mother and grandmother or women in general. Women were sacrosanct according to great uncle Ric.

The young men started calling Enrico Ric as teenagers which didn't go down well at all with the retired barber. He wanted to say, 'Show a bit of respect, gentlemen,' but never did.

'Are you going to be Santa again this year?' asked Sofia.

'Of course,' replied her brother. 'I told you that when the agency contacted me last month.'

'But what about your hip?'

'What about it?' he bristled. 'It works well when I walk on the flat and is still perfectly attached to my torso.'

'Yes, but for how long?'

He wanted to tell her to mind her own business but knew he *was* her business. She knew better than to argue. His GP said a hip replacement procedure existed with his name written on it, and she worried because she loved him, because he lived alone, and because she wanted him to keep busy.

'Santa sits most of the time,' added Enrico. 'The children love to sit on the sitting Santa, and my jokes and smiles are getting better with age.'

They were and the Christmas gig was a major incentive for Enrico to keep on keeping on. Not having children of his own meant entertaining youngsters in December gave his heart a solid serve of happiness—it was the best medicine around. His eyes sparkled at the faces of the little ones who came to meet and speak with Father Christmas.

'Have you been good this year?' he asked each youngster. The ability of a child to say "yes" with confidence never ceased to fascinate him, and to look behind the child at the mother and sometimes the father or grandparent and see their expression and head shaking, was the icing on his Christmas cake.

'So, when do you start being Santa?' asked Sofia.

'There's a costume fitting next week where we meet the new Santas.

'You must be the oldest one there.'

'No, no,' he scoffed. 'There's a bloke who's 80 if he's a day and, would you believe, they're taking young men these days, blokes in their 40s, even 30s.'

'Are they?'

'And wait for it; they're introducing ladies as well.'

Sofia gasped. 'Father Christmas is a woman! Tell me it's not true. This wake thing is ridiculous.'

'Not *Father* Christmas, *Mother* Christmas or rather Mrs Santa. And it's woke not wake.'

'I think the world has gone mad.'

'It means I'll finally get to have a wife although only for about a month.'

He chortled and she muttered, 'It's madness,' before ending the call.

Enrico *had* forgotten to take his tablets so shuffled around his kitchen, found the pill box, poured a glass of water and swallowed.

Costumes 4 U, the agency which hired actors, people who wanted a few extra dollars over the holiday season, was run by CEO Miranda, who contacted all last year's Santas asking if they were up for another season. Email was a foreign language for Enrico, the computer-less ex-barber, so he received a text on his phone. Santa replied immediately and phoned Miranda.

'Lovely to hear from you, Enrico,' she oozed taking a genuine interest in her charges and especially polite ones such as Enrico.

They chatted with the enthusiastic Santa hearing his heart begin to sing.

'See you on the 15th, my dear,' she said signing off leaving Enrico to daydream to his heart's content.

It was a Thursday, shopping day for Enrico, meaning a trip to the local shopping strip. He wanted to venture forth with his cloth bag and stick but needed a few extra items so opted for his four-wheeled shopping jeep. Dragging a two-wheeled model did nothing for his dicky hip. This way he grew confident about his posture and set off with vigour.

The old shopping strip struggled, fighting for life. The ancient milk bar, fish and chippery, dry-cleaning and laundry, and the newsagent with limited post office facilities survived only because the closest huge shopping centre was far enough away, meaning many shopped local. The small, independent supermarket charged more than the big boys, but Enrico wasn't the only one who enjoyed having the owners greet him by name.

'Morning Enrico,' they called, and other staff greeted him with 'Buon Giorno, Signor Salvatore,' which set his ticker purring.

He approached the store when a young mother came out of the milk bar pushing a pushchair. She was Ms Fecund having a 3-year-old holding Mum's free hand, the one not controlling the baby conveyance. Its rear was packed with goodies because in the front was infant number two.

The sight impressed Enrico; two under three must be a handful. But no, the roll call was incomplete. Across Mum's chest in a sling or papoose-like device lay a sleeping new-born—*three* kids! That's a lotta nappies!

Enrico slowed to admire the convoy. How long did the mother take to prepare her brood for a trip to the outside world?

The walking child adored licking an ice-cream in a cone when disaster struck. Her enthusiastic tongue proved too strong, and the scoop of the yummy cold stuff climbed out of the cone, proved the theory of gravity to be true, and took a kamikaze dive splattering face down on the footpath.

The little girl's wail saw heads turn and concerned citizens move to see if help was required. Enrico had a front-row seat. No bones broken, no fingers squeezed, but 98% of her prized ice-cream stuck to the footworn asphalt. Mind you it was swept clean every morning.

Two pigeons waddled in keen to strike. The early bird gets the churn.

The retired barber disappeared as Mum tried to pacify the mortified offspring. Her siblings, including the one asleep, came out in sympathy and soon the neighbourhood discovered their representative in this year's Best Bawling Babies bash.

Of course, motherhood has always been a soda. All this current Mum had to do was pacify all three without dropping the newborn, keep the purchases aboard the vehicle, and set off for home. As stated, a soda.

About to depart, the upset family stopped because Enrico blocked their path. This became the final straw for the exasperated mother.

Enrico bent from the waist, in itself a major achievement, and smiled at the oldest of the crying trio. From behind his back appeared another ice-cream, this time a frozen confection on a stick.

The crying stopped in a nanosecond. As if by magic, the siblings followed big sis with the one in the push chair thinking, *Anyfing f'me?*

The knight in shining armour offered the confection to the little girl. Her dumbfounded mother spoke.

'What do you say, Lily?

The child knew the routine, said 'Thank you,' and accepted the gift. Her eyes sparkled and her tongue tackled a new task.

'Thank you, kind sir,' said Mum. She fumbled for her purse. 'Let me pay you.'

'Don't be silly,' said Enrico. 'You deserve it doing a brilliant job with such a fine-looking family.'

The woman smiled, looked massively relieved and set off. She turned back and spoke with a soft voice.

'You would make a wonderful Father Christmas.'

She and her kids departed with the former barber grinning inside and out.

Chapter 2
Mum, you won't believe this; Grannie's getting married.

Many relationships skip a generation and 20-year-old Phillippa loved her paternal grandmother, Rosie, to bits. The feeling was mutual. Both women sported red tresses with Grannie mixing hers with the odd splash of grey.

Pippa's parents too loved their only child but with father, Malcolm, a long-distance lorry driver, and mother, Anna, operating her own beautician and hairdressing business, their busy lives didn't allow for much of a family life. Pippa spent much of her childhood being babysat by Grannie.

Every Thursday afternoon, Pippa arrived at Rosie's maisonette straight from her performing arts' studies, and the two had dinner and one heck of a gossip. Mum, Anna, cut hair late on Thursday night, and Dad drove somewhere near the Victoria-South Australia border.

The redhead conversation covered a thousand topics.

'What happened to that boy you liked?' asked Rosie.

'Which one?'

'Don't be a smart-alec, and did you get that role in *West Side Story?*'

'No but he did.'

'A boy's playing Maria?'

More laughter. Both women had show business in their blood with Rosie involved in community theatre most of her life. She was long divorced from her husband and kept busy with a book club and running the wardrobe at her local amateur theatre company.

The laughter flowed over dinner but screeched to a stop when Grannie dropped a bombshell.

'Pippa, I need to tell you something.'

This sounded serious and Rosie's expression spoke volumes.

'You're not ill, Gran, please. I won't allow you to be sick.'

'It's nothing like that.' She paused like a good actor milking the moment. 'I've been to an audition.'

'What?' gasped a delighted and much relieved granddaughter. 'I thought you'd given up acting to work on props and costumes.'

'A *professional* audition,' she boasted.

'What?' The young woman gasped. 'You're going to be a pro?'

Rosie paused again beefing up the tension. 'I answered an ad to be Mrs Santa this Christmas at the Eastland Shopping Centre in Ringwood, and wait for it, I got the job.'

'Mrs Santa!' beamed Pippa giving her beloved relative a huge hug. The granddaughter was super keen for details. 'But what's it all mean?'

'I work with a Santa on a morning or afternoon for a two-hour shift. I help the kids who might fear Santa, help the photographer and generally keep the place spick 'n span.'

'You're a skivvy,' announced the young woman with anger.

'No!' replied Rosie rejecting the claim.

'You run around picking up after an overweight slob who probably earns twice your pay.'

'Actually, the money's not bad and you know I'm saving up for that cruise next year.'

Pippa turned serious. 'No, Gran. Mum and Dad both said you're not to go. People get sick on those cruises. Many of the old folk die.'

'Are you calling me old?'

'Now who's being silly?'

'But those cruises are full of sugar daddies desperate for a gorgeous redhead like me.'

They laughed without conviction and the conversation paused. It was time for coffee and talk of the proposed Pacific cruise had faded when Anna, mother and daughter-in-law, arrived to collect Pippa.

'Mum, you won't believe this; Grannie's getting married.'

Both older women gasped, Anna's mouth opened to Luna Park size and fortunately the wind didn't change. Pippa continued.

'She's marrying Father Christmas.'

It took a few moments for the joke to be explained with neither of the redheads raising the subject of Mrs Santa's salary or the fact it might be used to buy a ticket on an ocean-going liner.

Going home, the conversation in the car proved interesting, especially when Anna asked if her mother-in-law was still planning a seafaring holiday. Pippa lied, dodging the issue.

On her kitchen table, Rosie opened her laptop and perused the web site of the company which provided Santa and Mrs Santa to shopping centres. The company referred to her as Mrs Santa.

Rosie looked at the photos studying the model posing as her character. *'Do I look as good as she does?'* she thought and reckoned the costume looked okay, but as someone with a lifetime of making, repairing and adjusting costumes, she knew she could provide something better; much better.

She wondered if they offered her the Santa job because of her dressmaking skills.

She continued to surf and landed on a site for South Pacific cruises. Reading the marketing patter, it did sound enticing. She studied the cabin interiors, the dining areas, the deck facilities and the entertainment spaces. Watching professionals perform and especially wearing dazzling costumes, fired her heart. The thought of meeting a lovely gentleman crept into a back corner of her brain. Getting married a second time never dominated her thinking but as she aged—63 next year, no, 64!—the thought of growing old with someone she loved and who returned the emotion, had a nice ring to it. Mind you, Buster, her Staffordshire/Retriever cross, a rescue dog, gave back twice the love she showered upon him.

Rosie put up her hair, stood in front of a full-length mirror and acted.

'Hello young lady and what's your name? Oh, that's a lovely name. Have you come to meet Santa? Well give me your hand and I'll introduce you. Walk this way.'

Holding an imaginary four-year-old hand, she walked with care to an imaginary big chair on which sat an imaginary man with a padded tummy, black boots and belt, a red suit, white gloves, cap, and white whiskers big enough for a cat and her kittens to sleep in. Mrs Santa was off and running.

Chapter 3
A woman approached wearing enough makeup for two faces.

Goodies, junk and more goodies filled every cupboard, wardrobe and box in the HQ of the warehouse of *Cossies 4 U*. Of course, the company did more than supply Santa costumes and blokes, the actors who wore them. You couldn't run a business on one month's trading a year.

Costume hire was their bread and butter relying on people going to parties as characters from movies, being famous stars such as Marilyn Munroe, or gangsters or creatures from the jungle, or even masks of famous politicians who many thought came from the jungle anyway. The runaway most popular mask belonged to Donald J Trump who, it was thought, employed a couple of lackeys to chase down what he claimed were infractions of his copyright.

Miranda, the CEO of *Cossies 4 U*, knew how to run a business, how to influence people and how to complete any business deal with a profit. She fussed over the room to be used today for a meeting of this year's Santas—oh and not forgetting their theatrical wives.

Soon the actors arrived. Former Santas greeted one another. Newbies impersonated wallflowers and Miranda and her offsider, Sandra, flitted around welcoming everyone getting people introduced. The fact that women were present gave the older Santas something to talk about. The females added a touch of class even mystique.

'Come now, ladies and gentlemen, take a seat, if you would,' called Miranda clapping her hands. The mob, nobody knew the collective noun for a group of Santas plus their better halves, moved to the seating area. Was it a sleigh of Santas?

As in every meeting room in the universe, people avoided the front rows and chose a space towards the back. Hardly pushy, Enrico moved towards the front.

'Good on you, Enrico, remarked Miranda. 'Tell them we don't bite.'

He headed into the second row and faced two empty seats with the third occupied by a woman. He thought it rude to sit in the first seat as if shunning the lady. Their eyes met and he indicated the seat next to her. 'Is this seat taken?' he asked with the question never being selected for any quiz show ever invented.

She spoke softly, 'No', their smiles bumped into one another, and the former barber sat beside her. The chairs offered room for ample bottoms—we're dealing with Father Christmas here—and so those seated weren't touching. Pause. A longer pause.

To break the silence the woman looked at Enrico.

'I'm Rosie O'Donnell,' she said and smiled.

'Hello,' replied the slightly flustered Santa. 'I'm Enrico Salvatore and pleased to meet you, Rosie.'

People continued to settle, and Miranda prepared to get cracking.

'Are you an experienced Santa?' asked Rosie.

'A little,' he said. 'This is my third year although there are a few men who've been doing it for many years.'

'You obviously like it.'

'I do.'

'Well, this is my first time as Mrs Santa.'

'And I'm sure you'll be excellent,' he said relaxed and enjoying female company. Before they could continue, the boss called for order.

'Good morning, everyone and welcome to *Cossies 4 U*. If you're a newbie, then we extend a special welcome. Now first we have our housekeeping to tackle. Sandra will pass around the clipboards with a pen and ask you to fill in the details alongside your name. We're not breaking any Privacy rules only asking you to confirm your preferred location and times, and please note the pens are all boomerangs.'

A few Santas laughed out of politeness. Miranda's script was recycled every year with the jokes not even being funny the first time.

Clipboards appeared and people started ticking boxes.

Rosie finished confirming her preferred location and times and passed the clipboard and pen to Enrico. He dropped the pen, and both bent to pick it up causing a gentle meeting of heads. Oh dear.

Mortified, Enrico apologized as if his life depended on it.

'I'm so sorry,' he gushed. 'Are you okay?'

'I'm fine, no damage done.' She retrieved the pen. 'You'll need this.'

Feeling foolish, he scribbled his details and passed the clipboard to the swooping Sandra.

Miranda took over and, pointing to a whiteboard, went through her lecture. She revelled in her position as the professor of her tin pot academy. The oldies knew it all and a few newbies reckoned she was in love with the sound of her own voice. True, but she genuinely wanted her staff to be happy in their work.

After questions and more stating of the bleeding obvious, the meeting ended and the Santas were sent for a coffee while the females awaited their unique instructions.

'Enrico!' boomed Big Graeme slapping the smaller, former barber too hard on the back. Being a gentle man, Enrico was too polite to tell the one Santa he knew well to tone it down.

'How are you, Graeme? Keeping well I hope?'

'Fit as a Mallee bull, and not needing any of that imitation padding,' he laughed at his own so-called joke patting his XXXL waistline.

'You're a real Santa,' said a grinning Enrico alarmed at the added weight of his workmate. *'If my hip is suspect, his must be under enormous pressure.'*

Making sure the females were out of earshot; Graeme turned his back on them and whispered. Mind you a Big Graeme whisper could blow out a cake full of candles at a dozen paces. He continued.

'Now listen, mate, wotcha reckon about this Mrs Santa malarkey? Will they help us get dressed?' Enrico's discomfort level climbed. 'I fancy having a randy old bird checking my inside leg measurement.'

He guffawed and only another Santa butting in saved Enrico from saying or doing something which might have ended his Father Christmas career.

The women broke up and joined the men. It looked like one of those old-fashioned Saturday night dances where the women huddled together with the males at the other end of the hall eyeing off who they fancied asking to dance.

'Now come on everyone,' called Miranda. 'Introduce yourselves. You know your shopping centre location. Hands up if you're at Northland.' Hands went up. 'Right, please move over there by the main office.' People moved. 'Who's at Ringwood?' Enrico and Big Graeme raised a hand. 'Over there by the door to the costumes,' she called and kept calling causing people to move and mingle.

A woman approached Enrico and Graeme and looked impressive wearing enough make-up for two faces. She asked if this was the Ringwood group.

'Yes, it is,' said Enrico. 'I'm Enrico and this is Graeme.'

'Big Graeme,' said the giant offering a large mitt.

The woman reluctantly took it. 'I'm Lorna Redgrave.'

'Have you ever been Mrs Santa before, Lorna?' asked Enrico.

'No, but I have a long career as a professional actress.'

'Oh, forgive me for not recognizing you,' he apologized.

'A professional?' queried Big Graeme with a serve of scepticism.

'Yes, I've done it all—theatre, film, TV, even ads.'

'Well, you should prove to be brilliant as Mrs Santa,' added Enrico who spotted Rosie and beckoned her forward introducing the women. He explained Lorna's thespian fame. She basked in her former glory and addressed Rosie. 'Have you been involved in theatre?'

'Yes; for years I trod the boards in my local company but today I work backstage looking after props and costumes.'

'Amateur?' asked Lorna knowing full well the answer but wanting to establish her so-called superior status. Enrico sensed tension but gave Lorna the benefit of the doubt hoping his two supporting performers would get on like a house on fire. From the off, Rosie picked Lorna as a stuck-up snob.

The fourth member of the Ringwood team inserted his giant girth and even bigger mouth, and the meeting went from bad to worse.

'So then,' he grinned with sleaze, 'which of you two beauties is my Mrs Santa?'

Despite their obvious differences in terms of personality, both women recoiled at the possibility of having to deal with Giant Gut Santa and froze. Enrico became a knight in shining armour without even trying.

'Do forgive me, ladies,' he smiled, 'but being a retired hairdresser,' (he lied using his sister's description), 'if you have any finishing touches needed to your coiffures, you only have to ask.

Big Graeme 0, Enrico 2.

Chapter 4
Every good lie contains a kernel of truth.

That night, Rosie's family wanted news with granddaughter Pippa oozing curiosity on the speaker phone. 'Come on Gran, tell all.'

'It went well,' replied Rosie.

Scoffing became the young woman's second nature. 'It went well?' she sneered. 'What the hell does that mean? Come on, what's your costume like? What are the other Santa ladies like? And most important, tell me about the Santas you're working with.'

Rosie hesitated and Pippa seized on the pause.

'Oh no,' sighed the young woman, 'it's a disaster. You've landed yourself with a bunch of losers.'

'No, I haven't!' fired back Rosie. 'One of the women is a former star of stage and screen, or so she says.'

'An old pro?' gasped Pippa. 'Wow, what's her name?'

'I don't know her stage name, assuming she had one, but she calls herself Lorna Redgrave.'

'What?' scoffed Pippa? 'She's pinched a theatrical name pretending to be someone she ain't and turned her minor roles into something they never were.'

'You don't know that; stop jumping to conclusions. And haven't I told you, every good lie contains a kernel of truth?'

'What's a colonel got to do with a lie?'

Pippa's parents rolled their eyes. Young people know everything and nothing. Rosie paused, tried to understand the confused question then ploughed ahead.

'There are two men I'll be working with. One is an overweight slob, and the other a perfect gentleman. Naturally I'm hoping I work with the nice one a lot more than the other.'

'Do you have a choice?'

'Not sure. We're given a roster, put in our preferences and I guess no correspondence will be entered into.'

Pippa grinned. 'You're a funny woman, Gran. I know where I get my red hair from and I reckon if I've managed to scrounge any brains along the way, Mum says they came from you as well.'

Rosie laughed. 'Enough about me. What's happening in your mad world, young lady?'

Pippa's news thrilled her grandmother but all through their chat, Mrs Santa kept thinking of her new partners in performance. She struggled to contain her fear when thinking about Big Graeme but remembering her time butting heads and chatting with the sweet smiling Enrico, gave her all sorts of other feelings—nice ones. Thinking about the retired barber made her smile.

Sofia rang as soon as she knew her brother would be home. He didn't need to look at the caller ID. He knew it was big sister and reckoned his phone gave a unique ringing sound whenever she called.

'Well?' she demanded. 'How did it go?'

She didn't need to add, "and tell me everything"—that was a given.

'It was lovely,' he said, 'nice people and new costumes. I'm looking forward to getting started.'

She didn't snap at him, but it was darn close to a blast. 'Enrico, what about the female Santas?'

''Oh, they're lovely. One lady is a professional actress and the other makes costumes for a local theatre company.'

'Are they married?'

'To one another?'

'Don't be crude, Enrico.'

He paused. He genuinely didn't know. He was not the greatest sweet talker in town and using his system of old-fashioned pretty much ancient manners, surely, he would never ask, 'Scuse me, love, is you married?' How rude would that be?

'I have no idea,' he said a tad miffed. 'And what has their marital status got to do with their work as a professional performer?'

Sofia grimaced. She needed to protect her baby brother. A grasping widow or divorcee would love to sink her painted nails into poor innocent Enrico and bleed him dry. She knew he would be easy pickings for any Jezebel and especially so for an experienced hussy.

'Don't forget Sunday lunch?' she said. 'Maria and the boys will be here. You can practise being Santa with your great nephews. Ciao.'

She hung up and Enrico imagined his great nephews, aged 22 and 24, sitting on their great uncle's lap. Now there's an impossibility.

Chapter 5

She watched him in her mirrors and liked what she saw.

Lunch at Nonna's was always an event. Starvation never appeared on the menu. Maria, her divorced daughter, brought herbs from her garden, and grandsons Michael and Joseph brought their fashionable clothes and louder opinions. Enrico brought fresh veg from his garden and hated being the focus of attention.

'Uncle,' said Maria, 'is it true you're getting married this Christmas?'

'Married!' exclaimed both great nephews always being far more interested in themselves than others.

Enrico waved his hand downplaying the situation. 'Yes, I'm Santa again and the company has decided to add a Mrs Santa. I think it'll be fun.'

'Is she hot, Ric?' asked Joseph with his usual disrespectful approach to women and to his great uncle, 'your Mrs Santa I mean?'

'That's enough,' snapped Sofia and even the loutish grandsons put a sock in it when Nonna gave an order.

The lunch was the usual fabulous feast and as Sofia gave her brother a fair chunk of the cooked food to take home for later in the week, Santa would not need to spend time cooking.

Both his niece and her sons always offered him a lift home and as always, he politely declined. He needed his stick but reckoned exercise might well delay any hip operation. Keep moving, my son.

Once home, he did his usual potter about before making a big decision—he would leave home. Not forever, not as a runaway but simply to rehearse the trip to the shopping centre where he pulled on his red suit, big black belt and boots, his gloves, whiskers and hat and spend his December days giving youngsters a thrill to remember.

He caught the train near his home, free for seniors on a Sunday, and from the Ringwood station, he wandered into the shopping centre. The set for Santa was already in place and he stood back and observed.

A few children studied the huge chair and decorations. Parents needed to explain the situation and then promise to return when Santa himself arrived via his sleigh.

Enrico smiled knowing Santa stood as good as next to them. He sat at a table of a nearby food outlet and ordered his favourite coffee. He enjoyed the crowd, the atmosphere of a fast-approaching Christmas, and sat there in his friendly stupor.

He blinked. His view narrowed because someone stopped a few metres away and stared at him. Bingo! The penny dropped and he sat up as Rosie, one of his December wives, came grinning towards him.

'Hello,' she said with a face that showered friendship and delight.

Enrico went to stand and struggled. Rosie moved quickly.

'Please don't get up, Enrico, stay where you are.' She knew his hip was not up to Olympic standard, and his stick rested beside him. 'May I join you?'

'Of course,' he said trying to move a chair. The waitress arrived with his coffee. 'Please allow me to buy you a coffee. What would you like?'

'How kind,' said Rosie feeling pleased she'd pushed herself to get out of the house to see her new workplace. 'Have we both done the same thing,' she asked; 'come to see the performing space?'

He nodded. 'Each Christmas, before the season begins, I like to see the set and try and soak up the atmosphere.'

'Do you get nervous?'

He didn't want to boast but shook his head. 'No because the children don't give me time to be nervous and besides, this year I'll have Mrs Santa to help keep everyone, including me, in order.'

She smiled and reinforced her early belief Enrico was a kind, caring and sensitive man. They settled. Her coffee arrived and they toasted their health and forthcoming project.

'I'm glad we're paired to start the season,' she said looking at him.

'So am I. Are you looking forward to performing?'

'I am. The excitement is starting to build and being here before the show begins makes it all so real.'

'I was nervous the first time, but it didn't take long to settle and I'm sure you'll be brilliant with the kiddies.'

'Thank you,' she said looking deep into his brown eyes. It seemed silly but she thought they sparkled. 'Did you say this is your third time as Santa?'

'My third and I'm still excited, can't wait till we begin in the morning.'

They continued drinking their coffee.

'Would you have any tips for the new girl on the block?'

His wry smile appeared. 'No,' he said, and she looked disappointed. 'You see I've never been *Mrs* Santa before.'

She laughed and he reckoned she performed the kindest laugh he'd ever seen or heard. Their conversation sparkled with both wanting the kids to start arriving right now.

They wandered over to the set with Enrico then showing Rosie the door leading to their dressing room, and other important venues such as the closest public loo and easiest access to the station.

'I drive,' said Rosie. 'Miranda explained the special parking ticket.'

'I'm close by so use public transport,' he replied, 'and speaking of which, my train's due in about fifteen minutes.'

'Where are you heading?' she asked and immediately wanted to bite her tongue. 'Oh, I'm so sorry, I didn't mean to pry.'

'No probs,' as my great nephews so often say. I'm in Blackburn.'

'Well, I drive through there. I'm in East Camberwell. You bought me coffee, so now it's my turn to return the favour. Come on, I'll give you a lift.'

He smiled, enjoyed peak happiness, and followed her out to the carpark. He wanted to throw his stick over his shoulder and pretend to again become the man who broke the bank at Monte Carlo but thought better of it.

Her car was spotless. He liked that. In fact, he liked everything about Rosie, his new Christmas wife. Once they took off, she could have been a driving instructor not that he'd know. He'd never once driven a car.

She chatted easily and naturally. 'Will your friends and family come to see you being Santa?'

'Oh yes, and they'll be quick to add their comments when they see me out of costume.'

'That doesn't sound nice.'

'Oh, they mean well, and you'll understand if you ever meet my big sister, Sofia. She's taken over the role of my mother making sure her bachelor brother is keeping on the straight and narrow.'

She laughed. 'You make it sound like you're a bit of a Jack the lad.'

He laughed. 'Hardly. I'm often teased about never letting my hair down but then how could I, I'm a former barber.'

She laughed at his dad joke. 'I remember. You told me when we first met.'

Did he? He often wondered about his memory and if it was fading. He raised a hand. 'This is my stop. I'm only a short walk down this road.'

She pulled in. 'Are you sure?'

'I'll be fine and thank you again for your kindness.'

She stopped and he struggled to get out. She wanted to help but saw how that could be humiliating for the man she found entertaining and endearing.

Leaning on his stick, he turned back. 'See you in the morning, Mrs Santa.'

'Till the morning, Santa' she called as he closed the door needing two attempts.

He strode off as if he were half a century younger. She watched him in her mirrors and liked what she saw.

Chapter 6

He discovered he could still dance, well, shuffle around his kitchen.

When shopping, Enrico walked the long way round. He couldn't bear walking past his old shop in the local shopping strip.

His parents arrived from Italy in the 1960s and settled in Carlton. His father found work in the fruit and vegetable world but in the 1970s the family moved to the suburbs, to Blackburn and bought an old, solid home on a large block. The straggly lawn in the front garden was soon replaced by thriving tomato plants and pumpkins boomed in the back yard beneath Enrico's mother's washing lines, plural.

The boy saw his father up at 4am or earlier and reckoned that life, carrying boxes of fruit and veg at the wholesale market was not for him. His uncle ran a barber's shop in nearby Box Hill, and soon the lad was sweeping the floor and learning how to cut hair.

Bloody hard work saw his employment skills flourish and his uncle gave him plenty of opportunity. He became a natural barber although his ability to cut hair far exceeded his ability to pull birds. In secret, his parents wondered if he was possibly not interested in the fairer sex. They were wrong as he was decidedly heterosexual and once met a girl. They were keen but after a year or two of dating, it all came to a crashing halt as she chose another. He surrendered. Faint heart, Enrico, never won fair lady.

Sofia knew that rejection hurt her teenage brother hard and knew why he seemed reluctant to look for love again. A few other attempts petered out and the longer he remained a bachelor, the stronger his single life became.

Sofia married and moved away. Enrico remained at home in Blackburn with his parents. When a shop became vacant in the local strip, Enrico was given the lease, and his business life took off. He cared for his ageing parents, walked to work, trimmed hair and life drifted by.

His father died and then his mother. Sofia called at the home on a daily basis and took over her mother's role as head of the family.

Time passed and a major change saw his retirement and the closing of his business. He'd cut the hair of boys who became fathers who became grandfathers. Men would call in, not for a haircut but simply to say 'G'day'. It gave Enrico a huge buzz. Handshakes, hugs, grizzly grins and happy, happy memories.

Today, it was all gone. Only the faded sign above the door remained.

E. Salvatore. Haircut and a shave

The sign writer questioned the wording but Enrico stuck firm. He was a product of those Italians who took to adding the indefinite article to many of their sentences. 'He would go', became, 'He would-a go.' So therefore, instead of 'Haircut and shave', it became 'Haircut and-a shave' at least sans hyphen.

Once Enrico retired, the family who owned the premises advertised for a new tenant. Where in the Universe would they find another Signor Salvatore, the perfect tenant?

A trendy couple opened a wine shop and finished up drinking their profits. Two sisters who loved knitting set up a wool shop and burnt through most of their parents' inheritance. Finally, a Chinese lady filled, and by filled the word is FILLED the space with her unusual goodies. Where the items came from remains a mystery and it's said she took the best part of a month simply packing the stock after the business collapsed. Mind you, it's hard to collapse when you're still horizontal in terms of sales.

No-one stepped forward and the shop remained shut and still does with a fading *For Lease* sign skew whiff in one corner of the grubby front window.

No wonder Enrico went the long way round to avoid his old emporium.

He arrived home from his exploratory trip to the shopping centre to be greeted by a ringing telephone. And yes, the unique tone could mean only one person calling.

He jumped in first. 'Ciao, Sofia, how are you?'

Distress and anxiety poured from the receiver. 'Where have you been? I've been ringing for ages. I was about to have Beverley,' (his next-door neighbour) 'or even the boys go round and check on you.'

'Didn't I tell you? I've been to Ringwood to test-run the Santa set ready for our first day in the morning.'

His explanation let most of the anxiety wind out of his sister's sails. 'You should have told me.'

'I met my wife there and we had a coffee, and she drove me home.'

Every one of those pieces of information proved explosive. Three pieces represented a potential cataclysmic catastrophe. Sofia struggled. Her brother referred to his wife, having a social encounter, and getting in a car with said woman. Where should she begin?

He jumped in and for once controlled the conversation.

'I think you'll like, Rosie. She's a kind and friendly lady with perfect manners and owns the cleanest car I've ever seen inside and out.

Sofia now needed a sizeable number of smelling salts. Enrico ploughed ahead. What could be driving his enthusiasm?

'Rosie will make the perfect Mrs Santa,' he said but finally Sofia got a word in edgeways. Mind you it was only the one word.

'Rosie!' she gasped.

'You must come to Ringwood and once she changes out of her costume, I'll introduce you.'

Sofia's blood pressure became confused. It wanted to soar but the latest news where her brother was talking about a woman taking off her clothes, albeit in private, meant new veins were required forthwith.

He became so smitten, if that's the word, with his new working partner, he didn't realize his sister was stunned. He reckoned the conversation was over and so moved to end the call.

Sofia, the leader of the pack, the family matriarch, the ruler of the clan whimpered her goodbye.

'Another coffee, Enrico,' said Santa to himself and discovered he could still dance, well, shuffle around his kitchen.

Chapter 7

I've used the garden for you know what so that means at least one extra treat.

Rosie arrived home thinking about the former barber she enjoyed a coffee with an hour or so earlier. There was something about Enrico Salvatore she couldn't put her finger on. His perfect manners danced around him with his smile giving anyone who saw it a lift. But since their two meetings, her life as Mrs Santa, in itself an interesting gig, the prospect of working with this senior gent gave her ticker a touch of palpitations: low-level admittedly but palpitations, nevertheless.

She parked in her driveway and entered her kitchen to be hammered with questions requiring her to answer.

'Yes, all right, I'll tell you, I'll tell you. Please be patient.'

Whatever else Buster O'Donnell was, he wasn't patient. 'Tell me now, now or I'll keep on pestering until you do.'

She gave the dog a look of impatience. 'I had coffee with Santa and then drove him home.'

Buster shook his head. 'I am not even remotely interested in a dog called Santa; all I want is my tea and a walk, treats and a belly rub. Oh, and I've used the garden for you know what so that means at least one extra treat.'

His eyes spoke louder than his bark and Rosie fed her best friend. Afterwards, on their walk in the park, Buster wondered why his mistress spent less time talking to him and more time daydreaming.

'I mean what's that all about?' he thought. *'What could be more important than me, her faithful, her one and only true friend?'*

He stopped and waited for Rosie to throw his ball using one of those plastic stick thingies. A terrible thought pinged in Buster's brain. *'She hasn't got another faithful and one true friend. Has she?'*

The flying ball saw him back on track.

Sitting on her sofa with Buster by her side, Rosie had an idea. It concerned her new friend, Santa the barber. She knew he was worried about one thing and reckoned she could help. Her mind raced as she sketched ideas on a pad while Buster dreamt of being not only the leader of the pack but, in fact, the entire pack.

As the dog dozed, Rosie went to her second bedroom where the cupboards and wardrobes held props, costumes and part-costumes because the storeroom at her local theatre company was fit to burst.

She found a collection of props, chose one, tested it then hunted for other items. Working late into the night she cut, stitched and glued then admired her Christmas present for Father Christmas.

'I wonder what he'll say?' she said showing the item to Buster before they both went to bed. Buster showed little interest.

There was no alarm needed for the morning. Enrico became like his old man and rose before the first trams and trains were even switched on in their sheds or stabling yards. Shaving was once his profession and facial hair his life's calling. Hairs stood resplendent awaiting their orders with the master's cut-throat razor and always-sharpened scissors on call. He daydreamed of being Santa with wife.

All Santas' costuming and prop requirements were delivered to the centres by *Costumes 4 U*. Enrico knew this, and despite a dicky hip, at home he started figuratively pawing the carpet, raring to go.

As he tucked into his toast and tea breakfast, he again studied a printed train timetable wishing he had gone digital when his niece and her sons urged him to do so. Checking timetables on his phone proved a nightmare.

Sending and receiving texts and calls he could manage, but finding let alone reading about train delays proved to be a viaduct too far.

He checked the weather forecast by looking out the window, shouldered his bag with thermos, sandwich and collapsible umbrella, and grabbed his unwanted walking stick. It was the only part of his Santa journey which gave him concern. Would his hip pass muster?

Will people, and children in particular, point out that Santa is a broken-down old man who should be put out to pasture? To the railway station he went.

On his first day, Enrico caught an even earlier train, alighting at Ringwood. In the huge shopping centre, he headed to the Santa set. It stood empty but looked impressive and he thought it smiled at him. A sign stood out front.

Meet Santa from 10am

He headed for the centre management office and waited at the counter as a member of staff approached.

'Good morning,' she said. 'Can I help you?'

A twinge of sadness pinged in his heart as the budding Santa needed to explain who he was. But before he could reply, a friendly voice was heard and another member of staff, Debbie, approached.

'Enrico, how lovely to see you again,' she enthused.

Debbie remembered him from last Christmas, introduced Santa to her colleague and then walked with him through the centre.

'We're all excited to have Mrs Santa on the set this year,' she said. 'Have you met your wife?' she winked.

'I have and they're both lovely ladies.'

Debbie teased, 'Ooooh, two wives, hey. I hope you'll behave, Santa.'

He smiled without laughing as they entered the corridor inside the complex. They reached a door marked *Private* which Debbie unlocked. This was the dressing-room Enrico used in previous years.

His splendid costume and props were hanging on the wall. He looked around. 'Where does Mrs Santa change?' he asked.

'I'm afraid you're all in together, Enrico but with you being such a gentleman, I'm sure the two Mrs Santas will be perfectly at ease.'

She squeezed his arm, gave him the key and prepared to leave.

'Let me know if you need anything and have a wonderful first day.'

She departed with a radio crackling in her ear.

Enrico checked his bits and bobs. Everything was present and spotless. He surveyed the room. Both Mrs Santa's materials were nearby but he worried. *Where will they change? They can't disrobe here with the men and especially not with the lecherous Big Graeme.*

A pile of cardboard boxes stood against a wall. They contained cheap Christmas give-a-ways and were not heavy. He started "renovating" the room. By pushing the boxes into a new position in a corner, he made two walls and thus a small room with a space for an opening. He found a piece of white card and a Texta, printed *Mrs Santa* on the card, bent it and shoved the top half between two of the boxes beside the "door". He went all warm inside.

He removed the dry-cleaning plastic on his outfit when someone tapped on the door. 'Come in,' he called and faced the sound.

Rosie O'Donnell appeared with her smile lighting up the room.

'Good morning. Is this the right place?' she asked.

He moved to hold open the door as she entered carrying a large well-wrapped gift.

'Indeed, and please come in.' Rosie looked around. He indicated the newly created female dressing-room. 'This is for you and Lorna. I'm afraid it needs a little interior decoration.'

'Did you do this?' she asked.

He nodded looking shy. 'I thought you and the other Mrs Santa would like a little privacy.'

'How thoughtful you are, thank you,' she said handing him the present. 'And this is for you ... Merry Christmas, Father Christmas.'

He froze. 'But ... you shouldn't have. There's no need.'

'You don't know what it is yet.'

His embarrassment took over as he carefully unwrapped the odd-shaped present. The gift, whatever it was, proved hard to define. Then he twigged. It was a beautifully decorated walking stick. It looked like a stick Santa would use when hopping around his North Pole workshop. It could be a pointing stick for Father Christmas and a natural accoutrement for his lifestyle. Secretly it would give him confidence and a new freedom of expression. It was perfect. Finally, he didn't know what to say.

'Do you like it?' she asked.

He struggled to speak. 'It's beautiful. I don't know what to say.'

'Try it out.'

He looked at her and the stick and then went for a walk around the storeroom now set aside for Santa and Mrs Santa. The stick was strong and the more he walked the more confident he became.

He stopped and couldn't control his smile. Both were grinning.

'I believed you would be the perfect Mrs Santa and now I *know* you are. Thank you, Rosie. You have made an old Santa incredibly happy.'

'Not that old, surely,' she said, and the mood bubbled.

Chapter 8
Mum laughed and steered her terrified toddler away.

Rosie slipped into the special space to change and become Mrs Santa. Enrico potted about testing his present. He gleamed. Making a grand entrance and, holding her dress outwards, she posed and asked a question.

'What do you think?'

He thought she looked terrific, no, better than terrific.

'Perfect,' he said and started a small wobble still getting used to his costume and all that padding. Not being the strongest Santa this side of the North Pole, Enrico found the hat and whiskers a little challenging. He remembered from previous years that standing quickly and without preparation was never wise.

'Slow and steady,' he kept reminding himself.

She approached. 'How is your new walking stick?'

He gripped it firmly and took on a new personality. This wasn't a walking stick, but a magic Santa wand created by his magical wife. He raised it in triumph.

She rejoiced with him when both were rudely interrupted. Someone entered without knocking steering a bucket and mop on wheels.

The cleaner realized he was not alone and used a dropped jaw as proof.

'Sorry, I didn't know there was anyone in here.'

'You're new,' said Enrico remembering the cleaners of previous years.

'Yes, I'm Anton,' he said. 'I'll get out of your way. Bye,' he called and departed leaving his equipment to one side.

Rosie looked at Santa. 'It's not the grandest of dressing-rooms.'

'No and it doubles as a storeroom for the cleaners.'

'I wonder what Lorna the former star actress will make of it.'

He raised his eyebrows, faked a grin then looked at his watch. It was hard to locate under his big red sleeves. 'I think we should make a start.'

'I'll follow you,' she said, and they followed the cleaner.

Dressed for Christmas, the two actors walked along a corridor never used by members of the public and came to a large swing door with a glass porthole near the top. You could peek into the outside world where shoppers moved back and forth. Mr and Mrs Santa took a cheeky peek outside. No-one looked back. Seeing potential clients gave both performers a new surge of excitement.

'Well,' said Santa, 'this is it, Mrs Santa.' She looked into his eyes, and they spoke silently to one another. 'As we arranged,' he said. 'I'll take off first, ring my bell and head towards the set. You follow. We never know who we'll meet before we get there or how they'll react. Are you ready?' She nodded as excited as a young child about to meet Santa.

'Good luck,' he said not knowing the showbiz mantra about not, about *never* saying those particular words to a fellow performer.

He took a deep breath, pushed open the door and gave his bell a good ring. The sounds of the shoppers together with plastic Christmas music washed over him. People stopped and stared. Enrico didn't hesitate.

'Ho, ho, ho!' he called and again rang his bell with his other hand, the one not holding his new Christmas present. If people weren't looking before, they sure were now. He loved the experience and reckoned it even beat the thrill of picking his gorgeous tomatoes.

Children pointed and moved towards him, several ran. Rosie followed at a distance admiring Santa's style. His voice sounded deeper, and his stick looked impressive. He was a natural.

A mother with a toddler in the top of a supermarket trolley floated towards him. She was about to give her little one a first—a meeting with Santa. He was experienced. No sudden movements, no frightening voice or gestures.

'Merry Christmas,' he said at a distance from the child. The world awaited the youngster's response, her first face to face with good old Saint Nick. Then the nightmare exploded.

Her mouth twisted, tears flowed, and her scream filled the vast space.

Mum laughed and steered her terrified toddler away.

Santa and Mrs Santa exchanged a glance and hoped that last incident was not an omen for the day and weeks ahead.

On the Santa set, Russell the photographer was checking his equipment. 'Morning Santa,' he said then spotted Mrs Santa. 'Oh, and to you Mrs Santa. I'm Russell.'

'Good morning, sir,' said Rosie exploring the set.'

'Good morning, Russell. It's me, Enrico.'

'Of course it is. I recognized your walk but not your fancy new stick.'

Enrico reached his special Santa seat, placed his new Santa stick to one side but within reach and sat. He surveyed his kingdom. Early bird visitors pressed forward against the surrounding fence. Santa was a magnet for all ages. Rosie looked to him for advice. He nodded to the clients, and she moved to the now growing line of children with beaming faces.

'Hello and what's your name?' asked Rosie of the first two siblings.

The older girl took control and baby brother was too entranced to do anything other than follow. Rosie brought them forward and introduced each child by name.

Enrico was in love. This experience, this time of year brought him happiness like no other. And now, the delight enveloping children was crowned by his new friend and Christmas spouse. What's not to like?

The patter flowed from the former barber. 'Have you been good? What do you want for Christmas? Do you promise to be kind to people and pets?'

The promises were strong and sincere and despite Christmas still being about three weeks away, the kids kept coming.

During a brief break, Rosie asked Santa a question. 'Is it always this busy?'

'Busy?' sounded a surprised Enrico. 'You wait till December 20. Those last few days are crazy.'

Rosie smiled but stopped when a familiar voice sounded. 'Good morning, Mrs Santa.' She turned to see her grinning granddaughter waving from behind the fence surrounding the set.

'My granddaughter,' said Rosie to Enrico.

'Bring her in,' said Enrico. 'There's a break in the line.'

Rosie's eyes widened. 'Are you sure?'

'Of course but tell her she's too big to sit on Santa's knee.' He smiled.

Rosie moved to Pippa and set off rabbiting. Next thing the young red-headed woman made her way to the entrance and was escorted onto the Santa set.

'Santa, this is my granddaughter, Pippa.'

'Hello Santa,' said Pippa accepting Enrico's extended, white-gloved hand. 'I'm pleased to meet you.'

'Hello Pippa. I'm delighted to meet anyone related to my favourite wife.'

That comment threw the ladies. But there was no stopping the man in the red suit. Maybe being in disguise gave him the equivalent of Dutch courage. Chatting up ladies was never his strong suit, but something changed.

'Now Pippa, I can see where your red hair and natural beauty comes from. Please tell me, what are you hoping Santa will bring you for Christmas?'

Pippa caught the mood. 'I'm so glad you asked me, Santa. I've seen these Jimmy Choo shoes I rather fancy, and a Chanel bag I could die for.' She smiled at him. 'How's that for starters?'

'For starters?' replied Santa with faux shock. 'You mean there's more?'

'You could throw in a return business-class flight to the Big Apple.'

'Or how about a bus ticket to Box Hill? It's my old hometown.'

Both women erupted. They loved his answer and sense of humour.

Russell interrupted. 'Customers, Santa,' he said.

Pippa departed. 'Bye Santa; lovely to meet you. Bye Gran. I'll call you.'

The young woman departed, and business resumed with big-eyed children fascinated by the man with the forest of white whiskers.

It was a wonderful first session, a steady stream of bubbling little humans with happiness in abundance. Rosie found the whole experience nigh on perfect. A happy audience always brings satisfaction but seeing the faces of the children and their overflowing joy gave her goose bumps.

Russell took over. His job of taking photos of the children with Santa, and now Mrs Santa, was full on. He wanted his break and that meant Santa and Mrs Santa were off as well. The sign out front changed to:

Meet Santa from 1.30pm

En route to their dressing-room, shoppers of all ages wanted to say hello. Children called from afar. Rosie admired how Enrico gave time to everyone.

The Christmas couple reached their exit/entrance door. He stood back allowing her to go first. Once in the corridor and away from the masses, they sighed and leant against the walls. Enrico's magic wand proved unnecessary.

'You were brilliant, Rosie,' he said leaving her speechless.

She recovered. 'Me? You do all the work and never stop.'

'Only three weeks to go,' he grinned. 'Come on, we need to change.'

They reached the door of their dressing-room and entered in high spirits only to crash and burn. The alternative Christmas couple were "in the house".

The giant Santa, Big Graeme, sprawled on a bench, struggling to pull on his boots. Sounds escaping from beneath his costume caused the new arrivals to freeze and then step backwards.

'Hello, Santa,' said Enrico trying to recover.

'These bloody boots,' snorted Gazza. 'They've given me the wrong ones.' He spotted Rosie. 'Hello darling,' he oozed. 'Fancy giving me a gentle tug?'

Enrico stepped forward. 'Allow me,' he said and fixed the boots.

'Is Mrs Santa here?' asked Rosie. Graeme nodded towards the corner and a certain former actress, a former star according to the woman herself, appeared. She drifted between unhappy and fuming.

'This is outrageous. I've never been so insulted in all my theatrical life. No lavatory or mirror with lights, not even a mirror, and a so-called dressing room behind a pile of boxes. Where are my agent and the union when you need them?'

Rosie and Enrico looked at one another and Graeme flashed a pathetic grin. And they haven't even appeared in public yet. Such fun.

Chapter 9

Please, my friend, tell me, when you are old can you still have sex?

Enrico changed and waited for Rosie. When she emerged, they left together. Neither fancied having to linger with the prima donna and her mammoth mate. Both Enrico and Rosie were buzzing from their first session and at their encounter with the alternative performers.

'Where is my agent?' mocked Rosie in a clever mimic of Lorna. Enrico joined in but without Rosie's finesse.

'I have no lavatory,' he whined, and they both drew attention to themselves. Onlookers had no idea what or who they were talking about and certainly no idea that now, being in mufti, they were the well-known characters who once dominated the nearby set.

'Should we stay and watch them?' asked Rosie.

'I used to when I got on well with the other Santa, but today I think I'd be embarrassed,' he replied. 'I feel sorry for Lorna.'

'Oh? May I ask why?'

'Well, if she was a top professional, it must be a bitter pill to swallow performing in such a non-glamourous setting.'

'You said *if* she was a professional. Do you think she's telling lies?'

'Does she convince you?'

Rosie grimaced. 'I'm not sure. I looked her up online and only found a few minor mentions of her name from long ago.'

'I have met people who talk about their skills and achievements, and I reckon they are trying to impress. She may have been a minor player but now exaggerates her experience to boost her own confidence or to impress others.'

Rosie looked at the man standing in front of her. He was like no other she'd met, and a million miles removed from her former husband.

'You are a most interesting man, Signor Salvatore.'

He hesitated. 'Is that a good thing?'

She smiled. 'It certainly is. Now can I give you a lift home?'

'Thank you but no. I'm meeting an old friend. We try to get together around Christmas and today's the day.'

'Well, don't let me hold you up. You meet your friend, and I'll see you in the morning.' She gave his arm a gentle squeeze sending a bolt of electricity through his body.

'I look forward to it and congratulations again, Rosie; you were a brilliant Mrs Santa. Bye.'

She blew him a kiss and left. He stood there his heart picking up speed. This was only the first day. What would tomorrow and the following weeks be like? Being Santa was fabulous but having a helper, a woman pretending to be his wife who was so kind and lovely and beautiful, wow, his thoughts ran amok. He was unsure about his situation. Was this an unexpected love tale? Could life get any better? What's going to happen next?

Alf, born Alfrid, and Enrico were friends, great pals since childhood. Their fathers were mates, and the sons met when their fathers dragged them out of bed to get a taste of working at the wholesale fruit and vegetable market. Neither son followed in their father's footsteps with Enrico cutting hair and Alfrid cooking pizzas. Both had been and still were darn good at their respective occupations.

For the third December in a row, their annual rendezvous was the Ringwood Lake, handy for Lilydale resident Alf who had set up the luncheon spot by the time Enrico waddled in using his "normal" walking stick.

'Ciao Signor,' called Enrico, and his friend rose, and they embraced. These men of Italian heritage found hugging and kissing foreheads and cheeks to be par for the course—normal and natural.

They settled and Alf revealed his typical repast—risotto, marinated cheese and more. Classic vino appeared as if by magic and the friends feted and regaled one another with their news and views. Between mouthfuls, Alf asked about the Santa story. 'So, you have started being a Father Christmas again, yes? How is it going?'

'I told you, my friend, we are called Santa. All the little ones call me Santa and I am already having the best time, but Alfrid you must understand; now it is different. Now there is a Mrs Santa.'

Alf exploded. 'What? You have a wife? Why do you not tell me?'

Enrico nodded as he chewed and still managed to talk. 'Her name is Rosie, and she is,' he exploded his fingers from his lips, 'Bellissima.'

Alf reacted with a mixture of delight and alarm. 'Wait, wait; what is this you are telling me? Your name is now changed from Enrico to Romeo?' Enrico laughed but not for long. He gushed in all seriousness.

'She helps me with the children and does a perfect job but, Alfrid, listen carefully.' He reached out to grab his friend's arm. 'I think she likes me.'

'She likes you or she likes Santa?'

'Both but certainly she likes *me*.'

Alfrid spoke with his mouth half full. 'You sly old fox, you.'

'She made me a special walking stick. It's decorated and I can use it as a prop when I'm Santa. Why did she do that for me?'

'Because your old stick is like you; falling to bits.'

Enrico turned serious. 'No, please, I ask you. Why did she do that?'

'It could be because she feels sorry for the old barber with the crooked hip and who looks like he's always about to fall over.'

Wow did that comment sting. Enrico had never considered such a scenario. His mind whirled. *'She's helping me because she feels sorry for me,'* he thought and cried inside. Alfrid saw his friend was upset.

'Listen you old fool, don't take any notice of me. You know my record with women; three wives and now a fourth, a live-in girlfriend.'

Enrico leaned towards his friend and spoke in an intimate voice. There was no need for secrecy as they were far from other people.

'I do not know what to say or do. Alfrid, my friend, you must help me.'

The friend caught Santa's serious attitude. 'Okay, so what's the problem?'

Santa hesitated again. 'How do I know if I am in love?'

Alf wanted to roar with laughter but knew his friend would be hurt were such laughter to erupt. Enrico kept on questioning.

'This is all new to me, Compagno. I have never thought about a woman like this before.'

'Never!' exclaimed Alf. 'How many times were you chasing girls when we were young? What about that dark-haired girl who worked in the chemist?'

'Gabriella,' said Enrico in an instant.

'You were madly in love with her.'

The retired barber nodded. 'But that was a lifetime ago and she married a footballer and had a team of babies. For the last fifty years, I've been a monk. I am the perfect example of a confirmed bachelor.'

'So, what, now you're going to become a Casanova in your old age?'

'Why not?' fizzed back Enrico. 'Can you only be in love with a woman if you are young or middle-aged? What is this rule about age and romance? Show me, please. Tell me I'm too old to be in love.'

Alf gave up arguing and joking because he could see how passionate, how determined his friend had become. The former chef spoke quietly.

'There is no age barrier, Signor, and I can only congratulate you on your good fortune.'

They hesitated before Alf raised his small plastic cup and made a toast. 'To Daisy,' he said.

Enrico copied the toast. 'It's Rosie,' he said not offended by the wrong name.

'And her too,' added Alf and they touched cups.

They resumed their luncheon and Alf decided to be brutal if only to help his friend.

'Now listen to me, Signor Salvatore, I am delighted you have found someone to love but there is a possible problem with your new romance.'

'My hip?' gasped Enrico. 'I tell you it is okay, and Rosie knows about it and has already made me ...'

Alf joined in and they spoke together. '... a special Santa walking-stick.'

Alf spoke alone. 'Yes, I know, you told me but in love my friend, it takes two to tango. You being madly in love is fabulous and at your age it's even better than wonderful but unless the feeling is reciprocated ...' He paused. 'I think that is the right word.'

'It is and I know what you are trying to say.'

'Unless Rosie feels the same about you, it can be a sad situation. A broken heart is mighty painful, and I should know, I've broken many.'

Enrico eyeballed his companion. 'Alfrid, I know she has feelings for me. I know.'

'How do you know? Did she tell you?'

Enrico fell silent, looked sad and slowly shook his head.

The former chef decided to drop the matter hoping like hell his friend was not infatuated with a woman who had nothing but friendship in mind when she looked at Santa.

This had been an interesting catch-up. As always, the food and wine were superb, but the conversation had gone on an unexpected journey. Soon it was about to veer right off the rails.

'Amico,' said Enrico. 'I need help; some serious advice.' He paused and the two old men stared at one another.

'I might be older than you but that doesn't mean I'm smarter,' said Alfrid.

'Yes, but you're up to wife number three,' argued Enrico.

'Four,' said Alf.

'Please, my friend, tell me, when you are old, can you still have sex?'

Chapter 10
Sofia's sense of humour had been lost in the mail.

Pippa couldn't wait to ring her grandmother wanting a full report on the first day as Mrs Santa. Pippa tried and got the message bank.

'It's your favourite granddaughter. Let me know when you are home. Byeee!'

Rosie listened to Pippa's messages and two others from friends all wanting to know how her day as Mrs Santa went. She dealt with the friends, and with Buster desperate for a walk, took off and called Pippa en route.

'Well?' asked the young woman. 'Tell me all.'

'It went well. The kids were great, and Santa is perfect.'

'Sorry?'

'I said the kids were great and Santa is perfect.'

Pippa made a fuss exaggerating her reply. 'Oh, sorry, I thought you were describing Enrico the man.'

'Stop that, behave yourself.' Rosie called. 'Buster, come here.'

'No, seriously, I thought he was a kind, nice man. A bit old for me but could be right up your street, Gran.'

'If you can't conduct a proper conversation, this call is over.'

Pippa became serious. 'Sorry, Gran, but seriously, you've found a perfect niche. They'll have you back there every Christmas. And think of all that money you're making.'

'I am. My winter cruise is looking better every day. Look, darling, Buster's going crazy, I've gotta go. I'll see you on Thursday. Bye.'

Buster *was* going crazy, but his owner's granddaughter was thinking overtime about what to tell her mother. This was a problem for Pippa; be true to her mother or keep her Gran's cruise plans secret.

It wasn't Thursday so Anna's hairdressing and beauty salon closed at a reasonable hour. With husband and father, Malcolm, away on his long-haul driving gig, Pippa and her mother never bothered with any fancy cooking. They were both keen on maintaining their slim figures and re-heating leftovers worked a treat.

'Well?' said Anna, 'how was Mrs Santa? A star I bet?'

'She's a natural, Mum. The kids loved her, and she and Santa worked hand in glove.'

'So, what's he like, big and fat I bet?'

'I met him. For a few minutes the queue to see Father Christmas disappeared and Gran called me onto the set.'

'And?'

'Santa's a darling, a normal older guy, quiet and friendly with the nicest manners in town. You could think he and Gran were a real husband and wife team.'

Anna stopped eating. 'That's nice. It would be a drag working with someone who was a pain.'

'You'd get on with him.'

'Oh. Why?'

'He's a retired hairdresser. He calls himself a retired barber but that's the sort of person he is.'

'Well, I'm glad. It gives your grandmother something to do and pick up a bit of pocket money at the same time.'

Pippa made the decision to tell all. Grannie was open about her proposed trip and didn't tell Pippa to keep quiet about it. 'It's more than pocket money, Mum. She reckons her winter ocean cruise is going to happen.'

Anna put down her cutlery in anger. 'Did she say that?' Pippa nodded. 'That won't happen or, if so, it'll be over my dead body.'

Pippa shook her head in disbelief. 'What is the matter with you and Dad? Why can't your mother-in-law spend her own money the way she wants to? Stop being such a wet blanket.'

Anna hated the reprimand mainly because her daughter spoke the truth, but her opinion was set in concrete.

'Look at those Covid cruises. Hundreds were infected and many seniors died. If even one person has the virus, it spreads like wildfire in those small spaces. It becomes a hospital ship for retirees.'

The meal continued in silence. Pippa remembered Enrico's Christmas gift.

'Gran made Santa a special walking stick.'

Anna struggled to speak with a mouth full and a dropped jaw.

'She what?'

'The old guy seems a bit shaky on his pins and uses a walking stick, but Gran pinched another stick from the theatre props and decorated it with Christmas items. It looked wonderful and he loved it.'

'I bet he did. Why is it women make a fuss over men they don't know?'

'What,' asked Pippa? 'Are you saying you never did?'

'With your father, yes, of course I did but that was different. I'd fallen for him and wanted to win his affection.'

The pause lingered. 'Maybe Grannie's doing that.'

Boy, did that comment produce a long and loud silence.

Sofia knew when Enrico started and finished as Santa. She knew all about her brother's reunion with his boyhood pal, Alfrid. She allowed two hours for their vino and gasbag lunch, and then 30 minutes for his train journey from Ringwood station and the walk home.

Of course she started ringing too early. He was still on the train when she delivered her first message to his machine. When he arrived home, he saw the blinking light and knew who the messages were from. He even knew, pretty much word for word, what Sofia had said.

He deleted the messages without listening to them and went for a pee. He was mid-way through when, surprise, surprise, the phone rang again. He returned to the kitchen in time to lift the receiver and listen.

'Is that you, Enrico?' she said having used that line since Noah crashed into Mt Ararat.

'North Pole? This is Santa Claus. How may I direct your call?'

Sofia's sense of humour had long been lost in the mail. 'I thought you would have been home by now.'

'I am home and about to have an afternoon nap.'

'Did you take your heart tablets before you left this morning?'

'Yes.

'And did you remember your walking stick?'

'Yes, but it was unnecessary.

'What do you mean?'

'I was presented with a special Santa walking stick to use all through my sessions until Christmas Eve.'

'I don't understand. What special Santa stick? You get a present at the end of your performances.'

'Ah but this was a special present, a stick beautifully decorated by a special and beautiful person.'

He teased his unhappy sister. Her solid ground became thin ice making her anxious and curious. Oh boy was she curious.

'What on earth are you talking about?'

'Mrs Santa made me a Christmas walking stick.'

'*Mrs* Santa?'

Well, her name is Rosie. Mrs Santa is the character she's playing in our performance.'

Sofia knew he was being cheeky. 'Enrico, I am not in the mood for your silly jokes.'

'It's not a joke. I've landed on my feet. Mum would be so happy. The woman I'm working with is not only beautiful and talented, but she's also a genuinely nice lady and I can't wait to get to know her better.'

It takes a lot to stop Sofia's train of thought let alone her verbal outpourings. At that moment she could not handle the number and variety of thoughts coursing through her brain. She couldn't decide which question to ask first or which command to issue. Before she even reached the runway, the take-off was aborted.

'I'm tired, Sis,' he said. 'I'll call you back after my sleep. Bye.'

He surprised himself with what he said and did. He rarely ended their conversations, but this time even went one step further and took the receiver out of the cradle. The line gave out an engaged signal.

Wow. That was unusual and big.

Usually, he sat on his bed and rolled or slowly fell to a supine position. Now he nearly threw himself. He thought. *Who needs a walking stick?*

He wasn't lying to Sofia about needing a nap and so prepared to fall asleep but struggled. His mind kept racing.

Did he ask his old pal about having sex with another person? That can't be right. He must have been dreaming. He pinched himself and it hurt. At that exact moment, Santa found himself in a right old pickle, and this was only day 1 of the season.

Chapter 11
I'll make sure she never gets within a kilometre of his privates.

News spread through the families. Grannie was making money to use on a cruise. Great Uncle Enrico has a new title—a fancy man.

With her degree in Gossip, Sofia earbashed Maria her daughter who showed less interest in Uncle Enrico than her mother but not so her sons. At a weekly meal, they bombarded their mother with questions.

'Ric has a girlfriend?' asked Michael more in disbelief than interest. 'Isn't that against the law?'

His brother turned sceptic. 'Anything Nonna says is subject to serious doubt. She controls poor old Ric like he's her son. Leave the old bugger alone.'

Maria persevered. 'Boys, you dismiss your grandmother's opinion at your peril. She's as sharp as anyone. Nothing escapes her eagle eye.'

Her sons stopped and stared.

'But so what,' asked Joseph? 'If great uncle Ric's found a lady friend, bloody good luck to him. It proves y'never too old for a bit of fun.'

'What if the fun gets serious?' asked Maria.

Michael scoffed. 'Oh, get real, Mum. He's been a bachelor all his life and now when he's 70 ...'

'71,' said Joseph.

'He's not gunna get hitched, not at his age.'

'But if he does, my darlings, you may have to wait a little bit longer for your inheritance.'

The bombshell dropped and you could be forgiven for thinking the ceiling collapsed with the air sucked from the room as the brothers stared at their mother and then one another.

'What do you mean?' demanded Joseph. 'Our inheritance is signed, sealed and will be delivered the day the old boy pegs out.'

'I told you years ago that your grandmother's estate goes to me, but your great uncle has left his estate to his version of grandchildren, his two great nephews.'

Michael shook his head. 'Right, so why raise the matter now?'

'Yes,' said his brother. 'How does Ric having a lady friend change his will?'

'I don't know,' said Maria. 'It may not make the slightest difference but if this unexpected romance does get serious, and great uncle Enrico pops the question and the lady says yes, you may have to wait until the widow passes away to get your hands on his estate, and who knows, she may outlive her husband by 10, 20 or even 30 years.'

Michael whispered in a controlled panic. '30 years!'

Joseph snorted and clenched his fists. 'That's not going to happen. Who is this bimbo? What's her name? Where does she live?'

'She's Mrs Santa,' said Maria.

'What!' exclaimed both brothers in unison?

'Her real address is probably care of the North Pole, but I understand for this month she's camped in Ringwood at Eastland.'

Maria went off to watch her favourite soap opera with lovelorn characters, eternal conflicts and cliffhanging endings, leaving her sons to get their own coffee. Michael turned philosophical.

'This could be nothing and anyway, who are we to stop the old guy enjoying his final years.'

Joseph simmered. 'I don't care about his love life, but I do care about a conniving woman flying in at the finishing post and grabbing the winner's cup. Who the hell does she think she is? *We're* his family. We always go to Christmas at Nonna's and give Ric a present.'

'Bought for us by Mum.'

'We always ring him on his birthday.'

'Once Mum tells us to.'

'Bloody hell, Michael, have you no sense of family? Blood is thicker than water, you idiot. Get with the programme.'

'Get with the programme? What's wrong with the language you spoke before you did that upmarket consultancy degree?'

'Please yourself, bro. But I'm going to check out this new chick and if she's taking Ric for a ride, I'll make sure she never gets within a kilometre of his privates and most definitely not his estate.'

Big brother stomped out to become intimate with his phone. He had a lawyer mate and wanted answers about a new spouse and last minute will changes. Michael finished his coffee, and he too handled his mobile. Both brothers found it easy to have their devices surgically attached to an upper limb.

Michael used his phone to romance a girl he'd taken a shine to, the third this month.

Chapter 12
She smiled causing Enrico's padding to itch.

Next morning, Enrico and Rosie were up with the birds, in their separate homes of course. Being early December, the weather helped, and their excitement at again becoming a popular character loved by children, gave them a boost. If Enrico could skip, he would.

Both showered, dressed and ate breakfast thinking about their character.

Rosie thought about the man playing Santa and Enrico thought about the woman playing his wife. She took Buster for a short walk and when ready to leave, left him inside with a chewy. The dog door meant he could go into the back garden and bark at the birds. After a canine hour or so he would miss his mistress but then find either of his two baskets inside, curl up and sleep.

Rosie headed for her new workplace quietly excited. Enrico grabbed his trusty walking stick and set off for the station. There was a spring in his step and the walking stick kept heading skywards to rest upon his shoulder.

At *Cossies 4 U*, Miranda struggled. Finding the ideal people to play Santa and this year, Mrs Santa, was no easy task. They had to be healthy, ideal employees, and great with all people, especially kids. When she chose wisely, the job worked a treat. If she picked a wrong'un, life sucked.

Big Graeme was a wonderful Santa with the one downside being his ability to offend his fellow workers. He'd been paired with the former self-proclaimed star actress, "I'm a pro" Lorna, and her true colours as a prima donna stood up and shouted on Day 1.

This was Miranda's on-going job, putting out spot fires and quickly. Lorna rang Miranda and complained about the dressing-room—what dressing-room? She complained about Santa making intimate remarks which were the equivalent of sexual harassment. They probably did meet the definition but had any woman told Fatso to get stuffed or worse, invited him to prove his manliness, the big boy would have run as far and as fast as he could, not that running was even remotely possible with the juggernaut known as Big Graeme. Clearly, he was all mouth and trousers—big trousers.

The only reason Lorna refused to walk off the set was the money. She was broke and refused to become a shop assistant or house cleaner. She added to her meagre Centre Link fortnightly income having found a few elocution students but a month's work as Mrs Santa was a godsend.

Miranda reckoned she had a solution. There was something minor she could do about the basic dressing-room, but she could make one simple major change. Oh, not that, please.

Enrico knocked on the storeroom door, heard no reply so entered. He was first. He checked his costume and props and dressed. He did so in the corner away from the female area and when undressed, he wore his vest, boxer shorts and of course his padding.

Mrs Santa tapped and entered.

'Good morning,' she said and smiled causing Enrico's padding to itch.

'Good morning,' he said. 'How did you pull up after your first day?'

'A bit tired but fine. And how did the lunch go with your friend?'

'Oh, we had a grand time. He's a former chef so his lunches are always superb.'

'Does he get his hair trimmed in kind?' she asked grinning.

'That would be impossible. His last hair count was six.'

Laughing, she headed for her area. 'I'd better get changed.' She entered her space and spoke loudly. 'Oh Santa, did you do this?

He headed to the space and looked inside. Two chairs and a small table were new additions.

'Not me,' he said, and the changes remained a mystery for a while. They came about because of Lorna's complaints. Miranda spoke to the centre management who ordered Anton the cleaner to find and set up the furniture.

Rosie changed and Enrico finished dressing. He picked up his Christmas stick and strutted about miming a Ho Ho Ho. A knock on the door saw him drop his character wondering if the cleaner was now using perfect manners.

The door opened and there stood his boss.

'Good morning, Santa,' said Miranda. 'You do look splendid.'

'Good morning, Miranda. This is a pleasant surprise.'

'Just popped in to see you have everything you need. Is Mrs Santa here?'

'Indeed, she is,' said Rosie stepping out in full costume.

Miranda took in a sharp breath. 'Wow! You've changed your costume.'

'I hope you don't mind,' said Rosie.

'Not at all; it looks superb. Well done you. So how was your first day?'

Rosie went to speak but was beaten to the punch by Santa.

'She was absolutely brilliant; Rosie is the perfect Mrs Santa.'

'I'm so pleased,' said Miranda finding her stomach churning and starting to tie itself in knots.

'And not only is she a whiz with costumes, but she also made me a perfect Santa stick.' He held it out for Miranda to inspect.

'That's wonderful. Thank you, Rosie. You're a real asset to the team.'

The happiness tried to flow freely around the room although the two actors sensed a pending problem. Something seemed out of place and Miranda knew it was time to bite the bullet.

Chapter 13
Enrico and Rosie sensed danger gurgling in their guts.

Joseph worked his phone. His consultancy work included networking, and he excelled at both. 'Maaaaate,' he said to a real estate agent he met once but spoke to now as if they went back years and were in one another's pocket.

The agent, Darren, studied at the same school for insincerity and started mentally recording the conversation to ensure there was something in it for him.

'Family business, Dazza, with a property to sell and who better to advise than your good self.'

Darren bathed in flattery and, never understanding irony let alone sarcasm, allowed the baloney to wash over him.

Joseph described Enrico's property giving as much detail as possible.

'I can look into that for you, pal, with natch you tipping me the wink as soon as the property even smells like it's up for sale.'

'As good as done,' said Joseph who lied even more naturally than he breathed.

Darren took a nanosecond to find Enrico's pad online. 'I've had a look Joe, and that area is definitely TT.'

'TT?' asked Joseph being ignorant and hating himself having to ask.

'Townhouse Territory, mate. The house is usually worth 50 cents and the block of land multi millions. Once the Council gives the developer the nod, he slaps in 2, 3 or hopefully 4 spanking new units and the buyers think they're on a winner.'

'Four townhouses!' exclaimed Joseph.

'And you reckon the owner's due to sell?'

'Ah, possibly but there's a prob. It's my great uncle who's nearly 80 and has a scheming bitch circling smelling big bucks.'

'Well, you wanna make sure his will's more watertight than a frigid clam and be ready to strike when the old bugger pops his clogs.'

'Sure, can do,' replied a now worried Joseph regretting having told anyone the fact that Ric is currently keen on a woman, a money-grubbing, black widow cum honey-trap princess.'

'Gotta 'nother call, mate,' said the agent. 'Bell me the moment you want to move. Later.'

Joseph's breathing changed. He needed air but the thought his great uncle was about to move an unknown woman up the pecking order while pushing the great nephews down, gave him a minor form of arrhythmia. He rang Michael.

'What's up?' asked the younger brother.

'What do we know about this bird Ric is keen on?'

'Nothing except she's Mrs Santa in his Christmas gig.'

'We need all the dope on her and especially if the old boy is even remotely serious.'

'Why?'

'Because I've discovered his joint is worth far more than I previously thought and if he changes his will, we are up a certain creek in a barbed-wire canoe. Now get out to Ringwood and start snooping, and make sure old Ric suspects nothing and never sees you. Got it?'

'Yes, but what if …' Big brother was gone.

In the anything-but-plush dressing-room with all its facilities including boxes and cleaning equipment, Miranda sweated. She wanted to lie and soft soap Mr and Mrs Santa but couldn't bring herself to do it. Mainly because she was a lousy liar and these folk were two of the last of the nice people.

'I need to ask a big favour,' she said, and Enrico and Rosie sensed danger begin gurgling in their guts.

'What's wrong?' asked Rosie genuinely confused.

'It's Lorna,' said Enrico and his boss nodded. He'd been in the job before and knew when the actors were happy and more so, when not.

'I can't afford to lose her, but I fear she might walk.'

'She won't walk,' said Enrico. 'Her pride and need for money will keep her in the job.'

Miranda had come to love and admire Enrico and now could see why. Apart from his kind and caring nature, he was smart. 'She expects to be treated like a star she claims to once have been,' said the boss.

'Are you saying she was never a star?' asked Rosie.

'She's had bit parts in a few long-forgotten TV shows and small parts in professional seasons touring regional theatres. But she hasn't worked professionally for ages and hates being anonymous.'

'You want us to swap,' said the clever barber and Rosie nearly died.

'Swap?' she blurted without thinking. 'But why?'

'Could we try it for a few days,' pleaded Miranda? 'Have Lorna stay on the second shift but work with you, Enrico and once she settles, we'll swap you back and hopefully by then she'll be happy in her work.'

Rosie struggled. 'You want me to be Mrs Santa to Big Graeme?'

'Just for a few days,' said Miranda close to begging. 'I can tell you he's all piss and wind, excuse my French, and you'll both be doing me a huge favour.'

Dressed in their full costumes, Enrico and Rosie looked perfect but inside were devastated. Neither had told the other their true feelings but the one thing that kept them excited in their new situation was the prospect of working together from now till Christmas. Neither knew what the future held beyond this gig, but hope proved a huge turn-on.

Enrico stood tall. 'I would like to be sure Rosie will be okay, and that you will look out for her,' said Enrico.

Rosie's heartbeat accelerated.

'I'll be fine,' she said, 'and thank you, Enrico for being so thoughtful.' She looked at Miranda. 'When do you want the change to start?

Miranda winced. 'How about we give it a go tomorrow?'

'I thought you said next week,' said Enrico fighting to keep his disappointment under wraps. He saw it was a fait accompli. 'So I switch to the afternoon shift working with Lorna and tomorrow, Rosie starts in the morning with Big Graeme?' He looked at Mrs Santa who barely nodded.

'Perfect,' she said feeling overwhelming relief. 'Well, I'll let you two get started and thanks again for being so considerate. Oh, and I'll tell the others.'

She left and the two costumed characters stared at one another in silence. This was not the plan they had in mind. The shock hit hard and hurt.

They paused at the porthole door and, without saying a word, Santa gave it a shove and strode out complete with ringing bell and fancy walking stick.

'Ho Ho Ho,' he called, and people stopped and stared with a few moving to the man in the big red suit. Mrs Santa waved to children and the party headed to the Christmas set.

Russell greeted them and helped them settle. It was time to pretend, to act, to play a role. Never mind your feelings, be the character and do so with enthusiasm and jollity. It's show time, folks.

The morning continued with the queue long and many chats between Santa and excited children. Not for a second could anyone tell Santa and Mrs Santa were sad getting sadder. When the queue thinned and they had a child-free minute or three, they whispered.

'I'm sorry about the change, Rosie,' he said.

'Don't be silly, it's not your fault.'

'Miranda should tell the selfish woman she's unprofessional and unless she stops being a prima donna, show her the door.'

'But aren't they short of actors?'

Enrico's disappointment showed. He was fond of Rosie and loved working with her but now, out of nowhere, he reckoned their friendship was under threat and all through no fault of their own.

He wanted to say more but a young family of two youngsters and a baby arrived desperate to talk to Santa.

Session over, they changed and left the dressing-room before Big Graeme and Lorna arrived. Enrico and Rosie waited outside in the shopping centre to see how their fellow performers performed. They moved to one side both not wanting to say goodbye and leave. They made small talk until Big Graeme and Lorna appeared. The first Mr and Mrs Santa watched unimpressed. The pressure built before Enrico came clean.

'I'm feeling miserable, Rosie,' he said, and she returned his gaze.

'It may not be for long. I think Miranda is under pressure and I'm sure you'll help Lorna settle in her role.'

'I'd much rather help you,' he said without thinking and placed his hand on her arm. She sensed a rush of something in her chest, but their brief moment of pleasure vanished when a child screamed.

The sound came from the Christmas set and with many shoppers, Enrico and Rosie moved forward. A youngster, in being handed from Mrs Santa to Santa had wiggled free and landed on the plastic grass and a toy sled fortunately made of cardboard.

The child's grandmother was sensible—she had eight grandchildren—and having checked and discovered the little one suffered no injury, wisely took the crying toddler away. Lorna seemed at a loss and instead of enquiring if the little one was hurt, kept pointing out how it wasn't her fault.

Enrico and Rosie exchanged glances. They both were now sure this Mrs Santa should never have been given the job.

Once normal service resumed, they headed for the exit.

'May I offer you a lift, Enrico?' she asked.

He hesitated. He hated depending on others and preferred his own company, but this woman was exceptional. He struggled to find an excuse. 'I won't bite,' she said and that broke the tension.

He laughed in his polite way and agreed, following her to the car park. He stood beside her as she unlocked her car preparing to open her door.

'I'm the one driving, Santa. You get in the other side,' she said smiling and he knew it. His endearing manners meant he only wanted to open the door for her.

They set off and approached the place where she dropped him last time. 'Now please let me drive you to your home,' she insisted. 'Do I turn here?'

'Yes,' he said giving in and she turned into his street. 'This is so kind of you.'

'It's not out of my way and besides, what are friends for?'

He muttered his thanks, and they approached his home.

'That's my place,' he said pointing, and she pulled over and stopped. 'What a lovely garden. Are you the gardener?'

'I am,' he said unlocking his seat belt. 'Would you like to see it?'

Enrico lost control of his normal thought processes. He was acting on gut instinct. His excitement levels kept climbing.

'I'd love to,' said Rosie turning off the engine and getting out. He waited for her to lock the vehicle and walk around to his side.

'The flowers are for show but as a true Italian and the son of a fruiterer, you will note the veggies in the front garden and, of course, there are more around the back.'

'I love them and wish I had a block even half this size.'

'Come and I'll show you the back garden.'

They set off but stopped when a voice rang out.

'Hello Signor. How are you going in your big red suit?'

Enrico smiled and called. 'Hello Beverley. All is good, thank you.'

'I will be bringing my grandson on Friday.'

Enrico stopped, wondering if he would be there at that time. 'Good oh. I'll see you then. Ciao.'

He led his friend down the drive much to the chagrin of his neighbour who was curious beyond measure to learn anything about the attractive woman by his side. *Who the hell is that woman? Enrico has a girlfriend. No!*

Santa and Mrs Santa entered the even bigger back yard. Enrico's vegetable production was seasonal and at this time of the year his tomatoes, pumpkins and onions were on the march. His apricot and peach trees groaned.

Rosie admired the tidiness of the property. A clothesline stretched into the garden and stood tall thanks to a large wooden pole with a V at its top. This was pre-Hills Hoist. Sheets flapped in the breeze. She discovered so much about this man. He was a gardener and seriously domesticated.

'Would you like coffee?' he asked, and Rosie could not have been more delighted.

He unlocked his back door and ushered his guest inside. She entered the kitchen and discovered the consistency of Enrico Salvatore. The interior of his house was spotless.

He pottered while she sat at a small round table. Instant coffee was, for him, a mortal sin and he prepared a quality brew.

'Forgive me being personal, Enrico, but I find it hard to believe a man living alone is able to run a garden and a house where everything is so perfect.'

'Ah, you haven't seen my bedroom, Rosie. It is ...' He froze. 'Oh, I am so terribly sorry, please forgive me. I was not suggesting you should enter ... I mean ...'

He stopped because she laughed so loud and for so long.

'Of course you weren't and I'm guessing that was your attempt at trying to be funny.'

Relief gripped him. 'Thank you, Rosie. Yes, it was a terrible attempt. Now, I need you to remind me how you like your coffee.'

He served it and of course opened a packet of Italian biscuits placing them on a plate which matched the coffee cups and saucers.

After a few sips and nibbles, she produced a twinkle in her eye and said, 'I bet you even have hospital corners on your bed.'

Now it was his turn to laugh and after their wonderful chat and coffee, he led her out via the front door with Rosie stopping by the main bedroom. The door was open.

'See,' she said and pointed, 'hospital corners.'

Again he laughed with delight and relief and walked her out to the car. He left his walking stick inside. For this woman, he determined he could stride about anywhere sans stick.

The neighbour hid and watched. Her fascination with the mysterious woman saw her eyes widen and her jaw keep dropping.

Chapter 14
'Not alone,' gasped Stepanie. 'He can't be alone with Timmy.'

Thomas Larsen was an ordinary bloke, born in Europe who, as a child, with his parents and younger sister, migrated Down Under. As an adult, he trained in surveying and found work in local government in Melbourne. At work he met Stephanie Gibson who worked as a clerical officer. He asked her on a date, she accepted, and their relationship began.

Her parents liked him, and his parents liked her. If this was love, play on.

In time they married, set up house in leafy Montrose and started a family. Their son Timothy was born and proved a happy and healthy little boy.

But a year or more later all was not well in Montrose. Why did the marriage hit trouble? Well, pick any of the usual reasons. The couple stopped communicating, one or both changed, they were not suited in the first place, they had no expertise in handling marital difficulties, or one met someone and reckoned they made a bad choice in the marriage stakes in the first place.

Stephanie had a girlfriend, Christine, and both were stay-at-home young mums caring for their infant. The women met regularly for coffee and a chat. The state of the Larsen marriage ranked high on the agenda.

Poor old Thomas copped a bashing, figuratively speaking, and remained ignorant of the plan being hatched to have him removed from the relationship and the property. He sensed his wife's unhappiness but being from an old-fashioned family where couples, for the sake of the children, stuck together through thick and thin, he ploughed ahead working longer hours continuing to avoid the trouble brewing at home.

The marriage continued to deteriorate, and soon little Timmy would fall asleep to a backdrop of the muffled raised voices of his parents.

It's difficult to pinpoint how and why a marriage first begins to fail but a failure to discuss and resolve a problem is a common starting point.

The snowball of unhappiness continued rolling downhill gathering size and speed, and conspiring with her friend, Stephanie made an appointment with a solicitor who dealt with marital disputes in the field of family law.

The female lawyer heard nothing new. She listened for an age not wanting to "lead the witness". When Stephanie had exhausted her case details having been prompted at times by her friend, the solicitor laid out the legal situation.

She discussed sharing of assets with the house being the primary item. She detailed the custody and care of little Timothy, payment for his upkeep as well as visitation rights for the lad's father.

'Do you wish to remain in the family home?' Stephanie wasn't sure.

'I do but I can't afford the mortgage,' she said close to tears.

'Do you wish to have custody of Timothy?'

'Of course,' blurted the mother.

'Will your husband have access at particular times?'

'Not alone,' gasped Stephanie. 'He can't be alone with Timmy.'

The room temperature dropped. In an instant the mood changed, and Stephanie's friend touched her pal's arm urging her to tell all.

The fascinated solicitor probed with gentle but specific questions.

'Has your husband been violent or threatened to use violence to you or your son?' The solicitor used this leading question knowing the answer might well be true, untrue or an exaggeration.

Stephanie broke down sobbing. The interview ended and the ignorant, innocent husband and father was unofficially stitched up.

That night Thomas was in for a shock, not so much because his wife was contemplating a divorce, but that she had done something about it and all behind his back. Armed with the details explained by her solicitor, Stephanie, as nervous as a frightened kitten and fearing his reaction, told her husband they needed to talk. She began and his shock was palpable.

When he recovered enough to speak sensibly, another bombshell landed. This was not the time to discuss and possibly seek therapy, mediation or any form of reconciliation, this was game over, sign here, go pack your bags and vamoose time.

Thomas experienced many emotions—anger, desperation, accusations and a break down. Sucking in deep breaths, his major concern was their son.

'Where will he live?' he needed to know.

Stephanie refused to answer his questions and now less timid, doled out advice as if to an immature and badly-behaved child. 'Thomas, you need to get a lawyer who can explain the procedures. Get professional advice.'

His face became red getting redder. 'That's a bit rich. First my wife dumps me, tells me nothing until the divorce is off and running, and then gives me advice on how to run my new single life.'

'I'm sorry,' said an unsympathetic Stephanie who wasn't sorry and knew her so-called fine words were never going to butter any parsnips.

'But he's my son,' he whined. 'You can't just cut me out of his life.'

'Keep your voice down. You'll wake Timmy and half the street.'

The deflated, despairing husband sat there speechless before dragging himself up and storming outside with Stephanie hearing the car drive away.

Weeks earlier she confessed all to her parents in private and they were at a loss as to what she should do. Her father pretended it wasn't happening, and her mother begged her daughter to try and patch up the union for the sake of their only grandson. For Stephanie, that was never going to happen.

Thomas returned in the wee small hours avoiding his wife. He went to his son and kissed the boy not being able to prevent a tear land on the little lad's cheek. The distraught father slept on a makeshift bed in his study.

At work, he put in even longer hours knowing he should find a solicitor but couldn't bring himself to do so. He heard they charge an arm and a leg. He stayed the night in a motel which produced even greater tension, and had the husband and father known his wife was taking notes, keeping records of his behaviour—all prompted by advice from her friend—the miserable dad would have been even more desolate.

Eventually he surrendered, moved out and into his old bedroom in his parents' house. They mourned as if someone had died.

Stephanie's pursuit of the divorce saw Thomas receive a registered letter card at his place of work. Looks from colleagues hammered home his embarrassment. He signed for the mail at the post office and learned of his fate and date. The court hearing was in six weeks.

Little Timmy became a toddler and his ability to walk impressed all. His maternal grandparents spoilt him rotten, Timmy being their only grandchild. Thomas and his parents saw little of the youngster. Stephanie left him with her parents for three hours on a Sunday allowing Thomas to visit his boy. The child bore no ill-will against his old man and his open arms while calling, 'Daddy,' bore deep inside Thomas's soul.

These visits made life worse and ill-feeling bubbled away beneath the surface. Thomas gave birth to an ulcer.

The boy's next birthday party was a weird affair. Timmy delighted in his gifts and the decorations for his party while the grown-ups in the room knew the dislike, even hatred between his parents could be weighed on a pair of scales. Every adult in the room was acting.

The father arrived long after the cake and candles were put away. His gift to his son turned out to be a damp squib. The child had been swamped with presents and Timmy's delight with so much and so many meant his acceptance of Dad's gift went unnoticed. Thomas departed not wanting to look back at his darling boy.

Chapter 15

Heir today, gone tomorrow.

The brothers sat in Joseph's Chevrolet Corvette, an ancient model but which Joseph loved more than any human. They fiddled with their phones.

'And you're sure?' asked Michael for the umpteenth time?

'Yes, I'm sure,' snapped big brother. 'Old Ric has pulled a bird defying every law and statistic known to humankind. This moneygrubbing bitch has obviously seen him as a soft touch, she's checked out his real estate and probably his bank balance and decided to strike.'

'So if he marries her, she replaces us as his main beneficiary.'

'Bingo.'

'And if she outlives the old boy, we could be middle-aged by the time we get our hands on the property?'

'At last, Mr Thicky twigs,' sighed Joseph and furious, slapped the steering wheel of his beloved Corvette.

'So what's the plan?' asked Michael.

'I'm still working on it.'

'If we can convince Ric his bitch is a low-life and only interested in his money, he'll dump her, and we'll be back as his rightful heirs and be quids in.'

'You don't say,' replied the sarcastic brother. 'But there's obviously one hell of a potential problem.'

Michael's face scrunched in ignorance. 'Which is?'

'Ric sees us on Nonna's birthday, Christmas and the odd lunch. Even if we prove the woman's a crook or invent stuff that convinces him she is, he will wonder why we're now in his face and on his case. He's not stupid.'

'How about we engage a third party?'

Joseph looked at his younger brother. 'Engage a third party? What are you, a poor man's Mafia bagman?'

Michael hit back. Both were snarky. 'Well, what do you suggest?'

'The first thing is to find out everything about the girlfriend. Where she lives? What's she worth? Does she have a past? Is she for real?'

Now the sarcasm switched siblings. 'Oh, so who's the private eye now? We know nothing about stalking and spying.'

'We can learn. We *must* learn. You'll be screaming if Ric marries the bitch and then kicks the bucket after the excitement of his honeymoon. For a 71-year-old virgin, that to me sounds like a real possibility.

'How do we know the bird's a virgin?'

Joseph screamed. 'Not her, *him!*'

They sat there silent, stewing. They could see their future financial prosperity evaporating before their eyes. Heir today, gone tomorrow.

'Okay, we have to do something but what, how and when?' asked Michael.

'We start with you following Ric to find and observe this woman. Get everything you can about her but don't let him see you, that's essential.'

'Yeah, all right, I know how to blend into a crowd.'

'There should be people working with Ric who might be able to give you details. I'll go to his employer and see what I can get.'

'How?'

'I dunno. I could be running a charity for sick kids, and we want to hire a Santa and Mrs Santa. Once we find her details, we can plan from there.'

Michael sniffed. He lacked his brother's desire for a quick buck but hated the idea his inheritance could be pinched at the death—that is, his great uncle's demise. Hell's bells, the adage remained; blood is bloody well thicker than water.

Of course Sofia was on the phone wanting to know all the news from baby brother's latest day as Santa.

'I have big news, Sis,' he said. 'The boss at *Costumes 4 U* has decided to switch performers and tomorrow I'll be working with the other Mrs Santa.'

'What? Why?' demanded the matriarch.

'It's nothing to do with me or Rosie. The other team are having problems so my boss Miranda thought mixing up the teams might be a good idea.'

'What does your current Mrs Santa think?'

'We haven't discussed it. I'm terribly disappointed as we seem to be getting on so well.'

'What does that mean?' enquired the widow Nosy-Parker. 'I hope you're not making a fool of yourself, Enrico.'

He might have been but didn't care. He hadn't felt like this since … well, since never.

'I need a nap, Sofia. All that smiling and talking to children is hard work.'

'Have you taken your blood pressure pills?'

'Just before you rang,' Enrico lied and wandered to the cupboard drawer.

'What are you having for your tea?'

'I haven't finished the casserole you gave me on the weekend.' He lied again. He gave the meat leftovers to next door's dog through the secret opening on their shared back fence.

It was another of Enrico's secrets. He loved his sister but subscribed to the adage that what you don't know can't hurt you.

'Goodbye Sofia,' he said and ended the call before she could continue.

He tried to doze but kept thinking about the meeting with his boss and favourite fellow performer earlier that day. Miranda later spoke to Big Graeme and to the woman she and her staff nicknamed Lorna Doom about the team switch starting tomorrow. The CEO gave a weak excuse about this being the first time her company had used a Mrs Santa and wanted everyone to get used to working with different performers.

Big Graeme didn't care, and Lorna reckoned it was her complaining which forced the change. It reinforced her self-belief she had power and relevance.

Chapter 16

'Are you insane? You never say "Good luck" to a professional.'

Michael was in his final year of a master's degree in computer science. He earned good money fixing computers for friends and designing web sites for anyone wanting a quality product at a competitive price. Paying cash helped Michael ignore the taxman.

The brothers spent an hour that night nutting out a plan or plans to thwart their great uncle acquiring a wife in these his sunset years. They both believed in the philosophy that old Ric didn't need a woman to nag him in his dotage and besides, sex was vastly overrated.

The thought of Enrico having a sex life triggered a feeling of disgust within his great nephews.

The first plan was simple. Michael would go to the shopping centre and spy. Who was this woman playing Mrs Santa with Ric? Find out anything and everything about her. The brothers needed data in order to scuttle any possible relationship. If such scuttling upset their great uncle, tough. He was knocking on the door of God's waiting room whereas his family, well his great nephews, needed financial support as they still had 50+ years of living to go.

In the Ringwood centre car park, Michael parked his fourth-hand MG near Lorna's battered Datsun with both having no idea of the other's identity. Michael went inside, bought an egg and bacon roll and a coffee and wandered the shopping centre. He was hardly in disguise, but his brother insisted he not draw attention to himself.

'Blend in with the crowd, look as if you're going Christmas shopping, and get photos of the bitch who threatens our future,' ordered big brother.

Even though he now performed the second shift, Enrico was always early. His heavy heart made his walking more difficult. He couldn't discard his usual stick, and he hoped like hell his hip would behave well with the other Mrs Santa. As she was a professional complainer, he worried she'd complain about Enrico not being up to snuff.

Big Graeme and Rosie's session neared its end. Enrico finished dressing when the door opened, and Lorna appeared. Enrico rose from his seat. 'Good afternoon,' he said with a forced smile.

'Good afternoon,' muttered Lorna heading for her dressing-room, the one without a star on its door, actually without any door.

He knew their relationship bore no resemblance to his one with Rosie, the perfect Mrs Santa. In fact, she was the perfect woman, a lady in every sense of the word. Lorna was the direct opposite.

Rosie and Big Graeme returned, and Enrico felt fantastic. The large Santa collapsed to recover. Rosie and Enrico enjoyed a quiet chat.

Eventually Lorna appeared with her wig a tad off-centre. 'Excuse me,' said Santa Enrico but I think your wig has slipped a little.'

She turned back in a huff. 'No make-up mirror, no lights, not even a hand basin,' she muttered before reappearing in better shape.

'Shall we make a start?' suggested Enrico.

''Why?' she snapped. 'We don't get paid for starting early.'

He got the message. 'As you wish,' he whispered.

The lack of conversation, the silence, apart from a few strange sounds emanating from somewhere inside Big Graeme, and the boredom pushed Lorna to react.

'Oh, all right, let's get it over with.' She started for the corridor ignoring Enrico with his fancy Santa stick. 'And make sure you only work the right hours, *no overtime.*'

Rosie smiled at Enrico, and as he passed Big Graeme the large Santa spoke. 'See how *you* like it.'

Enrico caught up with Lorna who waited at the door with the porthole. He smiled at her and whispered. 'Good luck,' he said falling back in fright when she erupted.

'What! Are you insane? You never say "Good luck" to a fellow professional.' Then under her breath she muttered, 'Bloody amateurs!'

He recovered, pushed open the door, rang his bell and started his Ho Ho Ho routine. She followed with the worst, or in fact the best plastic smile ever portrayed.

The session began well. There always seemed to be a good crowd ready when Santa first appeared. Maybe it was mothers not wanting to join a lengthy queue and having to calm their grizzly offspring. 'Are we there yet?' took on a new meaning.

Lorna performed well without any warmth or friendliness. Enrico tried even harder to give his Santa the biggest and warmest of hearts. The children loved the man with the huge white beard.

In the crowd with many onlookers stood a young man holding empty boxes he'd wrapped the night before. What a good lad he is, buying all those Christmas presents for his family and friends. Hardly, they were part of his disguise.

Michael used his phone to unobtrusively take pictures. Santa, his great uncle Enrico, was not important but Mrs Santa starred.

The great nephew moved back and observed from afar. A woman sat at a small table pushing her toddler in a stroller to keep the youngster quiet.

'Have you seen Santa yet?' he asked throwing in his version of sincerity.

'No because I think she'll scream,' replied Mum.

'You could try Mrs Santa. She seems a lovely lady and could help your little 'un prepare for the big man.'

The woman pondered. 'Not so sure about that. My friend was here yesterday and reckoned Mrs Santa was lovely but from what I've seen now, I can't agree.'

'Well, good luck,' said Michael, proving he was no Sherlock Holmes, and drifted away.

He had photos galore and two reviews about Enrico's bird—one good and one not so. He hoped big brother would be pleased.

That afternoon, Joseph slipped into his BS mode calling *Costumes 4 U*. Miranda was on the road putting out fires and her PA, Sandra, answered.

Joseph used his real name. 'I'm calling for a mate who at Christmas turns his huge garden into a party space for less-fortunate kiddies. He's asked me to see if I can find a Santa and Mrs Santa to hand out the presents.'

'You've called the right place. We have many brilliant people playing Santa and Mrs Santa.'

'My friend took her kids to Ringwood this afternoon and reckoned the two people you had there were brilliant. Santa was wonderful but Mrs Santa was perfect. She coaxed the kids into the right mood to meet Father Christmas.'

'That's nice. We're always glad to get good feedback. Can I take your details, and I'll have our boss, Miranda, call you back.'

'Perfect,' oozed Joseph. 'Look, my friend who opens his home doesn't care to be rewarded. If your boss would like to see the property, that could be arranged but he doesn't like the limelight.'

'We understand and good on him for all he does. We'll talk soon.'

Joseph gave his name and number and hung up pleased but in no way happy. He needed to discover the details of this Mrs Santa woman and then start work on exposing her as a gold digger chasing poor old Ric's estate, Joseph and Michael's inheritance. 'I bet she's a divorcee,' said Joseph to himself.

Back on the Santa set, Enrico Santa was on edge working with Mrs Prima Donna Santa. There were no dropped toddlers, but she kept looking at her watch and muttering. 'Last hour, thank God,' and 'There should be a law against certain women having children.'

When photographer Russell announced the end of the shift, Lorna couldn't have been more delighted and prepared to leave when Enrico made a stand.

'I'm sorry, Lorna, but we have to leave together; it's a company rule.'

She looked at him with enough venom to replenish half a dozen Eastern brown snakes. Her whispered retort was heard by Santa and the bloke with the camera.

'More amateurs,' she hissed, and continued fuming as Enrico found his Santa stick and bell and headed towards their storeroom. She followed with more fake sincerity than the great nephews combined.

Russell caught Santa's eye as they passed. 'Short straw, mate,' he whispered and the kind, hip-sore Enrico nodded and grimaced.

He could put up with her unprofessional behaviour, barely, but why must he be separated from the lovely Rosie?

Chapter 17
What a mess and all because he'd fallen in love.

Lorna and Enrico entered the storeroom. He collapsed and she left to change. He didn't bother to remove any part of his costume. Working with this Mrs Santa left him miserable. What could he do to restore the status quo? Neither he nor Rosie did anything wrong so why were they the ones to suffer?

Lorna came out dressed to travel. 'Staying the night, are we?' she said.

'No, but could we please have a chat?'

She stopped. 'I'm running late; maybe tomorrow.'

He called. 'No, wait!'

The tone of voice and delivery forced her to stop. She seethed.

'How dare you shout at me! I'll have you reported for bullying. You'll be out on your ear.'

Enrico turned humble. ''I'm so sorry, Lorna but I need to tell you something important.' This sounded serious.

'Well?'

'I don't think I'm the right Santa for you. I have no acting experience while you are a professional. I feel I'm letting you down, holding you back. If you ask Miranda to have me changed, I'll support your request and do whatever she decides.' He paused. 'Please.'

Whether he meant to be clever or not, his tactic was smart. She was thrown. He sounded and looked serious and sincere. He recognized her professional status, her superior ability. He knows he's an amateur. She breathed deeply and moved in close.

'I'll give you one more chance. Lift your game and I won't report you to Miranda. Tomorrow's the test.'

Another glare and she turned on her expensive heels and left.

He sat there, confused. What prompted him to do what he did? Was he so desperate to be reunited with Rosie? Will Lorna report him or ask Miranda to have him moved? What a mess and all because he'd fallen in love.

Still in costume, he snapped out of his reverie when Anton the cleaner pushed open the door and entered.

A short trip home with the train on time saw him unlocking his back door and collapsing on a kitchen chair. The phone rang.

'Bugger,' said the rarely swearing ex-barber. He knew who it was.

'Enrico?' asked his sister not even giving him a chance to say, 'Hello'.

'Yes, Sofia, I'm home and in need of a nap.'

'How was Mrs Santa?'

'Terrible,' he said causing his sister to pause—a rare occurrence.

'What do you mean, terrible?'

'She keeps looking at her watch, complaining about the parents and children, and the other day even managed to drop a youngster who, thank God, was not hurt.'

'That's dreadful,' replied big Sis feeling relieved and veering towards happiness. 'So, she's no longer the wonderful woman you first thought?'

'She never was or will be even remotely wonderful, and compared to the other Mrs Santa, she's a monster.'

Confusion reigned. Sofia, having forgotten his previous announcement of a staff roster change, didn't follow her brother's statements. She settled on the belief that this Rosie woman was showing her true colours, and her poor, deluded brother was now fully aware of the eyelid-fluttering wicked woman.

'I'm taking my nap, Sofia. Bye.'

He headed for bed.

She didn't like it when he ended the conversation but felt happy her baby brother had seen the light with Madame Jezebel.

Chapter 18

Michael made a face of disgust. 'It's like imagining your parents doing it.'

Michael arrived at his brother's rented flat in Hawthorn East. 'Come in,' said Joseph walking inside leaving his brother to close the door. 'Right, let's see those pics.'

On his phone, Michael opened the photos of Mrs Lorna Santa performing with their great uncle Ric. Joseph flicked through stopping to get a better look at certain ones.

'Shit,' said Joseph, 'she's a looker. No wonder old Enrico's hooked.'

'I heard mixed reviews about her.' Joseph looked at his brother.

'What's that in English?'

'I casually asked a mother if she'd taken her kid to see Santa, and she said a friend went yesterday, and Mrs Santa was wonderful but today, the mother I spoke to gave old Ric's bird a solitary 1 star.'

'So? Who cares whether she's good or lousy? What matters is, how far has she dug her claws into him?'

Michael couldn't help so turned the spotlight back on his brother. 'I'm working on it. What's *your* news?'

Joseph explained his fake Christmas party plan hoping that would get him the details of Mrs Santa. Both men were frustrated. This was not going to be easy. If they went too hard, they could show their hand and if Enrico found out, he could change his will there and then. A wrong move and they could shoot themselves in the foot. If the woman at *Costumes 4 U* twigged they were scam merchants, they'd create another possible landmine. It could mean their plan to grab Enrico's estate straight after his demise might crash and burn.

'I've had another idea,' said Joseph. 'You know that up-himself filmmaker, Simon McMahon?'

'You mean the wannabee Steven Spielberg of North Melbourne?'

'I put a grand in his last flop, so he owes me.'

'How can he help?'

'I'll get him to let me use his company name with matching web site, whip up a theatre agency business card and give one to Ric's bird.'

'And say what?'

'We're looking for experienced senior females and wonder if she's interested in a film role to be shot in Queensland. I give her my number but use Simon's business address. She'll look at his web site, see it's legit and be impressed. She returns my call asking for details. I spin a yarn but get her name and contact details.' Michael said nothing which annoyed big brother. 'Well have you got a better idea?'

'It might work,' he said.

'Until we ID the bitch, we can't stop her and Ric getting it on.'

Michael made a face of disgust. 'It's like imagining your parents doing it.'

Their distaste and frustration took root.

Pippa rang her grandmother, and Rosie was still recovering after surviving a session with that other Santa, Big Graeme.

'Hi, Gran. How did you go with the other Santa?'

Rosie went to speak but her voice croaked. She coughed and cleared her throat.

'Gran, are you all right?'

'Fine,' said Rosie recovering. 'I've had a tough day.'

'What happened?'

'Let's say working with Enrico is a sweet dream while working with Super-size Santa is a nightmare.'

'That's not on. Tell them you want to switch back and if you won't I will.'

Rosie scoffed. 'Thank you, my darling. I can look after myself. Now how was your day?'

'Dull and boring. So did you catch up with your favourite Santa?'

'We met briefly during the break and the poor man is unhappy.'

'Sorry?'

'That prima donna Mrs Santa is hard work, and I reckon Enrico will have found her more than a handful. I told him to go straight home and rest.'

'Gran, are you his secret girlfriend or his mother?'

They both laughed with the laughter covering serious issues of the heart. Rosie decided to censor her thoughts and deeds with the man she was now so fond of. She became nervous so strong were her feelings for the man with the walking stick. One thing was certain in her mind. She was 99% girlfriend and, at best, 1% mother.

Chapter 19
His work colleague looked up in alarm when Thomas collapsed.

It was D-Day for Thomas Larsen. The Family Court required his presence in the matter of the divorce from soon-to-be ex-wife, Stephanie. Silly-billy Thomas continued ignoring all advice and encouragement re hiring a solicitor. He represented himself. Big mistake.

He arrived alone, knew no-one and only when inside the court he spotted Stephanie with, surprise, surprise, her friend Christine.

The judge or magistrate or person in charge, Thomas had no idea, started speaking and Thomas struggled. When he was addressed by name the situation became overwhelming. He stood not even knowing if that was the right thing to do.

Stephanie couldn't bring herself to turn and look at him. Christine did and whispered to her friend.

Not having legal representation became a disaster for Thomas. He had no say in proceedings. The family home was to be sold, the mortgage repaid, and each party would receive half the remaining funds. At least he wasn't broke.

But the kicker, the thing he surely should have seen coming, was access to his son. Timmy was an energetic toddler starring at kindergarten. The child loved his father who sensed love pour from his body whenever he was allowed to be with his son.

But the ruling was strongly in favour of the mother. Timmy would live with her and Thomas would only have access on certain days and under certain rules and yet must contribute to the boy's upbringing.

The terms of the access decision hit Thomas hard, and when alone with his parents that night, his pain increased to record levels. Why was he being punished in this way?

'You should have found a solicitor,' said his father making Thomas sink even further into his morass of despair.

'Never mind, son,' said his mother trying in vain to help her boy. 'Timmy will grow up always seeing his father and knowing how much you love him.'

Even such loving words couldn't prevent more depression whacking Thomas in both his head and heart.

He made the decision to break out on his own. With his share of the money from the sale of the former marital home, he bought a plot of land in the Dandenongs and set about designing a house to be set among the gum trees. He would bring Timmy to this bushland retreat and the two would have wonderful adventures. Life would again be wonderful.

Pathetically and ironically, communication between the divorced parents was better now than when they were married. Thomas continued his job with local government and used his work address as his mailing address. Stephanie continued to use her solicitor's office as her mailing address. Thomas had no idea where she lived or with whom; Timmy obviously but was there a new partner, a new father for the child?

Thomas and an architect friend produced plans for his house in the hills and Thomas began applying to banks for a loan to build the new residence.

He wrote to Stephanie advising her of his plans and a week later, copped a sharp pain in his chest when he opened the reply from his ex's solicitor.

In short it stated that Stephanie objects to their son being taken away from Melbourne for any visitation times with his father, and certainly to a place far from medical facilities and where snakes and other wildlife could injure even kill a young boy or in which he could become lost. If you, Mr Larsen, persist in your plans, the matter will return to the Family Court seeking a ruling to prevent Timothy being taken to this place.

'This place!' the surveyor fumed then despaired. The pressure overwhelmed him, and his work colleague looked up in alarm when Thomas collapsed on his desk.

Chapter 20
He finished dressing wondering what on Earth had happened.

That night, Enrico slept well once he fell asleep. For an hour or so he tossed and turned thinking about Rosie and his unusual request to Lorna. He wondered if his words would come back to bite him, and if he would ever work with Rosie again. If so, would that destroy any future they might have once the Christmas event ended.

In the morning, he decided to perform simple exercises to help his aging legs and troublesome hip. 'Don't push it,' said the physiotherapist whose services came free as part of a Care Plan arranged through his GP. 'Slow and gentle,' was the command and Enrico obeyed, desperate to give himself every chance of keeping up with the younger Mrs Santa—the one called Rosie. He believed she was a good decade younger than him. It was not quite eight years.

That morning, a first-time visitor to the Eastland shopping centre was Enrico's great nephew, Joseph. He wasn't there to see Santa or the love of his great uncle's life. Joseph arrived in disguise to deliver a letter for the former "star" Lorna. In reception and wearing a Covid-style face mask and pretend Australia Post-style delivery jacket, Joseph told the receptionist he had a hand delivery letter for Mrs Santa.

'Which Mrs Santa,' asked the young woman?

'I'm told she's the one working with the walking-stick Santa.'

'Oh Enrico,' she said. Joseph nodded. Taking the letter, the receptionist said, 'That's Lorna. I'll take it to her dressing-room. She's performing this afternoon with Santa Enrico.'

Joseph handed her a clipboard with a fake letter detailing deliveries and the receptionist signed it proving the letter's acceptance. Joseph smiled behind his mask and left. He reckoned the charity event offer and now the film offer, neither of which was real, would flush out the gold-digger trying to rip off his poor old great uncle. Joseph would soon have Lorna's personal details.

Outside in the shopping centre, he removed his disguise and, from a distance, watched the large crowd surrounding the Santa set.

He put his extra clothes in his car then went in search of lunch. When he returned, the morning session was about to end. He moved closer and caught sight of a young woman with flaming red hair.

Pippa skipped her morning class on Interpretation and caught the train to Ringwood. She didn't tell her grandmother she wanted to see her working with the other Santa. Big Graeme and Rosie were in full swing when she arrived towards the end of the morning session. She used her zoom lens on her digital SLR to snap a few close-ups. Not too close because Santa's size required a wide-angle lens.

Studying the young woman taking photos, Joseph moved to get a better look deciding she was hot. He watched the redhead and when she stopped taking photos, made his move.

'Hi,' he said feasting his eyes on her tight sweater and its shape.

'Hi,' replied Pippa with less enthusiasm.

He indicated her camera. 'Do you do that for a living?'

She scoffed. 'No, it's more a hobby.'

'I'm Joseph. I work for a film company. We're always looking for young professional freelancers for special shoots. Here's my card.' He produced another of the film company cards and scribbled his number.

She took the card and studied it. 'Thanks.'

'My number's on the back. If you're after part-time work and you're good at what you do, give me a call.' He turned on a charm machine. 'What's your name?'

'Pippa.'

'Well Pippa, I'd like to hear from you.' The charm machine slipped into overdrive. 'Ciao,' he said, flashed his eyes and left.

She discovered her blood started moving faster, again looked at the card and wondered if the good-looking man and his offer were genuine. He was interesting and wore fancy threads. If that was an enticing pick-up routine, it worked.

'Mrs Santa,' called a voice and Rosie saw her granddaughter standing against the picket fence surrounding the set.

'My granddaughter,' whispered Rosie to Big Graeme.

'Nice,' he said and by adding, 'Santa's knee is always available,' he drove Rosie as far and as fast as she could move from the giant sleaze.

'I wanted to see how you perform with another Santa,' said Pippa giving a cheeky grin to her gran. Rosie dropped her voice.

'He's horrible. The kids love him but he's a sexist slob and I can't wait to change back to working with Enrico.'

People moved in to be closer to Mrs Santa and Rosie knew she couldn't be heard being critical, saying anything not in keeping with her character.

'I took a few terrific photos of you, Mrs Santa. You look great.'

'Lovely,' said Rosie and saw Russell giving her the nod. 'Must go, darling.'

Pippa's news burst out. 'Oh Gran, I got a job offer from a film company.'

Rosie's face said it all before she turned back to the set.

'Come on, Mrs Santa,' teased Big Graeme, 'we have children to see.'

He sounded like a man dismissing his wife and ordering her to get on with the housework. Pippa sounded excited but her grandmother was dead set bored, miserable and approaching anger.

'I'll send the photos,' called Pippa as she waved and disappeared.

Soon after Joseph and Pippa's disappearance, Rosie and Big Graeme were done and dusted, and Russell was on the empty set when Enrico arrived. 'Good afternoon,' said the photographer. 'For a man who is always early, aren't you cutting it a bit fine?'

Enrico grew tense upset by the truth of his question. 'Thank you, I'm okay,' he said and prepared to head off to get dressed.

'So you're back with the lovely Lorna.'

Enrico stopped, nodded and the two men exchanged a glance.

'Good luck,' said Russell returning to checking his equipment.

Enrico knocked, heard nothing and assumed Lorna was not there. But nor was Rosie or Big Graeme. He was dressing when Lorna entered.

'Good afternoon,' she spoke in the voice of a polite human being.

'Good afternoon,' replied Enrico in shock. She stopped beside him.

'Do you need a hand?' This time the shock hit hard.

'No, thank you, I think I can manage.'

'Well, let me know if I can help,' she said and disappeared.

He finished dressing wondering what on earth had happened. The answer appeared when Miranda arrived.

'Good afternoon, Enrico,' she beamed and stepped forward to give his cap a small adjustment. 'How is it all going?'

'It's going well, thank you. Rosie has been wonderful and I'm now working well with Lorna.'

'So I hear,' she said, grinning.

Enrico's shock was replaced by curiosity. He spoke with hesitation. 'I'm not sure I understand.'

'You and Lorna have been spotted by a rep from a charity. They hold a Christmas party for underprivileged kiddies and have asked if they can hire the two of you for a one-off appearance when you're not working here for *Costumes 4 U*. Congratulations.'

He nodded. 'I see.'

'I told Lorna last night but couldn't seem to raise you.'

He switched off his phone last night and now understood the personality change from his current Mrs Santa. Now she'd never report him for unsubstantiated bullying. That might upset this latest offer.

'It's extra money, Enrico, and usually these philanthropists are known to tip generously, especially at Christmas.'

'That's nice,' he replied and with money involved, knew his current theatrical wife would be in this extra performance like a rat up a drainpipe.

Speak of the devil, Mrs Santa appeared in costume and the two women greeted one another. This was a win-win situation for the boss. Lorna was happy and that happiness washed over Miranda like a luxurious bubble bath. The odd one out was the fellah. He wondered if this meant the end of his days working with Rosie. Not happy, Ric.

Miranda hung around making small talk and noting how co-operative Lorna had become. Incredibly, it was Mrs Santa who indicated time was up for the couple to greet the world of excited children outside. What a turnaround.

'Let's go, Santa,' she said. 'We can't keep those little angels waiting.'

There were no dropped kiddies or complaining about the job or the hours as Enrico worked with Lorna now on her best behaviour. When they hit a quiet time, she raised the charity booking.

'You made the right move to swap to me as Mrs Santa,' she said. 'You and others have twigged my theatrical experience means a top professional can be part of their show. Stick with me, Santa, and the sky's the limit. Oh, and you can thank me later.'

Enrico prepared to speak his mind, how he wasn't interested at all in the charity offer and, more importantly, how he wanted to switch back to working with the lovely Rosie. He opened his mouth to respond when Russell bobbed up with, 'Kiddies on deck, Santa.'

Russell once trained with the Sea Scouts, and the chat with children and photograph routine re-started.

The shift progressed well and when it ended, Lorna offered to help Enrico handing him his special walking stick. What a revelation. They returned to the dressing-room where Enrico's heart skipped two beats.

Rosie sat there in one of her classy outdoor outfits.

'You're early,' said Lorna. 'The morning shift starts tomorrow.'

'Hello Mrs Santa,' said Enrico thrilled to bits.

'Good afternoon, Santa,' she said. 'How did it go?'

'Brilliant,' said Lorna calling as she left, 'You tell her, Santa.'

Rosie explained. 'A friend in Lilydale is recovering from an op so I drove up to see her. Driving home I thought I'd pop in and see how you're getting on ... with Lorna.' She whispered the last two words. 'What did she mean, "you tell her, Santa"?'

Enrico shook his head. 'She and I have been invited to appear at a separate charity Christmas party.'

Their conversation froze when a scream erupted from Lorna. She appeared holding a letter. 'It's happened again. I'm on a roll.'

The others stared at her. Lorna waved the letter. 'A film company has asked me to audition for a role in a new Australian movie.'

'Congratulations,' said Enrico and continued. 'Does this mean you'll be quitting your role as Mrs Santa?' He sure hoped so.

'I forgot to tell you,' said Rosie. 'Someone from the front office brought an envelope in for you after I arrived.'

'I knew this would happen,' said the upbeat Mrs Santa continuing to wave the letter in triumph. 'As soon as the entertainment world discovered I'm back, the offers come rolling in. Once this crummy gig, no offence, is over I'll be back performing and this time for the masses.'

She disappeared to get changed leaving the good friends stunned.

Chapter 21
She went a tad clammy.

Joseph rang his brother. Michael was trying to finish a thesis for his post-grad degree. 'Big news, bro,' said Joe. Baby brother hated that shortened name. 'I've well and truly hooked the bimbo. The charity gig and the fake movie audition are both in play and I'll bet she'll ring any time.'

'Great,' replied Michael with limited enthusiasm.

'Well don't sound so excited,' snapped the senior sibling.

'I'm trying to finish this effing thesis,' said baby brother.

'And I'm trying to make you rich, or have you forgotten?'

'No, I haven't but I've been thinking.'

Joseph groaned. 'Don't start getting soft on me you weak prick. This bitch is conning old Ric into a marriage which sees our financial future shafted. Stick with me, Michael or it's not only your fortune that's dead.'

The threat sounded real. 'Meaning?' demanded Michael.

The reply was an engaged signal.

Joseph fumed but changed in a nanosecond when his phone rang. He used a musical theme suggesting James Bond; macho BS being his mantra.

'Joseph speaking,' he purred not recognizing the number.

'Oh hello, Joseph,' said a female. 'This is Lorna Redgrave. I received a letter today from the Compact Film and Video Company and …'

'Miss Redgrave, thank you for reaching out; it's lovely to hear from you.' He saved her number.

Lorna purred. She couldn't remember when she was last called Miss Redgrave.

'Your letter mentions an audition for a new movie.'

'We're only at the early stage but the director, Simon McMahon, is keen to cast as soon as possible.'

'May I ask how you found me?'

'I think you'll find your reputation precedes you, Miss Redgrave.'

She glowed with happiness. Her emotion pushed aside any thought of a scam. 'Thank you but I'm curious to know who recommended me.'

Joseph's basic research kicked in. 'To tell you the truth, Miss Redgrave,' (he wouldn't know the truth if it bit him on the bum) 'I can't remember. As you would know there are many outstanding but sadly out-of-work actors today and we cast our net wide. The director gave me a list of performers to contact, and someone said you were working at the shopping centre in Ringwood. I wish I could be more specific but I'm glad we've been able to hook up.'

'So am I,' she said.

'I'm responsible for drawing up a short list of possible cast members with the director obviously having the final say. Can we meet somewhere for coffee for a preliminary chat?'

'Of course.'

'Do you have an agent, Miss Redgrave?'

She paused and hated the embarrassment the question created.

'Not now. He died.'

'I'm sorry to hear that. Was it recent?'

She caught his skill at telling porkies. 'About a year ago,' she said. Not exactly true as the agent is still alive and working and they parted company when he dropped her.

'What suburb are you in, Miss Redgrave?'

'I'm near Canterbury,' she lied not wanting to mention Chadstone.'

'Great well let's meet in Maling Road at Bernie's. Do you know it?'

She didn't but there was no way she would admit to same.

'Perfect,' she said, 'but I'm busy performing at the moment.'

'Of course. But I need to submit this short list by Monday.'

She answered in a nanosecond. 'I can make it tomorrow at 5.'

'Brilliant. I'll see you tomorrow at Bernie's at 5. I'll be dressed all in black. Ciao.'

He hung up not wanting to say anything else which might cause her to doubt his preposterous and non-existent scheme.

She went a tad clammy.

Chapter 22
'In your dreams, pal,' she said and left.

Enrico slept badly—again. Phone calls from you know who were especially frustrating. The Santa season he so looked forward to now became annoying, frustrating and sad. What to do? He dragged his feet.

Working the afternoon session with Lorna gave him the creeps or the willies or both. He wanted to arrive early and watch Rosie and then catch up with her when she finished but dreaded that prospect. What if she enjoyed working with Big Graeme? Was she jealous that he and Lorna were invited to perform at a special event? He left it as late as possible and when he arrived, Rosie and Big Graeme were on their last few minutes.

He passed a florist and, without thinking, entered smiling at the owner.

'Hello,' she said. 'How can I help?'

'I'd like a beautiful bunch of flowers please.'

'Certainly; we have a variety. Does anything take your fancy?'

'I think quality rather than quantity is appropriate.'

'Of course; how about this bouquet?'

He thought they were beautiful.

'They are for a lady here in Eastland. Can I pay to have them delivered?'

'There'll be no delivery charge. What are the details and here,' she handed him a card, 'you can write a message on this.'

He did and wrote, *To my favourite Mrs Santa from an admirer.*

He paid. 'They're for the lady playing Mrs Santa right now,' he said pointing in the direction of the set. 'She finishes at 12.30 so a delivery before then would be wonderful.'

'I'll deliver them myself,' said the florist. Her smile boosted Enrico's heart and, if he was honest, even his soul.

He walked away from the Santa set to the other end of the centre and waited and never once needed his stick.

Big Graeme and Rosie were kept busy with Russell taking photos galore. His boss told him less is more, but he found by offering a greater choice, many buzzing parents and grandparents ordered extra copies. 'Get all three,' was a common expression from the mother to be followed by Grannie who said, 'No, get all four.'

As usual in the early days with Santa, there were short breaks when the queue thinned. Santa wheezed as his colossal frame needed to rest. Rosie fussed straightening anything out of place but stopped when someone called.

'Mrs Santa,' said the florist holding a gorgeous bunch of flowers.

Stunned, Rosie stared. She mimed, 'For me?'

The florist nodded. Rosie looked around as if to see who might be watching then moved to the trader. She gasped at the beauty of the blooms then read the card.

'But who are they from?'

The florist shook her head. 'I'm sorry, I couldn't possibly say.'

'Did he have a walking stick?'

The florist's face changed with a mini smile appearing. She spoke with the same pitch and tone. 'I'm sorry, I couldn't possibly say.'

Her smile blossomed before she left. Rosie lifted the blooms and breathed in the enchanting aroma. Big Graeme saw her and reacted.

'Oi, oi, oi, what's all this then? It's not Movvers' Day.'

Rosie put the flowers behind the mighty Santa chair and checked her watch. They were close to the end of the session, and she wanted to get these flowers home and in water. She decided she would split them in two with one vase in her kitchen and the other in her bedroom.

Most important she wanted to see and speak to the person who gave them to her. If that meant she would express her gratitude in public, then so be it.

She entered the storeroom with Big Graeme wheezing along behind her. Damn, no sign of Enrico. She worried because he was punctual to a fault. In the female dressing-room, Lorna re-applied make-up.

'Enrico not here?' asked Rosie.

Lorna found it hard to apply lipstick and speak at the same time. 'Am I my Santa's keeper? And look,' she said pointing to the sign Enrico made; *Female dressing-room*.

Rosie decided a conversation with Ms Rudeness was useless so changed. She went outside and saw Big Graeme struggling to remove his boots.

'Give us a hand, darling,' he grinned.

Given a choice of Lorna's sarcasm or Big Graeme's lechery, she chose to exit. It was one of those near misses in the course of true love. She couldn't stay with those two unpleasant people and left. Thirty seconds later, the man she desperately wanted to meet and thank arrived in a rush. He wished he hadn't delayed his arrival and hated having missed Rosie. He changed and couldn't bring himself to ask about the woman with the bunch of flowers.

Lorna appeared early, ready for action. 'Come on, Sunshine,' she said to the struggling Enrico, 'get a move on.'

She headed to the door and as she passed the whale disguised as St Nicholas, he requested her assistance. 'In your dreams, pal,' she said and left.

Lorna's behaviour now reflected her change of fortune. Two offers for possible paid work set her juices flowing meaning Russell and Enrico survived the latest session. Enrico would investigate the crowd hoping to spot his favourite Mrs Santa. Alas, she'd gone. The session ended, Enrico returned to base, changed and left as soon as possible.

From his train window, he always sat facing the driver knowing it afforded the best view. He stared. Not for a second did he stop wondering about Rosie's reaction when she received his flowers.

A terrifying thought involved her possible ignorance. She wouldn't know who sent them. He berated himself. *Of course she'd know it was me!*

His walk from the station was like his walk to the Ringwood station 20 minutes ago—no stick and a small to medium spring in his step.

As he opened the back door, his phone rang with the unique tone whenever Sofia dialled his number. Sometimes he thought she saw him as her six-year-old baby brother. 'Have you wiped your nose, Enrico? Did you wash your hands, Enrico?'

He moved to the phone. She could be a serious pain but without her constant checking, he could die in his sleep and remain there for a week. No chance today with big sister on the prowl. Besides he needed reminding about his heart medication and her cooking beat his hands down.

'Hello Sofia,' he said.

'Are you tired today like yesterday?'

'No, I'm feeling fine, thank you.'

'How did you go being Santa?'

'Pretty good, in fact, the second Mrs Santa has become much friendlier and better behaved.'

Sofia worried. 'Are you telling me you now have *two* girlfriends?'

'No,' he laughed.

'One is more than enough, Enrico, two will be the death of you.'

This time he did laugh. 'You're sounding ridiculous, big sister. I'm enjoying my work even though I'm not working with Rosie. And I like her so much, before I started my shift, I sent her a bunch of flowers.'

'You what?' gasped Sofia. 'You're throwing away your money on a woman you're not even working with? I'm going to make an appointment for you with Doctor Finlayson.'

Enrico gave as good as he got. 'No, you are not. Apart from my rusty hip, I'm perfectly healthy and my mind has never been in better working order. I've taken my tablets and am about to have a cup of coffee. Goodbye Sofia.'

The phone hit the cradle with force leaving his sister stunned and bewildered.

If ever she needed proof her brother had lost his marbles, this was it. Buying flowers for a woman he barely knew meant this ludicrous romance must be stopped. She rang her daughter.

Maria secretly admired her uncle for having a girlfriend at his age. Decades younger than her uncle, Maria longed for a lover of her own—any age, preferably male, and thus enable her to no longer live vicariously through the on-again off-again love stories revealed on her favourite soap opera.

'Tell my grandsons I need their help to stop my brother from making a fool of himself. Tell them please and have them ring me as soon as possible.'

'Yes Mum,' said Maria and groaned in silence.

Enrico's phone rang again but without Sofia's unique ring tone. He picked it up with hand shaking and pulse accelerating.

'Hello, Enrico speaking.' His heart started jogging.

'Is that the famous Santa who gives beautiful flowers to his stage wife?'

His heart started running. 'Hello Rosie; how did you go this morning? Is Big Graeme behaving?'

'I can't remember and couldn't care less about the other Santa. I am still coming back down to Earth since receiving your fabulous flowers. Thank you so much, Enrico, and when next I see you, I will thank you in person with an appropriate kiss.'

Both his hands now shook. 'I'm glad,' he said. 'I wanted to let you know how much I like you, and I thank my lucky stars we met when we did.'

'So, I gather Lorna is behaving herself.'

'She is. Something happened, it's these new work offers I think, and her whole personality has changed.'

'I'm glad and especially for you.'

'But I'm going to ask Miranda if she will allow the two of us to work together again. Do you mind?'

'Of course not but perhaps you should wait until the end of the week in case life gets a bit rocky again.'

'You're right. But I won't be put off.'

'You're a remarkable man, Enrico Salvatore. Now please have an early night and I'll see you between shows tomorrow. Bye.'

He said, 'Bye,' but kept holding the phone. She ended the call as he kept listening to the dead phone. He loved the sound of her voice.

Chapter 23
She smiled allowing her new lipstick to start a chorus line routine.

Thomas sold his land in the Dandenongs and moved out of his parents' home. His misery increased having his mother and father tell him he was badly treated, should have taken legal advice, and needed to invest his divorce funds in something sensible. Thomas wished they would change the record.

He left his parents' home, rented a basic flat and struggled to live day by day. His work colleagues avoided him finding his depression depressing.

Every fortnight he would travel to his former in-law's home for his visit with son Timmy. The boy obviously loved his father but the adults in the room could see a gradual softening of the child's affection. The youngster spent more time with his toys than relating to his father. To Thomas, it appeared as if he was a stranger.

It became so heartbreaking for the father, he wanted to abandon the visits, in effect to abandon his son. Knowing this would delight his ex-wife only made the sadness even more painful. It caused him to visit a GP such were his physical pains. The visit didn't help.

Driving back from a visit to a cousin across town, he pulled into the vast Chadstone shopping centre to buy a specific camera lens. He walked with purpose through the centre knowing the shop he wanted. Bang. He froze. Ahead of him to one side but walking towards him were his wife and child.

He turned his back and pretended to window shop. He waited. Looking over his shoulder his former wife and child were now past him but only then did the arrow plunge deeper inside his heart.

Stephanie held little Timmy's left hand, but the child's right hand clung to another person's hand, a male person's hand.

This gave Thomas a real kick in the guts. He watched Stephanie's new man, her boyfriend, her lover and worse, far worse, his son's new father. While the boy's father saw his son for an hour or two once a fortnight, this new man possibly had access on an unlimited basis.

Forget the camera accessories, Thomas headed for the nearest exit and his car. Driving home he found himself begin to cry. The tears appeared of their own freewill.

He always considered himself rational and sensible. Now, desperate thoughts crept into his mind including a reaction to his wife's behaviour, any sort of revenge or legal challenge and finally, a reason to no longer go on living. For Thomas, this was unchartered territory and scary.

Maria rang Joseph and told him about his grandmother's concern. 'Can you please ring your grandmother? She thinks her brother is about to be seduced and defrauded by this Mrs Santa woman who fluttered her eyelids at him and now he's besotted.'

'No problems, Mamma. I'll give Nonna a call and sort out the old bugger.'

'You know your grandmother panics at the drop of a hat but I'm sure you can say something to calm her down.'

'You know me, the family problem solver. Ciao Mamma.'

He hung up yet spoke aloud. 'Everything's under control and the Christmas bimbo will soon not even know what hit her.'

He rang Sofia and assured her that her baby brother was never going to make a fool of himself over any woman, greedy or otherwise. 'Leave it with me, Nonna. Great Uncle Enrico is family and me and Michael love him and will always look out for him.'

Nonna improved believing her grandsons were the salt of the Earth not knowing that in this case, blood was trickier than water.

Joseph went over the spiel for his meeting with Lorna. He needed as much background about her as possible and obviously her address. He had her phone number. He prepared audition material for hopeful actors for the non-existent film. His sole motive was to protect his inheritance and, if that meant stiffing a desperate out-of-work and forgotten actress, then so be it.

Next day around noon, Lorna was even bubblier than the day before. Enrico struggled to believe the change in his colleague. She bounced into the storeroom dressed to the nines and Enrico, despite his poor hearing, was sure she was humming.

'Hello, Santa,' she beamed. 'How are you today?'

'Good afternoon, Mrs Santa.'

'Oh please, you can call me Lorna.' She posed for him. 'What do you think of my outfit?'

It was as if she spoke a foreign language. Enrico was not and never had been a fashionista. She sported a silky green dress with a belt helping highlight her slim figure, a hint of cleavage, plus stilettos, bangles, and earrings which could double as knuckle dusters.

'Very nice,' he demurred hoping that was the right answer.

'I've scored an important audition with a casting director and want to make a good impression.'

'I see. Well …' He froze.

She pointed at him. 'Good boy, you're learning. What do you say?'

He spoke softly in hope. 'Break a leg?'

'Excellent,' she replied departing for her hideaway and continuing to hum.

He heard the others returning and butterflies started dancing in his gut. His worry beads worked up a sweat. There would be an audience to witness that promised kiss because of his flowery gift.

Rosie entered first and despite being tired from working with the giant, her face lit up when she saw Enrico standing tall without a stick.

She proved true to her promise on the phone last night, moved to him and gave him a powerful smooch. He knew what he wanted to do in return but with Big Graeme already present and with Lorna stepping out of her dressing room, he hesitated.

'What's all this?' demanded the whale planting his broad Kardashian bottom. '*I* never cracked a smooch after all my hard work.'

'It's no use, my dear,' said Lorna to Rosie. 'He's *my* Santa and we're doing the charity gig together.'

'Charity gig?' bellowed Big Graeme. 'What charity gig?'

'Thank you again for the beautiful bouquet,' said Rosie preparing to depart and change.

For Enrico the kiss was spine-tingling but the fact it happened in public, so to speak, had him thinking his walking stick might even be put out to pasture.

Lorna demanded the spotlight. 'I have big news, folks,' she announced. 'Tell them, Santa.'

The kissing spotlight was replaced by another requiring Enrico to spread this so-called good news.

'Oh,' he said looking at Rosie and wanting to tell her he loved her. He thought. *'Is that the news I should announce, my love for Rosie? Wow, now that would put Lorna back in her box.'*

Lorna couldn't wait so became the emcee. 'Have a guess who cracked an audition with a casting director of a major film company this afternoon?'

There was never any mention of the word *major* but hey, embellishment costs nothing.

'Congratulations,' said Rosie.

'Are you leaving us?' growled Big Graeme. 'I thought professionals saw out their contract.'

Lorna wagged a finger at Titanic Santa. 'Touch of jealousy, darling?'

Enrico and Lorna's session went smoothly with Mrs Santa falling over herself to be a star. The kiddies came to see Santa, but this Mrs Santa reckoned she was the centre of the universe and behaved as such.

Enrico didn't object as this later version of Mrs Santa rarely grumbled or checked the time, and never once dropped a client. Photographer Russell only cared about the number of photographs being ordered.

Lorna found Bernie's coffee shop, looked inside for any male dressed in black, saw no-one and entered.

'I'm meeting someone,' she said to Bernie's partner who indicated a table.

Joseph took his time, deliberately being late. Dressed in black he arrived in style complete with trendy black shoulder bag. He spotted his quarry as seen in his brother's pics. He gave his suave smile and headed for her table.

'Lorna,' he greased, holding out his hand. He took hers and kissed it, sat and placed his bag.

Bernie's partner arrived. Joseph addressed her as if they were old pals and ordered coffee.

'It's lovely to finally meet you, Lorna,' he said. 'I love your dress.'

She wanted to swoon but smiled allowing her new lipstick to start a chorus line routine.

'It's most kind of you to think of me.'

'Call me Joseph,' he said producing papers.

'It's most kind of you and Simon to think of a senior actress. We seem to be forgotten these days.'

'Quality will always out, Lorna.' He handed her a screed. 'This is the prospectus with a script synopsis we give to our angels. And here's an audition screed if you'd be kind enough to complete same. And here's a pen.'

'Thank you,' she said handing him a photo album. 'Here's a little of my work.'

She read and wrote while he looked at her scrapbook. The coffees arrived. After juggling and sipping they continued working.

It was classic irony writ large. Both were on the make. Both were frauds with a capital F. There was no movie, and she was not Enrico's girlfriend. Neither could mock the other as both were equally ignorant and foolish.

He skimmed through the photos and stopped with a thud. He stared at photos of Lorna in a bikini. She looked stunning.

She surreptitiously observed and knew why he'd stopped turning pages. He sensed her awareness of his ogling.

He tapped the page. 'You look great in a bikini.' Their eyes met.

'I still do,' she said; 'it's a bit further on.'

He turned the pages and found what she meant but here she was no longer 20 more like 50. 'Wow!' he whispered now thinking about how he could wreck Enrico's marriage plans but still give himself a chance to keep company with the woman in front of him.

Could he save his inheritance by seducing the woman thus screwing two birds with the one moan?

They chatted until he announced he had another interview. Lorna believed she was not the only horse in training.

'I'll keep in touch, Lorna. I'll tell Simon you're definitely on his short list.' He squeezed her hand. His final smile had letch written all over it.

Pippa arrived at her gran's house. It was Thursday takeaway night, and the two redheads had plenty to discuss. Proceedings began with their usual enthusiastic greeting, a hug and a kiss.

'So how did Mrs Santa finish up today?' This became a running question from the granddaughter.

'Good.'

'Good? What the heck does that mean?'

'You know I'd much rather work with Senor Salvatore, and I'm hoping we can hook up next week.'

'Hook up? Do you know the alternative meaning of that phrase?'

'You can make the coffee, Miss Know-all while I serve the Chinese.'

'You may not like my latest pics. They feature your least favourite Santa.'

They tackled their respective tasks. 'So tell me about this job offer for a film company.'

'Yes, you're not the only star in this family.'

An interested Rosie wanted details. 'Okay, spill the beans.'

'When I was shooting pics of you and Big Graeme, this tall, handsome stranger sidles up and gives me his card, from a film company no less.'

'A film company?'

'He said they're always looking for talented freelancers and to give him a ring if I was interested.'

'Was he good-looking?'

'He was actually.'

'And?'

'Give me time, Gran. You're the one preaching the play-hard-to-get line.'

She laughed and they started on the food.

'So how are you and Enrico getting on?' asked Pippa.

'Don't change the subject.' Pippa waited and Rosie hesitated. 'He gave me a beautiful bunch of flowers.' She nodded to the ones in the kitchen.

'Wow,' gasped the granddaughter. 'This sounds serious.'

Rosie found it hard to speak. Pippa nailed it as the relationship Rosie now enjoyed with Enrico dominated Mrs Santa's life.

Chapter 24
Gravity kicked in and he hit the floor.

Joseph luxuriated in hedonism. He would never consider himself a chauvinist, in fact would rail against any such charge. How could he be prejudiced against women when he loved them so much?

Clearly, he fancied women because they satisfied his carnal desires and boosted his need to prove he was God's gift to those he called "the weaker sex". But at this point in his life, marriage sat way beyond the horizon for Joe the Go-to Man. Let's face it; he had far too many female conquests to make before even thinking about settling down.

At present, his main task was to preserve his inheritance. Keep Great Uncle Ric's estate tucked away unharmed. Keep that scheming Mrs Santa away from Joseph and Michael's pot of real estate gold.

To win the financial war, he planned to sabotage Ric's romance with a woman Joseph came to know as Lorna Redgrave, the has-been actress, the also-ran in the world of minor league theatre and forgotten TV.

Having met the lady in person, he found himself peering or rather perving at old photos of her wearing a minimum of clothing. For a leer like Joseph, the study proved more than interesting. At their chat over coffee in Maling Road, Canterbury, he had no idea how he might thwart her romance with Ric. Mind you, the idiot Casanova kept chasing the wrong woman proving, for now, ignorance is indeed bliss.

Thinking back to the time he enjoyed the photos of the bikini-clad Lorna, especially the recent ones, he hit on an idea. How about I seduce Santa's missus? She'd be keen thinking such a union would boost her audition chances and stoke her self-confidence proving she could still pull a man which, in this case, would be a young man, young enough to be her grandson. Naturally, he'd be keen full stop.

Apart from enjoying the seduction, he would use her fling with a toy boy to destroy Ric's blissful relationship. This to Joseph was a win-win situation. He'd get his leg over with a cougar, and lock up his inheritance in one fell swoop, although such action might better be described as one foul swoop.

As he planned how he might enact his sexist and sneaky plan, his phone rang. He thought he remembered the number.

'Hi, Joseph here.'

'Hi, Joseph, it's Pippa. We met at the shopping centre where I was taking photos of Santa and Mrs Santa.'

'Pippa,' he oozed making it sound like he knew exactly who she was, and he was super keen to hear her voice. 'How's it goin', babe?'

'Fine. I've been thinking about the possibility of your job offer taking pics for your film company.'

'Great, I was hoping you'd be interested. Can we meet up and discuss details.' The grass found it impossible to grow under Ric's size 10s.

'Sure, so when and where?' she asked.

He loved it when women chased him. Not only did it grease his ego, but it also made the later seduction to be effortless. He thought in a Texan drawl. *'Joseph done good today.'* Two women, both attractive, one 60 one 20, and both keen to use him to get what they wanted— work. Naturally he would use them for what he wanted or rather craved.

He suggested the Electric Bar in Chapel Street, Prahran and Pippa happily agreed the time and place. 'Oh and bring your portfolio,' he added.

She ended the call, excited. He ended the call, cocky.

Enrico finished his evening coffee and sat on his favourite chair in his den. It was here he read, watched TV and pondered death. As a septuagenarian, he knew he was running the penultimate if not the final lap of life's race. He didn't dwell on morbid thoughts but going to funerals on a regular basis helped water the seeds of mortality in his brain.

Tonight a more recent thought occupied his mind. One of his favourite TV shows was due but he chose to leave the telly untouched.

Rosie O'Donnell, her smile, her voice, her perfume and images of her body filled his mind.

The kiss in the storeroom thanking him for his flowers, especially in public, still tingled. Thus far he refused to wash his cheek so as to not remove her scent.

The fact they were no longer working together, although mightily sad, didn't faze him. He'd met the girl of his dreams and better still, she liked him.

His bedtime came and went. He needed sleep. He'd be grumpy tomorrow without sufficient shuteye.

'What is Rosie doing right now?' he thought. 'I'd love to ring her. But am I pushing too hard? Does she love or only like me? I know I'm in love but is she only kind and friendly and worse, am I making a fool of myself?'

Too much thinking didn't help his mood. It's time for sleep, Santa. He struggled to push himself out of the chair, stood but found his hip twinge, his legs began to surrender and next thing, gravity kicked in and he hit the floor. En route to the ancient carpet, his head whacked the nest of tables his parents bought in 1971. Nighty-night, Enrico.

Chapter 25
The doctors will think you're an old drunk. Not so much of the old.

A few minutes later he came to and endured a thumping headache. He was lying awkwardly but managed to free a hand to touch the side of his noggin. Ouch! And worse his fingers were moist. Claret appeared. He wanted and needed to get up but couldn't. His bladder whispered in his ear.

The physical pain hurt but far greater the mental anguish, the thought his Santa days were o'er which meant his hours spent working with Rosie were finito. Such images plunged a metaphorical dagger in his heart. Bugger!

He drifted to sleep on a hot December night and, surprisingly, slept well. Maybe he needed a harder mattress because the floor lacked any give.

Next morning, Sofia was early. Was she prescient? Her ringing tone brought baby brother back to reality. There was no way he could rise and romp to the kitchen to use the Alexander Graeme Bell. It rang out. He could hear his big sister speaking via the answering machine.

'He's dead. He's had a heart attack and gone to sleep and never woken up.' Enrico grinned enjoying a moment of humour in his hour of misery. But that happiness vanished the moment his thoughts returned to his favourite job and colleague, a certain Mrs Santa. Not the other Mrs Santa; good God no.

Still daydreaming, he heard his back door being knocked.

'Enrico, are you all right? Hello?'

You must give Sofia a bit of credit. She met Enrico's middle-aged neighbour years ago and asked her to keep an eye on the former barber. As Enrico kept Beverley in top quality tomatoes and pumpkin, the sort Sofia and Enrico's old man would have been proud to sell, she, the neighbour, was next door in a flash.

Beverley had a spare back door key and hurried inside to find her neighbour prostrate in his snug. Her heart jammed thinking Sofia's brother to be no more, but she enjoyed enormous relief when he spoke.

'Good morning, Beverley. What kept you?'

She knelt and bent over him. 'Enrico, you gave me a terrible fright. You've banged your head.'

'Thank you, Doctor. Do you bulk bill?'

'Let's get you up in the chair.'

He went to protest. 'I've been here all night, so another minute won't hurt.' Beverley sized up the situation and produced her mobile. 'Please ring Sofia and tell her to cancel the undertaker,' he said with a twinkle in his eye; the black one now turning a lovely shade of purple.

His neighbour smiled knowing all there was to know about the sibling turned matriarch.

'But first, if you can't get me up and pointing towards the lavatory, kindly fetch the potty from under my bed.'

She sat him upright, helped him stand, gave him his stick, and the penny he spent was the best investment he ever made.

On the phone, of course Sofia demanded a detailed medical report giving her something else to worry about. Beverley explained the basics promising to call back later once she'd help Enrico recover.

He returned and sat. She found his ancient bottle of brandy and poured a snifter, handing him the glass.

He improved but crashed mentally realizing his Santa gig was a few hours away.

'I need to ring my boss,' he said, and Beverley grabbed her phone. He struggled with a different device. Technology survived without Signor Salvatore.

'What's your boss's number?'

'It's on the wall above my phone. Miranda at *Costumes 4 U.*'

Beverley dialled the number; he appeared and was handed the phone. Miranda looked at the number which meant nothing to her.

'Hello?'

'Oh Miranda, it's Enrico.'

'What's happened?' she said knowing this must be an emergency.

'I've had a fall at home and whacked my head.'

She spoke sincerely. 'Are you all right?'

'I'm fine but I ...'

Beverley snatched the phone from her neighbour and hit the speaker button. 'No, he's not fine. I'm Beverley his next-door neighbour. I've found him and he's spent the night on the floor with a bruise on his head the size of an egg—a double-yoker.'

'Oh, that's terrible.'

Enrico listened, remaining mute, helpless and sad.

'I'll take him to Box Hill Emergency to make sure he isn't concussed or broken any bones.'

'That's very kind of you, Beverley. Tell him not to worry about his Santa job. Did you know he's Santa at Ringwood?'

'Of course, and I'm taking my grandson as soon as Enrico's back on deck.'

'Will you please let me know how he gets on at the hospital?'

'I will.'

'And please give him my love.'

She ended the call and stared at Santa. 'You heard. She sends her love.'

'That's nice. She's a lovely lady.'

The sticky-beak neighbour grabbed her chance. 'Is she the lady you brought home the other day?'

He realized and slipped into dreamland. 'No, no that was Rosie the lady I'm going to marry.'

'What!' replied Beverley with far too much aggression. 'Marry?' He nodded with a serious grin. 'Does Sofia know?'

Enrico panicked. 'No, nobody knows, not even Rosie.' He begged. 'Please, Beverley, you mustn't breathe a word and especially not to my sister.'

'All right, you dark horse, your secret's safe with me. Oh, and remember what your boss said, you're not to worry about being Santa.' She took the glass. 'That's enough brandy. The doctors will think you're an old drunk.'

He stared back. 'Not so much of the old, if you don't mind.'

She grinned. 'Come on, Santa. I'll have to drive you in my *car* as my licence doesn't cover sleigh and reindeer.'

Keith Arthur, retired gent and man of leisure, played Santa last year but when Miranda asked him to give it a go again this year he declined. He wanted to play lawn bowls and spend more time with his grandkids.

'Would you be interested in sitting on the interchange bench?' asked Miranda. As he was a mad Collingwood supporter, she knew he would understand the lingo. 'Only a few performances and good money with a bonus for last minute jobs.'

Keith liked the offer and agreed. He planned to play bowls that day but instead found himself heading to Ringwood for the afternoon session. Enrico problem solved.

Miranda and the rest of the world wondered how the prima donna would handle the change, *another* Santa. Little did anyone know Lorna was preening and dreaming about her new movie career. Dream on, kiddo.

Using his stick and Beverley's arm, Enrico walked into the Emergency room at the Box Hill Public Hospital. Without bleeding or calling for help and walking reasonably well, he made it unaided to a seat. His black eye grew becoming a feature and talking point.

Beverley approached reception and explained the would-be patient's situation. Enrico was clerically admitted and sat awaiting a medico.

Sofia developed a mini panic wondering if her brother would last the morning. A phone call from Beverley allayed big sister's alarm by a modest amount. Once the call ended, Sofia rang her daughter, the third time in the last hour, and advised the mother of the great nephews that they, Sofia and Maria, were due at Box Hill as soon as possible.

Maria reckoned her mother must be over-reacting, i.e. acting normally, but did as the mater wished. Maria found a parking spot nearby, a miracle, and helped her mother out of the car. They headed inside and found Enrico resting on a bed in a large ward with curtains creating a little privacy for the patient. He relaxed while sporting a sticking plaster on his forehead. Beverley explained the situation. No concussion, no broken bones and, after approval from the doctor on duty, the bruised but not beaten Santa would be discharged with powerful over-the-counter headache tablets.

'Well, that's the end of Santa,' said Sofia. 'And at your age, Enrico, you've said "Ho Ho Ho" for the last time.'

He froze and clenched his fists. 'Stop being ridiculous,' he hissed at his sister and all three women automatically widened their eyes and mouth in surprise. Sofia reacted to this unusual and feisty response.

Beverley became the peacekeeper. 'You need to rest, Enrico,' she said, and led his family outside the surrounding curtains. Before the visitors could re-set the conversation and their mood, a woman, having received directions from a nurse, approached and interrupted the gathering.

'Excuse me,' she said. 'I've come to visit my friend, Enrico Salvatore.'

On the bed behind the curtains, the patient with a tinge of deafness, partly heard the new voice and enjoyed a surge of happiness. His mind came alive. *'Is that who I think it is?'* Sofia and Maria froze and stared or rather stared and froze.

'Hello,' said Beverley who recognized Rosie as the woman given a tour of Enrico's garden, front and back, the other day. 'I'm Bev his neighbour.' She didn't say, "I know who you're going to marry," but reckoned old Enrico was a fine judge of a bride.

'I'm Rosie, his wife at Ringwood.' She saw horror and confusion from two of the women so tried to allay fears. 'I'm Mrs Santa.'

'I'm Maria, Enrico's niece and this is his sister, my mother, Sofia.'

'Hello,' replied Rosie. 'I heard Enrico took a tumble. Is he okay?'

'I'll check,' said Maria and popped into her uncle's 1 star suite. She whispered to the patient.

'Mrs Santa's outside.'

Enrico panicked. 'Which one?' he gasped now thinking he misheard the visitor's voice.

Maria's eyes widened. 'You have *two* wives?'

'Her name's Rosie.'

'That's her.'

Maria was about to ask if her uncle would agree to see her, but he jumped in quickly.

'How do I look? Am I presentable? What's my bruise look like?'

Maria smiled. 'You look dashing, the wounded warrior look suits you,' she said and disappeared.

Sofia couldn't decide if she was standing beside her brother's friend or girlfriend, surely not the latter. Rarely lost for words, the matriarch stared, lips unable to move. Rosie smiled.

'Enrico has told me a lot about his wonderful sister and how you look after him. Without Sofia, he said, I wouldn't be here today.'

The flattery knocked Sofia sideways. Before she could reply, her daughter appeared. 'Santa would love to see his wife,' she said with a big smile.

Rosie came alive and Sofia didn't. Maria pulled back one of the curtains revealing the patient, still in yesterday's outfit, but with an excitement new to him and not experienced since the last millennium.

Watched by his sister and niece, Rosie moved to the side of the bed with love in her heart and face.

'Buon Giorno, Signor Salvatore,' she beamed and taking hold of his nearest hand, raised it to her lips and kissed his fingers.

His niece wanted to say, "Ahhhh", while his sister looked around to see if a spare bed was available; for her.

'Buon Giorno, Mrs Santa,' he replied. 'It's lovely to see you, and I'm so sorry to have let down both you and the team.'

'Don't be silly. Of course we all miss you but I'm sure you'll be back in costume tomorrow.

Sofia's true colours exploded. 'No, no, no, the doctor said he must rest.' Everyone witnessed tension join the party.

'But I'm being discharged this afternoon,' protested the patient.

'So, you can go home and rest,' argued big sister.

'Well, I can keep an eye on him,' said Beverley being fond of her kind elderly neighbour with green fingers, and even more so now being privy to a romantic secret not even the would-be bride knew.

'No, no, no,' said Sofia again and desperate to regain control. 'This is what families are for.' Enrico silently groaned.

The tension continued to rise but the current conflict would become a garden tea party dispute over scones once Rosie spoke.

'I could look after him.'

The nuclear explosion, although on mute, caused the curtains around Enrico's "room" to flap like a terrified bird's wings.

Rosie explained her offer. 'I have a spare room and as we'll soon be working together again, it's a practical and common-sense solution. We can arrive and leave together, and once Enrico is feeling better again, he can return to his lovely house and garden.'

If Sofia was a steam locomotive, the gauges in the cab would be screaming to the driver and fireman urging immediate action. Abandon ship or rather, jump off the footplate!

'Are we going to be back working together?' he asked in hope.

Rosie explained. 'There's a new Santa called Keith and Lorna is happy, strangely happy to work with him or Big Graeme. Miranda told me the old team will likely be back in harness as soon as you're back on deck.'

Actually, Miranda copped serious pressure and as Enrico and Rosie were two of her best and favourite performers, she wanted to reward them both.

'That's wonderful,' said Enrico with a face broadcasting his delight and genuine affection for Rosie. The other three women were in no doubt. This is serious. Santa's in love. Even Sofia could join the dots.

Rosie addressed the group. 'Well, I must be off. I'm Mrs Santa in about an hour. I'll leave you to decide the best place for Enrico to recover but I'm happy to chauffeur him to work and home wherever that may be. Lovely to meet you all,' she said before addressing the patient. 'Get well soon, Santa.' She blew him a kiss then made a theatrical exit leaving the audience stunned.

The others spoke ignoring the patient. Sofia began, slowly regaining her true position. 'Well, I never,' didn't do justice to her outrage. 'Fancy thinking our family can't look after our own.'

Beverley spoke her mind. 'Now Sofia, are you upset because someone else offered to take your place or because your brother might be in love?'

The stunning question floored the matriarch. She couldn't answer and worse, the possibility her brother willingly entered a romantic relationship, and with a striking and friendly woman, sent the hairs all over her body, and there were many, springing to attention as in, "Stand by your beds!"

From his bed, the wounded barber ventured an opinion. 'Has anyone wondered what the patient would like to do?'

'I think we already know, Uncle,' said Maria. 'Your doe-eyed expression positively beams bright despite that gorgeous shiner.'

He grinned and couldn't stop. What headache? He felt fantastic.

Rosie drove herself from the hospital in time for her morning shift with Big Graeme. He was ready when she arrived.

'Oi, oi, where's your late pass?' he asked.

She ignored him, dressed super quickly and off they went. She said nothing to Big Graeme about Enrico. Despite this silent treatment, their shift went well with not even photographer Russell noting the couple's cool demeanour.

When the session ended, it always took Big Graeme a minute or three to return to his maximum height. While he did so, Rosie located her bag, concealed on the set, and discretely checked her phone. There was one message from Beverley.

Hi Rosie. Enrico's care was decided by you know who. Sofia agreed to him going home to be nursed by Moi, Nurse Bev. Feel free to call or drop in. Well done you. I've never seen the old boy so happy. Talk soon. Bev

Rosie flushed with joy. A great result in the circumstances, and Beverley's comment about Enrico having a new zest for life thrilled her.

Goliath announced he was ready for the trek back to base.

In the storeroom as Rosie and Big Graeme were finishing, Keith the fill-in Santa, unpacked his bits and bobs and started dressing. Larger than Enrico and smaller, much smaller than Big Graeme, he strutted about admiring himself in the mirror borrowed from a store in the centre. He was in the middle of a Ho Ho Ho warm-up when Lorna arrived.

'Are you the understudy?' she demanded rather than asked.

'Good afternoon, madam and yes, I'm Keith your emergency Santa. The skipper, Captain Miranda, has listed Enrico under the Weather column, and for the foreseeable you're stuck with me. It's Norma, isn't it?'

'Lorna,' she snapped and headed to her dressing-room.

Rosie and Big Graeme returned with Goliath ignorant of Enrico's condition. Rosie had told him nothing but now, meeting Keith, she explained her secret boyfriend and his fall at home.

'I saw him in hospital this morning and he looked fine.'

Big Graeme's eyes widened. 'You saw him in hospital! What is this? Be kind to Santa week?'

Rosie stood her ground. 'Enrico's a dear friend, not that it's any of your business, and if there's anything I can do to help him, I will.'

'Wow! So if I stub my big toe, will you give me a foot massage?'

'No, I'd move to the position of toe-*cutter*.' He gasped realizing she meant it. 'But first I need to change.' She departed with steam escaping from her wig.

All went well for the second session. Keith had Santa experience to burn, and Lorna could have turned on a prima donna performance par excellence, yet the old chap wouldn't have batted an eye. In fact, Lorna kept busy dreaming of a date with a certain young film executive. Keith could have been a prat, and she wouldn't have cared or noticed. Lorna had other fish to fry.

At her rented unit in Chadstone, Lorna surveyed the garments in her only wardrobe. She'd become a regular at charity shops buying Toorak socialites' hand-me-downs. She wanted to make a powerful impression on young filmmaker, Joseph. A thought popped into her mind and stayed there.

Should I seduce him or rather, allow him to seduce me? Was that my ticket to getting this role and thus back into the big time? Is the old casting-couch routine still in operation?

Her phone rang. 'Hi Lorna, it's Joseph.'

'Hi Joseph. I've been thinking about your film and from reading your fascinating synopsis, I know this will be a brilliant movie.'

Had she over-sauced the goose? Was her desperation on show? Yes, and yes but her behaviour was exactly what he wanted to hear.

'Listen darl, I told Simon about our meeting, and he's keen for a get-together.' Lorna struggled to control her breathing. 'He's out of town until next week but how are you placed for later this month?'

'I'm free,' said Lorna cursing her exuberance.

'Great. I'll give you a call as soon as the director's available. It'll be best at night if that suits you.'

'Nights are fine. I'll look forward to your call.'

'Thanks Lorna. I hope we can make this work.'

She knew what he meant and liked what she heard.

Chapter 26
'Oh God, she's here. Where will I hide?'

Bev drove Enrico home and helped him settle. Sofia had been there earlier filling his fridge with various dishes. Of course she did. Bev opened Sofia's written instructions.

'Wow, your sister sure runs your life, Enrico.'

'You don't say,' squeaked the injured Santa. 'Whatever gave you that idea?'

She moved to him and plumped a cushion behind his back. 'And you know your romantic secret's safe with me.' They stared at one another, and she winked before heading to make a cuppa.

'It needs to remain a secret until I pop the question,' he said worried about Rosie's possible answers.

'Have you bought the ring?'

He didn't answer and she stopped sorting cups to look at him.

He shook his head. 'Bev, this is all new to me. I'm like a fish out of water.'

'You could always ask your sister.'

There was nothing to hand so Enrico's wish to hurl something at his neighbour was replaced by a glare.

Before the cuppa, Bev approached with a glass of water and a small container of headache pills. He popped one in his mouth, took a swig and swallowed. He looked to his new nurse for approval.

'*Two* tablets, Signor,' she said.

He forced a grin and repeated the procedure. He liked the nurse and the feeling was reciprocated. But he knew trouble lay ahead.

'Now Santa, about that ring; tell all.'

His face dropped and she wished she'd left well alone.

Joseph eased into the Chapel Street bar. It was his territory, his patch, his hunting ground. He spotted Pippa against a wall and sidled up to her.

'Pippa, you look great. What can I get you?'

She'd been warned about sharks from lifesavers, her mother and a grandmother, and plumped for mineral water.

He returned. 'Don't drink it all at once,' he said taking the mickey while at the same time planning how he could get her back to his place.

'Thanks,' she said. 'I brought my portfolio.'

'Great.'

They sat and he flicked through her photos. He wondered if there might be any of Pippa in a bikini. Hardly, they were the subjects of her hobbies. He made idle conversation but stopped turning pages when he came to those at Ringwood. Big Graeme sat on stage with a woman, Mrs Santa, the photographer's gran. As great uncle Ric was absent, Joseph moved on.

'I could have a possible gig for you.' Pippa's ears pricked.

'Tell me more.'

He forgot the photos to concentrate on her.

'I have a mate who turns his enormous garden over to underprivileged kids for a Christmas party. He's asked me to find a Santa and Mrs Santa. It's a sort of emergency as the party's next week.' He tapped the photo. 'What do you know about the actors playing Santa and Mrs Santa?'

'Nothing.' She worried about her instant lie.

'Then why all the photos?'

She sensed danger. Nothing specific but a feeling Joseph was not being up front with her and this situation.

'I was in the centre Christmas shopping,' she lied, 'saw the crowd and took the pics.'

'Well these are great. Are you interested in this kids' party? It's a sort of trial and you can meet the boss, Simon, who chooses our freelancers.'

'I'm definitely interested.'

'And I can recommend you.' He left the last sentence hanging and tapped a photo. 'And you don't know the actors?'

She panicked but tried not to let it show. 'No, I just took their photos.'

'It's important we get the right people. The agency reckons they're okay but any tips from other sources can often prove super helpful.'

There was definitely something not right about Joseph and that hint of danger appealed to Pippa. The male students at her drama school were not in his league. They were her age and not seriously interested or interesting. He was older and interesting. She found him to be, well, sexy.

She kept talking. 'If I hear anything I'll let you know.'

'Great. Now I've gotta fly, babe. Where can I drop you?'

Talk about controlling the situation. Pippa thought fast. 'I'm fine. I'm meeting a girlfriend.

'Cool,' he said, stood and drained his beer. 'We must do dinner. I'll bell you. Later.'

He was gone leaving Enrico's girlfriend's granddaughter lost for words.

Bev had warmed one of Sofia's meals and Enrico insisted his neighbour stay and join him.

'Whatever you do, Enrico, do not tell your sister I was here for a meal.'

He laughed and they tucked in. They finished their meal but were interrupted when the front doorbell rang.

'Oh God, she's here,' said Bev. 'Where will I hide?'

He laughed and pointed out that Sofia would never ring any doorbell in this her former home. 'She has her own key anyway.'

Bev walked to the front door and Enrico could hear voices then footsteps.

'Look who's come to see the war-weary soldier,' said Bev leading a certain Mrs Santa into the kitchen. It wasn't the one in a bikini.

Enrico experienced joy and embarrassment in equal measure.

'Rosie,' he exclaimed, tried to stand and dropped back onto his chair.

'Enrico,' she scolded. 'Stay where you are.' She moved to him and when he moved a chair ever so slightly, she sat. 'How is your head?'

'I'm fine and all the better for seeing you.'

Bev had to control the urge to say, 'Ahhh.' Instead, she offered Sofia's finest cooking.'

'Thank you, I've already eaten but I won't say no to a cuppa,' replied Rosie. She turned to Santa. 'I wanted to ring but I knew you wouldn't tell me the truth so here I am.'

'Are you calling me a liar?'

She saw the twinkle in his eye and squeezed his arm then recoiled in fear. 'Oh Enrico, that's not injured too is it?'

Before he could reply his phone rang and Bev answered it.

'Hello. … No, it's Bev his neighbour and he's right here.' She handed the phone to Santa. 'It's Miranda.'

He hit the speaker button and placed the phone on the table.

'Hello Miranda, how nice of you to call.'

'How are you, Enrico? Feeling better I hope?'

'Feeling better and being waited on hand and foot.'

'Good for you.'

'I have Bev my lovely neighbour and Mrs Santa my lovely wife.'

Bev gulped and Miranda stalled. Rosie stepped into the silence.

'Hello Miranda, it's Rosie. I popped in to see if Santa needed anything, but Bev is a superb neighbour.'

'Hello Rosie. How nice of you to keep an eye on our favourite Santa.'

'Hang on a minute,' interrupted the male. 'I'll hit Record, and you can say that again.'

Everyone laughed but Enrico turned serious.

'Now please, Miranda, when am I starting work again? Morning or afternoon on Monday will both suit me fine.'

His enthusiasm flooded the room. Miranda came under pressure.

'How about I check again on Sunday, and we can decide then.'

'I'll be here waiting for your call, and if you don't ring me, I'll ring you.'

More laughter but no-one doubted his sincerity.

'Oakey-Dokey, I'll talk to you on Sunday afternoon. Bye Enrico and all the members of your harem.'

They all laughed and called their goodbye. Enrico buzzed. Bev, being privy to her neighbour's romantic situation, decided to delicately retire.

'I'll leave you two to discuss Christmas tactics. I'll see you in the morning, Santa. And don't forget to buzz me if you need anything. Remember it's Bev first and second and Sofia third.'

She started clearing away dishes and Rosie took over. 'Leave those, Bev. I'll fix it.'

Bev thanked Rosie and left to the voice of her neighbour calling. 'I'll have more tomatoes for you this week!'

Rosie tidied up then came to sit beside the man who made her heart beat faster. His heart was already working overtime. He wanted to propose but faced two obstacles. He had no ring and if he knelt, in his current health situation, he knew he couldn't stand again without a crane or his sweetheart doing the heavy lifting.

'Thank you for coming to the hospital and now to my home,' he said looking fondly into her eyes.

'It's my pleasure, Signor. In case you hadn't noticed, I've become fond of you and with only a short time to go, I want us to be together again in our Christmas costumes.'

He took a deep breath and struggled to speak. 'Thank you,' he whispered, and a tear appeared and paused ready to descend.

'Now what can I do to help? Any cooking, cleaning or gardening tasks, although I'll never be up to your outstanding green fingers standard?'

'Don't be silly,' he said being unable to control his thoughts and say exactly what he thought of her. He looked at her and decided without a ring and while sitting, he would ask Rosie to marry him. In the second he took a deep breath, his phone sounded with the well-known sisterly ring.

Rosie reckoned he was about to say something important, saw his face start to crack and hopped up to answer his phone.

'Hello,' she said.

Sofia attacked. 'Beverley, why are you still there?'

Rosie recognized the caller. 'Sofia, it's not Beverley, it's Rosie. We met at the hospital.'

Enrico gripped the arms of his chair. Sofia gripped the arms of her chair to maintain her sanity. The siblings were in possible freefall. 'Is Enrico there?'

'I'll put him on,' said Mrs Santa and handed Enrico the phone.

He paused and sensed his sister's breath and anger seeping from the receiver. He looked at Rosie and made a face.

'Hello Sis. I'm still here, feeling much better and being spoilt rotten by Bev and Rosie. How are you?'

Not well, obviously and Sofia found herself panicking mainly because her brother was slipping out of control, *her* control.

The call ended and Rosie replaced the phone. They looked at one another. Rosie decided.

'I should go and let you rest,' she said.' He wanted her to stay but thought begging would be demeaning. 'I'll give you a call in the morning.' She moved to him and Enrico thought his heart would burst.

She bent and gently kissed his mouth, squeezed his arm and left. At the front door, she called. 'Sleep well, Santa.'

He heard the door close and spoke to no-one, 'Good night my darling.'

The curtains in Bev's front room twitched as Rosie headed to her car.

Chapter 27

Her chosen underwear was for special occasions.

The weekend dragged. Sofia, Bev and Rosie all rang to check on the patient. Bev popped in at lunchtime. Apart from being stiff all over, he felt fine and by the afternoon he kept thinking about ringing Miranda. She rang him.

'Good afternoon, Santa,' she said. 'How are you feeling?'

'Never better, and you can take that as official.'

She laughed at his enthusiasm. 'And headaches?'

'All gone and I was up at 6 watering tomatoes. I'm ready to don that big red suit, Miranda, and I shall no longer regard you as the perfect employer if you keep me locked up in my own home.'

She laughed. 'All right, you win, you can start in the morning.'

He wanted to cheer. 'Thank you, Miranda, thank you so much.'

'But there is a slight problem.' Air expelled instantly from his body. 'Your problem, Enrico, is you are too popular. Both your ladies wish to perform with you.'

'But ...,' he said before being interrupted.

'Lorna is adamant she must partner you. She is convinced you are her good luck charm.'

He panicked. 'Miranda, please, you must never say "Good luck" to Lorna.'

More laughter from the boss. 'I managed to calm her by saying next week she can work with you in the morning but for the rest of the season she will partner Big Graeme.'

She paused waiting for him to speak.

'Can I have that in writing?'

He couldn't see her grin. 'You have my word, Mr Popular. Now, do you want me to call Rosie and tell her the arrangement?'

'No thank you, I can do that.'

'I'm sure you can, and I know it's safe for me to say "Good luck" to you for your magical return tomorrow. Bye.'

He stared at the phone. Good news followed by great news. Rosie waited for his call as excited as him.

'I was hoping it'd be you and you're sounding sprightly.'

'I'm feeling sprightly.'

'So what's your news?'

He hesitated and she worried. 'I start tomorrow but all next week I will be working with Lorna in the morning.'

'Oh,' said a disappointed Rosie.

'But for the rest of the season, we are to become a pair again.'

'That's wonderful, Enrico. And how are your headaches?'

'No headaches only heartaches we won't be working together tomorrow.'

Her body gave a slight involuntary shudder. 'But soon and I can't wait for the final week. I'll see you tomorrow, my darling.'

He froze. *What did she say?* He knew what she said but its impact hit hard and lingered. Then he couldn't decide if the noise he heard was a phone click or a kiss. *Bloody hell, Enrico, this is serious.*

Thomas Larsen and the black dog were best pals. He was sure he couldn't sink any deeper in his pit of desperation. Losing his boy hurt so much he contemplated leaving the state or even the country. His German passport was still valid. Being geographically apart and starting a new life appealed more than his present morass and suffering.

He went to see his parents where the despair caused them to age even faster. 'Why don't you take a break, son,' suggested his father?

'Get away somewhere nice,' added his mother. 'Do something you find enjoyable—photography, fishing or bike riding.'

'Why don't you see if you can take Timmy for a holiday? You're his father. You have rights. Apply to the court for a one-off exemption for an annual holiday with your son. We can come with you.'

He nodded and promised to think about it. The family went from happy and content to constant misery. It wasn't a death in the family atmosphere but certainly similar.

Thomas decided, took a fortnight's leave and left the day after his fortnightly visit to see his boy. They caused him more pain than joy.

On the first day of his "holiday" he went online and bought a non-firing imitation replica pistol. It was a spur-of-the-moment decision. He headed to the bush and camped under the stars. He planned to have time with his son—it would be their time together.

Joseph rang Lorna. He needed to kill her relationship with his great uncle. His plan was simple. Seduce her and tell Ric his true love is a tramp.

'Hi Lorna, it's Joseph.' They small talked before he cut to the chase.

'Listen, lovely lady, Simon is still out of town and won't be back till Christmas. I would hate for him to find someone else for that part and have you miss out.'

'I'd hate that too especially as I know I can be brilliant in the role.'

'Here's an idea. You read for me, and I'll tell Simon he'd be mad to not cast you. What do you think?'

'Will you do that for me? Really?'

'It'd be my pleasure. I can come to yours or you can come to me.' He left the sentence hanging.

There was no way Lorna would invite the striking, young and powerful executive to her basic, clean but plain unit in the less salubrious part of Chadstone.

'I'd be happy to come to you.'

'Great and the sooner the better. What about tonight at say 9?'

'Suits me.' He gave her his address. 'And I really appreciate this, Joseph.'

'My pleasure, babe.'

She showered, powdered and perfumed and wore what she thought was both revealing yet classy. Her chosen underwear was for special occasions.

He opened the door to his swish East Hawthorn pad, she entered, and he kissed her cheek. He indicated his lounge with its sultry lighting. She sat and crossed her legs. With G & T in hand, she sipped and flicked through pages of the scenes involving her character, a middle-aged woman; all created by the unknown playwright, Joseph.

He read the other lines and when done, he praised her work. Desperation gripped her body. Here was her chance to get back on the stage and screen, to become a pro again. Fame was what she craved and of course the money, my god yes, the money.

She asked to be excused, and he directed her to the en suite in his bedroom. When she came out, he was lying on his bed obviously expecting his upfront fee for getting her the part. She wasn't going to surrender without at least a promise.

He hopped up, made the false promise, and they moved willingly into the scene they both expected and wanted. Joseph had a discreet camera in place having used same on other occasions. Full of class was our Joey.

She wallowed in his flattery and only left when he gently reminded her she was on duty tomorrow. Driving home, this Mrs Santa revelled in her ability to pull a toy boy and the belief she was about to be offered a role in a new movie.

The spoiler alert is superfluous.

Chapter 28
I seduced the director's partner who's half my age.

Bev insisted on driving Enrico to work. 'It's your first day back and you need to be in tip top condition.' She kissed his cheek.

He didn't argue and was grateful. She walked with him into the centre. 'Thank you, Bev, you're a true friend.' He kissed her cheek.

'Ooo,' she said. 'I've never been kissed by Santa before. Did you know there's a sprig of mistletoe at my place?'

He laughed, they parted, and he dressed ready for action. Lorna arrived looking and sounding like she'd won the lottery.

'Good morning, Santa. Don't you look gorgeous?' He scored a kiss from another woman and reckoned he should fall over more often. She'd changed, seriously so.

Miranda popped in to see if her team were both shipshape and Bristol fashion and yes, Enrico found himself being kissed by a third woman and that before he'd even started work.

Santa led his wife to the porthole door. He looked at her and remembered his line. 'Break a leg, Mrs Santa,' he said, and she smiled with feeling. As they left, he felt his bottom being patted. Bloody hell!

Russell was pleased to see him back and the queue of excited children soon grew. Lorna behaved in a new and remarkable way. No grumbling or groaning, no dropped little ones, and plenty of praise for Santa's efforts. Remarkable indeed.

Time flies when you're having fun. Their shift ended with everyone happy. As they walked to the storeroom, Santa heard a familiar voice.

'Ciao, Santa. Fancy a sandwich?'

It was Alfrid complete with grin and carry bag. He lifted the bag pointing at it. Enrico nodded but kept talking to children keen and excited to speak to their hero.

Inside the storeroom, Enrico's heart caught fire. Rosie was there but not yet in costume. There were greetings all round and Enrico's scorecard of cheek kisses chalked up another tick.

Rosie wanted to know how her favourite Santa had performed and of course, his current health. He could have been exhausted but being beside his girl caused him to describe his condition as top notch.

Rosie squeezed his arm and departed to change. Big Graeme arrived and made a fuss over the returning Santa.

In their dressing-room, the women chatted. Rosie's delight at Enrico's return caused her to sound excited.

'He did all right,' said Lorna, 'but I did better.'

Rosie's face changed. She stood up for her friend. 'He's been in hospital, Lorna. It's a huge effort just to be here let alone perform. How can you say you're better?'

'Not out there,' she scoffed. 'I'm talking behind the scenes last night at my movie audition. I seduced the director's partner, who's half my age, and have landed a top role. Let me tell you, lady, I've still got it.'

Many males who commit murder can't resist telling someone of their deed. Last night did not involve a homicide but Lorna suffered the same irresistible urge to boast of her achievement.

She swanned out leaving Rosie gobsmacked.

Enrico waited for Rosie to appear in costume, wished her well and whispered an invitation to call in to his place on her way home. She smiled and nodded.

'Oi, oi, what's goin' on over there,' growled Big Graeme struggling to dress. Enrico gave him a hand, winked at Rosie and left.

Outside he spotted Alfrid and joined him. They wandered to an area where shoppers could take the weight off their feet. Out came the thermos flask and sandwiches. Perfetto.

'This is a pleasant surprise,' said Enrico.

'Your sister told me you went to hospital, so I came here to see if you is still alive. I even watched you perform.'

'That's kind of you, my friend.'

'And to take a look at this woman you've fallen for. I must say, she looks a goer, Sunshine. Are you sure you can keep up?'

'That's not her,' hissed Enrico. 'That's the other Mrs Santa. My girl will be on stage any time now.'

'Oh, fair enough. And is you still keen?'

'Of course, but now I'm desperate. You've gotta help me, Alfrid.' Enrico's face backed up his words.

'All right, okay, keep y'shirt on.'

'I want to propose but don't know how.'

'Is that all? Look, Signore, it's simple. Buy a ring then ask her.'

His painful whispering attracted attention. People wondered what the two old men were so demonstrative about.

'Yes but what about sex?'

Alfrid despaired. 'Are you serious? You don't know what sex is?'

'Of course I know. But do we wait till we're married? Do I let her undress in private? Can you only have sex at night with the lights out? What about birth control? Alfrid, I need help.'

This time Alfrid laughed causing even more people to stare. Enrico dropped his head. He hated his ignorance even more than he hated possibly harming or embarrassing the woman he loved. He wanted everything to be perfect.

Alfrid continued whispering. 'Enrico, women have a condition called the menopause.'

'I've heard of that.'

'If your lady is over 50 ...'

'She's over 60 ... just.'

'Then her days of getting pregnant are over.' He spoke each word with emphasis. 'You do not need birth control.'

The old men looked at one another. Enrico spoke.

'You think I'm an idiot.'

'No, I think you're a kind, single man who's led a sheltered life and is now, as a pensioner, finally fallen madly in love.' Enrico couldn't speak. His lips locked hard. He nodded. 'So when am I going to meet the blushing bride?'

Enrico finished his coffee, returned the cup and referred to the beverage. 'Beautiful as always, Amico, and thank you for the lunch and advice. Now come and I'll show you my lovely Rosie.'

From a distance they watched Santa and his wife thrilling kids.

Alfrid turned to his friend. 'You have excellent taste, Signor.' Enrico smiled delighted his friend appreciated his choice of possible future wife. 'But tell me, does she have a sister?'

Chapter 29

It was an interesting pitch; the scammer using a scam to scam.

Joseph was getting close to snuffing out his great uncle's possible nuptials. His sneaky photos of the lovely Lorna in all her glory cheating on her wealthy, old boyfriend proved Enrico was being duped by a scarlet woman. She didn't love him; she loved his money and other men. Joseph's photographic evidence was the smoking gun. Will locked. Case closed.

His problem though was when to strike. He needed the right time and now that Lorna was a living character in his play, he couldn't allow her to run free and certainly not to get engaged to the former barber.

The great nephew needed to keep her inside the tent and rang Simon the small-time movie director. 'Mate, I need a favour.'

Simon wanted Joseph's financial contribution to help get his latest B grade movie off the ground and constantly needed to keep all his backers sweet.

'Sure man, what's happening?'

'I'm doing a favour for one of my grandmother's friends. She's a former actress, a bit player from years ago on forgotten TV shows but this lovely older lady is desperate to get back into show business even if for only a finale. Can you give her anything?'

'I'm making a commercial soon and there's a part for a grandmother.'

'Perfect,' said Joseph, 'I owe you one. I'll text you her details.'

An hour later Lorna could not believe the text she received from Simon. It wasn't an offer for the movie she auditioned for sans clothes, but it was work and money and the chance for her face to be seen. She purred, accepted the job, sent Simon her CV with a cheeky photo, and Joseph a text with a huge emoji of blood red lips. Joseph clenched his fist pulling his elbow towards him.

But now it was on to his next conquest and Pippa, the red-headed photographer provided a different challenge. He could tell she was interested in him, the chick magnet, with the bonus, the hook of offering her possible work, all fake of course. He called.

'Hi babe,' he crooned down the line. 'I know you'd like me to help you get freelance work and I will but how about we mix business with a little pleasure, and I take you to dinner.'

She buzzed with a mixture of pleasure and concern but agreed. He would collect her from home that night.

'Smart casual, babe,' he added, 'although you'd look great in anything.'

Pippa told her mother but not her grandmother. Anna was pleased but Rosie would require more details. She'd be told *after* the event.

Joseph arrived early, met the Mum and charmed her as well. Pippa looked fabulous and the meal was a treat.

'Listen, babe, there's a problem. I'm helping a mate stop his grandfather being scammed and I reckon you can help.'

It was an interesting pitch; the scammer using a scam to scam.

'Me?' asked Pippa, again spotting a red flag. 'How?'

'Those photos you took at Ringwood could be the key to helping the old pensioner. Let's swing by my place for coffee where I can explain the problem before I drop you home.'

It did sound interesting even if alarm bells warmed up in the background.

Pippa discovered his spotless flat which showed off his taste in fine things. There was no sight or mention of his debts. His possessions, as they used to say, were on the never-never. He offered her a glass of wine instead of coffee and Pippa relaxed in the same spot where Lorna sat. Would there be the same outcome? He gave his spiel.

'The Santa in the photos you took is wealthy and one of the women acting with him is trying to scam the old bugger.' For Pippa, several red flags popped up everywhere.

'I don't follow,' she said as the hairs on the back of her neck rose.

'You know there are millions of scams today, and the elderly are often the ones who get screwed. The woman in your photos has her claws into poor, old Santa and I need to help save the pensioner from losing his life savings.'

A worried Pippa sipped her wine. 'I'm not sure how I can help.'

'Come on, a gorgeous, smart girl like you is sure to think of something,' he said reaching in to take her glass.

He was sure the prey was ready to commit to an amorous encounter but miscalculated, badly so. His fatal error came when he revealed his interest in her grandmother's boyfriend, a kind and friendly gentleman. She met him. No way was he a scammer.

Escaping became her goal. 'Do you have any other photos of Santa and his nasty scammer girlfriend?'

'I do,' he said heading to his bedroom. 'Hang tight, babe.'

He wanted seduction but having her help save his inheritance appealed even more. He looked through a box of blackmail goodies, found what he wanted and headed back to the lovely photographer.

'Take a peek at …' he stopped mid-sentence as his sofa sat empty. 'Babe?' he called thinking Pippa had slipped into the other bathroom. He heard nothing so approached and tapped gently. 'You okay?' Still nothing so Don Juan opened the door half hoping his latest bimbo might be in a state of undress. He was all class.

At that moment, Pippa was fully dressed and phoning an Uber to meet her at the nearest main intersection. She fled and when Joseph called, she was on her way to Grannie's and didn't bother to answer.

Travelling to Rosie's maisonette, Pippa called and caused her grandmother to worry. 'I have news, Grannie, I'll be there in fifteen.'

'What news?'

'And I've eaten but coffee would be wonderful. Bye Gran.'

Rosie wondered what Pippa's news might be and greeted the young woman with coffee, home-baked biscuits and a large serving of intrigue. When Pippa dropped the bombshell about Enrico and his femme fatale, this Mrs Santa opened her eyes in genuine shock. The following conversation was worth bottling.

'Tell no-one,' became Rosie's command. 'I'll sort this.'

'Do you think Enrico knows?'

'Tell me everything you know about this Joseph guy. I want a detailed description, and I think the other Mrs Santa and I need a serious heart to heart.'

Chapter 30
'You bitch,' she hissed, loud enough for the men outside to hear.

Rosie arrived for her session, surprised at an absent Big Graeme. She changed and waited for Enrico and Lorna. They arrived and the retired barber was thrilled.

'Hello, Mrs Santa,' he said with his best natural smile on show.

She replied with concern. 'How did you go? Was everything okay?'

Lorna brushed past. 'Of course it was. I carried him as usual.' She left for the female room and before the lovers could speak, Big Graeme arrived looking worse for wear.

'My bloody car wouldn't start.'

Sporting enough perspiration to drown a rat, he collapsed on a makeshift chair which instinctively tried to move.

Rosie looked at Enrico. 'I need to check my make-up. I'll see you soon.' She headed to the female dressing-room.

Lorna regarded the female space as her own and spread out making it difficult for Rosie to do anything. She reached for her make-up case and annoyed Lorna.

'Do you mind, I haven't finished my face.'

Rosie stepped to one side and spoke quietly. 'Lorna, look at me.' This sounded and looked serious. Lorna turned, intrigued. 'Are you planning to scam Enrico?'

'What?' The question made no sense, and a flustered Lorna glared. But Rosie's next question stopped the former TV actress dead in her tracks.

'And who is this young man called Joseph?'

Silence. Lorna couldn't believe her private life was anyone else's business, and her first reaction was that Rosie was trying to gazump her plan to get back into the world of entertainment.

'You bitch,' she hissed loud enough for the men outside to hear.

'Hello, hello,' called Big Graeme. 'Is there a cat fight in there?'

Lorna pointed at Rosie and snarled. 'Cross me, darling, and you will regret it, big time.'

A shocked Rosie saw serious intent in her colleague's eyes and decided a tactical retreat to be the wisest action. Both men looked at Rosie as she stepped into their space.

'Rosie?' asked Enrico worried for his first best friend.

'I'm fine. Sorry Enrico but I need some fresh air. I'll be back in a couple of minutes.' She headed for the door.

'Hey, we're on soon,' added Big Graeme. 'What's going on?'

Before Rosie could respond, the door opened, and Miranda entered.

'Good afternoon, all. How are we? Is Lorna here? I need a quick word.'

The furious prima donna appeared. 'I'm here and wishing I wasn't because someone is jealous of my success in returning to the movie world.'

Her words, body language and tone of voice gave the atmosphere a swift kick, and the other three performers froze wondering how the boss would react. Miranda ignored Lorna's latest performance and fell back on the pacify-the-selfish-woman approach.

'Hi Lorna. How would you like another session on Friday night? It'll mean more money of course.'

Lorna switched instantly once the word *money* appeared.

'You mean after hours?'

'Yes,' said Miranda. 'The couple I hired for the dog show are now minus a Mrs Santa. Keith is fine but the lady has pulled out and Rosie has already asked to be excused so she can bring her pooch.'

'If this is after hours,' said Lorna; 'it means time and a half.'

Miranda anticipated such a demand. 'Exactly and thank you for kindly volunteering. Doing the morning session means you'll have a free afternoon before the dog show at night.'

'Okay,' mumbled Lorna then threw away, 'never work with children or animals.'

'Now Graeme has asked if he can be excused on Friday afternoon so Enrico will you please switch to the after-lunch session on Friday?'

'With Rosie?' he asked too enthusiastically.

'Yes and remember we'll all change partners for the Christmas week. Enrico and Rosie before lunch, and Lorna and Graeme after lunch.'

Enrico and Rosie glowed inside.

'Suits me,' said Lorna as I'll be working all weekend on my advert.

'Your advert?' queried Miranda.

'Yes, I'm starring in a new ad and filming all weekend.'

Enrico took control. 'Well before next week or even Friday night, there's a session due to start here in about ten minutes.'

He was right and Big Graeme finished dressing and he and Rosie took off. Miranda looked at her other performers. 'Everything going well?' she asked in genuine hope.

Lorna and Enrico muttered their replies, their lies.

'Good, good, good,' said Miranda. 'Well, I'll leave you to it. Bye.'

Enrico wanted to quiz Lorna about the heated words he overheard between the two Mrs Santas. 'Lorna, may I …'

Lorna walked past him. 'Mind your own bloody business,' she spoke in a spiteful voice which, combined with her menacing look ended any hope of an explanation. Enrico changed as the Mrs Santa he didn't remotely care for, stormed out leaving him with questions aplenty.

Lorna went home and continued fuming about Rosie's question. *'And who is this young man called Joseph?'* The bit about scamming Enrico meant nothing but pinching her toy boy and his influence in getting her an audition for a movie role, and definitely a TV ad, was red-rag-to-a-bull to Lorna.

The retired barber wandered the shopping centre and was late getting home. He arrived to a ringing phone. 'Hello Sofia. I've …'

'Enrico, it's me, Rosie.'

'Rosie,' he gasped. 'Are you all right?'

'I'm fine. How are you?'

'I'm worried about you and what sounded like an argument with Lorna.'

'It was nothing; a misunderstanding over make-up.'

He wasn't convinced and she wasn't sure what, if anything, to tell him. She decided to not mention the story Pippa told her. It might not be true, and Rosie would do anything to protect the man she loved. She couldn't bear to upset him.

'I'll be there on Friday night as I want to meet your family.' This threw her. He explained. 'I want to have a good chat with Buster.'

She laughed more from relief than happiness.

'We will not be Mr and Mrs Santa so we can behave as the people we are.' She loved his words. 'Will Buster be upset if I hold your hand?'

This time she knew she loved him. 'Buster will be happy, but I will be happier.'

Neither spoke. They wished they were together now, in person and in love.

'Sleep well, darling lady, and I'll see you tomorrow in our favourite storeroom.'

Both paused before Rosie whispered. 'Goodnight my love.'

The build-up to Friday passed without incident. Rosie desperately wanted Pippa's tale to be fully explained. Pippa wanted nothing more to do with Joseph. He hated failing in the seduction stakes but returned to his treasured philosophy of, "There are plenty more fish in the sea".

The Friday night session would happen when the usual Santa visitors, the children, were at home in bed dreaming about the old bloke and his sleigh bursting with presents on Christmas Eve. The shopping centre, wanting as much foot traffic as possible, advertised a *Have Your Dog Meet Santa* session and dogs in local parks soon barked the gossip to other pooches.

'Have you, woof, heard about, woof, this Meet Santa session, and woof?'

The news spread and dog owners soon found the pressure so great they agreed to their canine's demand. 'Yes, yes, all right, I'll take you.'

Rosie told Buster who couldn't wait. Enrico declined Rosie's offer of a lift with Buster in the back. 'Thank you, my dear, but Buster doesn't like distractions. I'll see you there.'

They arrived on Friday for the afternoon session to work together. This was a bonus with both eagerly anticipating being back together for the final week. Enrico arrived first and was dressed when Rosie entered the storeroom. The cleaner was fussing with equipment which put a dampener on their greeting. They longed to simply but discretely touch. Rosie retired to dress and when she appeared, Lorna and Big Graeme arrived.

Like a broken record, Lorna told everyone she was part of a TV advert being shot on the weekend.

'What's it about?' asked Big Graeme still struggling to undress.

'All I know is I'm on screen for virtually the whole time.'

'Wow, you *are* a star.' She gloated.

Enrico and Rosie worked the afternoon session and were a hit. The way she spoke to her husband was kind and loving with no-one guessing they would love to be husband and wife in real life.

Russell grew suspicious. 'You two are either brilliant actors or something else is going on here.'

The couple from the North Pole glanced at one another and Enrico wanted the subject changed.

'Have you lined up your doggy bags for tonight?'

The photographer groaned. 'Oh please, don't remind me.'

The session ended and Rosie gave Santa a lift home. She pulled up outside his large and much coveted block. He looked at her and found his body start to tingle. 'I can't wait to see you tonight; oh, and Buster as well.'

She smiled. 'Will you come out with me tomorrow night?'

Shock whacked his face. 'Tomorrow night?'

'Yes, tomorrow night, on a date?'

'But I thought it was the man's job to ask the lady on a date.'

'Back in Victorian times but not so much today.'

'I should be asking *you* to dinner.'

'This is not to dinner. It's to the final performance of a play staged by the theatre company I belong to. I would love you to come and meet my friends.'

Enrico smiled enjoying the thought of becoming a public lover before worrying if people would like him or possibly even laugh at him. Right now, his Don Juan status never appeared shakier.

'Thank you, I would love to come,' he spoke with nervous enthusiasm. 'What do I wear? Is there a dress code? I haven't been to the theatre since I was a child. And where can I buy the tickets?'

She laughed. 'You always dress well, Signor and as I'm a life member of the company, I'm given comps.' He didn't understand. She explained and squeezed his arm. 'I'll see you tonight *with* Buster and pick you up at seven tomorrow night with*out* the world's greatest pooch. He hates live theatre.'

She leant across and kissed his cheek. He wanted to continue the romantic activity, but a family approached on the adjacent footpath. He hopped out. Hopping was an accurate description but with his stick for stability, he closed the door and waved to the driver.

Of course, Sofia rang not long after he arrived. 'How did you go?' she asked with a hint of demand.

'It went well and soon I'll be back working with Rosie.'

'Oh,' replied his sister fearing the worst, 'and for how long?'

'We start on Monday and then for the rest of the season.'

'Is that wise?'

'And we're going tonight but only to watch.'

'Tonight? There's Santa at night?'

'It's for dogs and their owners. Rosie's taking Buster.'

'Buster? Who's he? Is he her boyfriend?'

Enrico laughed. 'Buster's her dog and he's going to meet Santa. And tomorrow I'm taking Rosie to the theatre or rather, she's taking me.'

This was too much information for Sofia. Working together for the rest of the season meant anything could happen. And going on a date where the woman, she refused to say Rosie, asked *him,* set off alarms.

'I must go, Sofia and you'll be pleased to know, your baby brother has never been so happy in his entire life. Bye.'

He might be happy, but his sister fretted and worried. This was serious. She rang her daughter, Maria.

'Yes, Mamma?'

'Your uncle has gone mad. He's back working with that woman and now she is taking him to the theatre.'

'She's taking *him*? Wow, times have changed. Mind you, Joseph and Michael might be right. She's probably after his money.'

Sofia exploded. 'Which is why you must tell them! They must save their dear great uncle from making a fool of himself and losing everything.'

Chapter 31
You will now need a bigger shelf for your pumpkins, beans and tomatoes.

Enrico entered the packed shopping centre and headed towards the Santa set to find the joint was jumping. The usual Christmas music played throughout, and the sound of barking dogs gave the place a showground or agricultural atmosphere.

He became lost in the crowds around the performing space and squeezed around people to get a better view.

The dogs didn't expect an individual meeting with Santa but were up for a whole mob en masse photo with the old man in the red suit.

Enrico couldn't see Rosie. Where is she? Keith, the fill-in Santa, and Laura as Mrs Santa were doing next to nothing. Only children wanted to chat. Laura was clearly not a dog person. Russell moved back and forth setting up the one big photo. There were happy dogs, excited dogs and the odd confused and timid canine.

Enrico discovered Rosie. She was sitting or rather lying on the set buried behind her dog and several others. Owners were not the star; their beloved pets were downstage centre and hopefully looking at the camera when Russell called, 'Cheese' or 'Treat'.'

Fortunately, he didn't say, 'Walkies' as that might have set off a stampede with the hounds running carefree throughout the shopping centre.

The large crowd loved the scenario. Children spotted their family dog and called to it. The dogs were excited anyway but a familiar voice stating their name ratcheted up their happiness.

Finally, Russell was ready. He stood behind his tripod and raised a hand. This was the signal previously explained to the humans. Santa was centre stage grinning like a Cheshire cat which was risky in a mass gathering of dogs.

Russell took several photos in the hope at least one would not feature a dog with its bottom staring at the camera.

Then it was over. Owners stood and chatted to their pet. Santa joined in although Lorna couldn't wait for the allotted finish time to arrive.

Enrico pressed close to the set and tried to catch Rosie's attention. He called with decorum. 'Rosie! Rosie!' The din was such she didn't hear. He saw Buster looking at his owner and reckoned another approach might work. He upped the volume a bit then more than a bit.

'Buster,' he called; 'Buster, here boy.' Enrico whistled.

This worked. Did it ever? Rosie's Buster knew his name and turned in the direction of the Santa in mufti.

Rosie looked where Buster looked and spotted Enrico. She waved and he smiled and waved again. Now he wanted to join what he hoped would soon be his new family. He called even more loudly.

'Buster, here boy,' he yelled with affection.

Enrico didn't know he would soon be responsible for a chain reaction. Recently, Buster had become a popular name for canines. Their super hearing kicked in. In waving to Enrico, Rosie held Buster's lead with only one hand and he, the pooch, reckoned responding to the kind old bloke calling meant he should set off and greet his owner's friend. He did.

He dragged Rosie off balance. She dropped the lead. Buster bounded away and three other dogs, also called Buster, decided to copy him.

Dogs encircled their owner locking human legs. People struggled to break free, dropped their dog's lead allowing Buster play time to begin.

Owners called their dog who reckoned this was a fantastic game. Many non-Buster dogs started barking, several demanding a name change, and the great idea of the centre management turned into a free for all, a circus.

Dozens of shoppers whipped out their phones, and videos and still photos were recorded en masse. Soon social media came alive and even one TV station included a story towards the end of their bulletin.

Santa gets tails wagging this Christmas!

In the pandemonium, Rosie fought through the crowds and found Enrico holding her Buster's lead. She looked around and glimpsed Russell scrambling to rescue his equipment, set up a display of his pics, and take orders from dog owners many of whom reckoned the event proved a smashing success.

'I think we should go,' said Rosie and took off for the car park.

'Don't you want a photo of Buster and your feet?'

She saw he was grinning. 'Ha ha,' she said and kept walking. They reached her car, put Buster in his back seat bed, and hopped in the front. They closed their door and stared at one another.

'Did I do the wrong thing?' he asked now worried.

'Of course not but it might be better if you weren't able to make it tonight.'

'But ... oh, you mean I was never here and need an alibi.'

She smiled and drove Santa to his non-North Pole home. She stopped outside said property apparently now worth a small fortune to any developer.

'I'm ever so sorry, Rosie. You must know I didn't mean any harm.'

'Stop apologizing as the night was a great success. Now I'll pick you up tomorrow at 7.'

He paused. 'Right, that sounds wonderful.' He paused again.

'Is something wrong?' she asked.

'I'm not sure of the order of events.'

'Sorry? What events?'

'Which comes first; patting Buster or kissing the driver?'

She laughed. He leant into the back and patted the tail-thumping dog then leant across and kissed Rosie sweetly on the lips.

'Good night, Mrs Santa,' he said and struggled to exit. Before he closed the door, she spoke.

'Good night, Santa. Sweet dreams.'

He couldn't sleep. The crazy dog event made him smile, cringe and then smile again. But his love for Buster's mother soon dominated his thinking. He wanted and needed to take that all-important step and come the morrow he decided he would.

Telling Sofia would be the right thing to do but doing so was the equivalent of telling the world. No, for now, he would wait.

He knew she would ring at her usual 9am and because he wanted to go shopping, he rang her. For him to not be home when she rang would cause no end of trouble.

'What's wrong?' she asked when he called.

'Nothing, I'm going out for a spot of shopping and didn't want you to worry when I didn't answer.'

'You're going out? It's Saturday morning. You shop on Thursdays.'

'And I'll be out tonight too. Remember I'm taking Rosie to the theatre.'

She hesitated. Wanting to say "that woman is after your money" could annoy him and push him into doing something even more extreme. She settled for a reminder about his tablets.

He could have gone shopping in the Ringwood shopping centre, but he might be seen and that was a recipe for trouble. 'Did I see you in the jeweller's shop on Saturday?' would be a disaster. No, he would shop as far from his suburb as possible.

He went next door with two firm, ripe, home-grown tomatoes, interrupted Beverley doing her daily vac. 'Good morning, stranger. Come in, come in.'

'Something for your salads,' he said, and her gratitude was fulsome.

She made him a cuppa. 'So how did the dog show with Santa go?'

'I think it went well.'

'You think?'

'I may have caused a bit of a commotion when a few of the dogs wanted to party.'

'What!'

'But Bev; I have a problem and need your help.' His face, body language and voice screamed concern.

'Of course. What's up?'

'Can you use your computer and help me find a jeweller's shop in the city?'

Her smile appeared and he knew she knew. Without speaking she moved to her elderly neighbour and gave him a fierce hug. 'That's wonderful news, Signor. I couldn't be happier for you both.'

Bev turned on her laptop and searched for Melbourne jewellers. She jotted down their names and then opened their web pages. He sat beside her amazed at the technology.

'I've no idea what to buy,' he said. 'And what if she doesn't like it?'

She looked at him. 'Would you like me to come with you?'

Shock and relief whacked him. 'Oh Bev, will you?'

She closed her laptop. 'Of course I will. Give me five to add some lippy.'

And that was how Enrico went shopping for an engagement ring. His neighbour was assumed to be his intended. The assistant made a total mess of the deal. I mean how many septuagenarians purchase an engagement ring with the help of their middle-aged neighbour?

Beverley performed the perfect role as wedding planner cum engagement ring adviser. She even negotiated a discount pointing out the age of the bride and groom. All the way home, Enrico kept feeling the little container resting in his jacket pocket.

At their driveways, he kissed her cheek and said, 'You will now need a bigger shelf for your pumpkins, beans and tomatoes.'

The wannabe bridegroom was over the moon.

Chapter 32
They weren't wearing much at all.

He took an age getting ready for his Saturday night date. Choosing his attire proved a nightmare. A tie, of course he would wear a tie, but a suit seemed too much. His sports jacket bought from Fletcher Jones in the last millennium would do and his grey slacks, also from FJ's, completed his ensemble.

A small box containing a certain piece of jewellery sat in his bedside tabletop drawer. He needed time to build up the courage to pop the question. Tonight, that small box would stay at home.

He kept looking at his watch as the pick-up time drew closer. He went for a pee and ten minutes later went again. Going on a date with a woman was a first this century but asking said woman to marry him was, well, arriving in a foreign country unable to speak the local lingo.

Rosie's car arrived and he was out the door and walking as if his walking stick was superfluous. She walked towards him.

'Good evening, Signor,' she said and kissed him.

'You look marvellous,' he replied and meant it. He loved her perfume.

Again he wanted to hold the door for her but waited by his door until she settled. Beverley watched and purred.

The couple chatted freely until Rosie popped a question. Not *that* question. 'And what did you do today, Enrico? Anything interesting?'

Oh Lordy Lord, he groaned inside. 'I'm sure you could guess; Sofia and gardening,' he said, and she laughed. His nerves became uncontrollable.

Rosie's amateur theatre company had enjoyed success for many decades. Being a life member, she was afforded much respect and love but even she became nervous bringing the man she wanted to marry to meet her circle of friends. None of them had any knowledge of her current beau.

They entered the theatre foyer with Front of House staff greeting her like a diva. She kissed so many people, Enrico was thrown.

In-between kisses, Rosie introduced Enrico. He made sure his extended hand established his preferred form of greeting.

A bell sounded and Rosie took Enrico's arm. 'Time for the play, sir,' she said, and they entered the theatre. Rosie always received the same two seats, and she cursed the fact they were in the centre of the row. With nearby patrons already seated, she worried the man with the stick might struggle. He made it, the house lights faded, and the play began.

Rosie kept sneaking mini glances at her beau. He found the theatrical experience fascinating. The play, a comedy, grabbed his attention with his smile constantly on show.

He took coffee at the interval with Rosie shepherding him to one side where he could place his cup and maintain his balance with relative ease. He found another reason to love this Mrs Santa.

The second act was even better, funnier than the first with the cast receiving prolonged applause during their curtain calls. In the foyer, people gushed. Cast members, on a high, greeted their relatives and friends. Rosie knew most of the cast and they were thrilled to greet the lady who made them look good. Her costumes were always perfect for the period.

Enrico survived the throng and audience members drifted away. Rosie wondered if her guest had seen enough and would prefer to go home.

'The cast and crew always enjoy an after-show party to celebrate the end of the season. We can pop in for a few minutes or we can leave now. What would you like to do?'

He could see it would be wrong for Rosie to leave without congratulating her friends. 'I think we should stay,' he said, and she smiled.

The furniture on stage became the furniture for the party. Drinks and laughter flowed freely. Rosie performed a juggling act as she joined the party while introducing her friend to all and sundry. One gent approached Rosie giving her a huge hug and enthusiastic kiss.

'Darling,' exclaimed the effeminate middle-aged man dressed in an OTT fashion. No Fletcher Jones slacks and sports jacket for Gavin.

'Gavin,' said Rosie, 'I'd like you to meet my friend, Enrico.'

The former barber's hand was extended before Rosie's introduction ended. Enrico's limit of hugs and kisses from total strangers was already way past his accepted level of zero.

'Lovely to meet you, Enrico,' said Gavin. 'Don't tell me,' he added pointing at a certain sports coat, 'Fletcher Jones.'

Rosie explained. 'Enrico's a retired barber. What he doesn't know about cutting hair and hairpieces isn't worth knowing.'

Gavin shrieked. 'Marvellous! Wonderful! You're the man I want.'

'Gavin's in charge of our make-up, wigs, hairpieces and moustaches.'

The theatrical wigmaker with a head so bald he combed his hair with a towel, took hold of Enrico's hand, the one not controlling his stick. 'I need an expert's advice, darling. Please walk this way.'

Enrico looked pleadingly at Rosie who gave a pathetic smile and Santa found himself being taken off-stage, down a flight of stairs and into a dark underground room packed with costumes, props, tins of paint and anything else a theatre company used.

Gavin hit a light switch and stopped at a glass-topped display cabinet filled with wigs. 'Don't ask where they came from or I'll be sent to the naughty corner but please, Frederico, I need to know what I can save and what is likely to fall apart.' Gavin opened the glass top. Frederico, playing Enrico, examined the wigs.

He knew quality when he saw it, and these were the best. Gavin thrilled to the advice he received and was already planning which wigs he could use in the first show next year.

Enrico picked up another wig when a strange sound was heard. He froze and Gavin fumed.

'Stephen,' he hissed and moved along the row of men's suits. Enrico half followed and saw Gavin pull apart the suits to reveal another performance, a current, one-act drama.

A man, the lighting designer and operator, and a woman, the wife of the stage manager, were not wearing any of the costumes in the costume store. In fact they weren't wearing much at all and could well have been life models although neither was posing.

'Jesus, when are you two gunna grow up,' exploded Gavin and turned on his heel and left. 'Come on, Valentino, we're outa here.'

The retired barber stood transfixed, feeling overdressed. The man amongst the costumes spoke. 'Come on, Chiko. This is your lucky night.'

The woman smiled. 'Ever had a threesome, Grandpa?'

Enrico came alive, turned and ran out of the storeroom. He didn't need his stick as he "bounded" up the stairs and instead of turning left and entering stage right, he opened the side door and headed for the street at the front of the theatre.

He could see the nearby intersection and a tram. He hurried and after a short wait, climbed aboard. It was heading to the city, and he knew a train with his name on it would be close at hand.

Back on stage, the party warmed up and Rosie helped the others celebrate. It was only when she saw Gavin drinking with a couple of actors that she panicked. Where's Enrico?

Gavin didn't spare the fruity language in explaining what he and Emilio discovered.

'But where's Enrico?' she gasped. Gavin shrugged and Rosie went searching. She looked everywhere before heading downstairs to the costumes. What she heard was enough to send her skywards. She grabbed her phone and called Enrico.

On the tram, he looked at the number and turned off his phone. His heart kept beating like mad and questions flooded his brain.

'Do I really know Rosie? Are my sister and niece right when they doubt my romantic friendship? And can I get a refund on that ring?'

Rosie suffered panic and pain. *'What has happened? Why won't he answer? Is he all right? And where is he?'*

The two love birds made their own way home. Both travelled thinking constantly of the other. He couldn't get the sex scene he confronted at the theatre out of his mind. *Were those people friends of Rosie? Did she approve of their public behaviour? Did she engage in this type of activity? Have I fallen for a woman who is not the person I thought she was? Have I made a terrible mistake? Thank God I haven't proposed marriage.*

Rosie struggled to drive home alone as tears kept filling her eyes. *Enrico is obviously upset.* She reached home, went inside and Buster immediately saw her distress. He pawed and nuzzled her leg as she found him a midnight snack. She rang Enrico's landline and froze unable to leave a voice message. Then she sent a text to his mobile. Full of apologies, she hoped this would never upset their friendship and could he please tell her he was home safe and well.

He arrived and saw his message bank flashing. He didn't want to speak with Rosie and so ignored it. Not to worry as Sofia was the message giver.

He put away his 1970s outfit, last worn at a cousin's funeral, and prepared for bed. He checked his mobile phone and saw the text from Rosie. At least he didn't have to speak to her. He read her text and replied.

Rosie. I am home and will see you on Monday at Ringwood. Enrico.

If anything, his reply made her worse. By chance she had met a lovely man and their blossoming romance unexpectedly hit a wall. She should never have taken him to that damn play.

Chapter 33
What do you want; a medal or a chest to pin it on?

It was the longest Sunday of their lives. Both remained at home, neither contacted the other and misery washed over them like an incoming tide. They were back working together in the morning and that alone scared them.

Enrico arrived at Ringwood way too early. He thought he would get dressed and then hide somewhere in the centre and avoid meeting Rosie until just before they were due on set.

His confusion bubbled and doubled, and he couldn't go through with such a move so waited until she arrived.

'Good morning,' he said.

She moved and stood near him. 'Good morning,' she replied then the moment she wanted to tackle their issue head on, the cleaner entered, apologized and fussed with his equipment.

Rosie left for her room and changed. She waited until their departure was imminent and appeared with Enrico ready to roll. He opened the door for her as he always did, and they walked in silence.

He pushed open the porthole door, rang his bell and shouted, 'Ho, Ho, Ho.' Rosie followed, and both smiled at children while crying inside.

Soon it was back chatting to the little ones and although the Santas' behaviour was impeccable, Russell sensed something. 'What's happened, folks?' he whispered. 'Somebody die?'

'We're fine,' said Rosie killing Russell's curiosity.

Enrico ignored the photographer, and he knew his, Enrico's reaction to Rosie was worse than him being rude or angry.

They survived the session and as they walked along the corridor, Rosie stopped and looked at him. Her tears were real. She begged.

'Can we talk, please, Enrico? I can't go on like this. We seemed to be best friends and now we're …' She cried and Enrico became sad and embarrassed. To make a bad situation worse, Big Graeme arrived for his afternoon shift.

'Oi, oi, oi, what's goin' on 'ere?' he blundered towards them.

'The lady is not feeling well,' said Enrico. 'A little more respect please.'

'Sorry,' said Big Graeme, made a face and left. Rosie felt instantly better with Enrico reverting to type, caring for her, protecting her.

'I think you should go inside and change,' he said.

He followed her, they avoided Big Graeme, and she settled in her space.

Enrico changed not knowing if he should wait. Before he could decide, Lorna appeared and seemed on fire.

'Goooood afternoon, gentlemen; no need to stand for the star of a new ad soon to hit our screens.' The males offered a mute reaction. Big Graeme reckoned she was a temperamental windbag and Enrico had other fish to fry.

She entered the smaller room where Rosie had changed and was fixing her face. Lorna continued boasting.

'I've only seen a few rushes, but this ad is going to be big.' Rosie didn't respond and with all fellow actors showing no interest, she sneered and changed. 'Well, be snooty, see if I care. This pathetic amateurish gig is my last before the big offers start rolling in.' She pulled on her wig. 'And not only am I back in the professional world, but I've also even done what so many senior ladies *can* never and *will* never do.' She dropped her voice. 'I've still got it, sweetheart and yes, it's true. Last week I did indeed pull a guy young enough to be my grandson.'

'Congratulations,' said Rosie continuing to work on her make-up.

'Jealous, are we?' added Lorna in full flight.

Without turning, Rosie finally spoke. 'What do you want; a medal or a chest to pin it on?'

Wow did that get a reaction. Lorna moved close to Rosie and hissed. 'You bitch. I saw him first, he's my ticket to fame, so back off or else.'

Rosie stood, gave the other Mrs Santa a grim smile and left. Lorna fumed. Silence packed a powerful punch.

The men were fascinated having heard snippets of Lorna's speech with enough to make them seriously curious.

Rosie looked at Enrico, held his gaze then left with her heart in pain.

Lorna appeared and headed for the door. Passing Big Graeme, she muttered, 'Come on Fatso, get y'arse into gear.' She left.

Enrico looked at the gobsmacked Santa and spoke. 'She's a lady is our Lorna.'

Enrico arrived home and spent the afternoon alone. He was watering his front garden when Beverley came wandering along his drive.

'Good afternoon, Romeo,' she said then nearly died. His face and body language screamed sadness. She thought the worst. He's popped the question and been turned down.

'Hello neighbour,' he said mopping his brow.

She didn't want to ask romantic questions so plumped for non-controversial ones. 'Are you okay, Enrico? And why are you watering in the hottest part of the day?'

'Come inside and have a cold drink.' She accepted, desperate to hear his news. The explanation included a toned-down version of that hanky-panky below stage. 'We haven't been arguing but maybe we've become too close. I became upset with what happened at the theatre, and now I've got doubts about our friendship.'

Bev reckoned this was baloney and decided to become an Agony Aunt. 'Listen Enrico, Confucius say, "A good barber can help you lose weight".'

He stared at her, confused. 'Confucius said that? And what does it mean?'

'It's nonsense I made up, but what *is* true is that you'll always regret not going to Rosie and having a serious chat. Sort it out, my friend, and the sooner the better.'

They hugged and she went to leave. 'Thank you, Doctor, what do I owe you?' She grinned and left.

He picked up his phone and called Rosie. Before it connected, he cancelled the call. He had a better idea.

That afternoon, Joseph and Michael met in a pub. 'This is getting serious,' said big brother. 'Mum says Nonna says Ric's about to propose.'

Michael shook his head. 'If that's true we're sunk.'

'Unless we jump in and show him his girlfriend getting it off with her toy boy. We can't wait. He could do the business in a registry office, and we'll be out of the will and short a small fortune.'

'How will he react when he sees the sex pics?'

'I don't care how he reacts so long as he dumps the bird. Now let's get serious and start a stalking show.'

'What? You want to stalk our great uncle?'

'You take the shift tonight. I'll do tomorrow. Sit outside his place and see what he does. With him not having wheels, his darling girl will probably visit him. Take notes and we'll set the perfect time to hit the bugger between the eyes.'

Michael hated the cloak and dagger routine but hated the idea of being cut out of the will. The brothers toasted their plan in sombre seriousness.

With daylight saving, it was still light when Enrico walked from his front door that late afternoon sporting his trusty walking stick. Great nephew #2, Michael, was parked a good fifty yards away in a parking bay beside an oval. He slipped from his car and followed Enrico on the other side of the road.

He worried about being on foot but the old relative with a dicky hip was never going to outpace him.

Then panic set in. Enrico headed for his local station with Michael following while staying out of sight. The train to Melbourne pulled in and Michael waited until the last moment before boarding two carriages apart.

He watched at each station with no movement from Enrico. East Camberwell was the stop. Michael waited for Enrico to alight then did so at the last moment and stood beside the fence. The station platform curved providing better cover. Once the retired barber left the station, Michael was on his toes and followed at a distance. Enrico reached a maisonette in a nearby tree-lined street, opened the gate and walked to the front door.

Michael started looking for a place to keep watch while not looking suspicious.

Rosie opened her front door and thought her heart would burst. 'May I come in?' said Enrico, and Rosie hugged him with such ferocity he stumbled, his Bank of Monte Carlo magic walking stick proving useless. She broke her hug, helped him steady and helped him inside.

Michael didn't fancy standing in the street holding a camera. Someone with a twitching curtain would call the cops, especially in this suburb. He walked away with the occasional look back then turned and walked back. He cursed his brother for sending him on what might be a wasted trip.

He was on his third wander back when he saw activity. He hurried behind a tree, grabbed his camera and started filming.

Enrico stood outside the door with his back to the street. He and a woman embraced with Great Uncle Ric dropping his stick and using his lover for stability. They kissed with passion and Michael's camera whirred.

The passion on parade stopped and Michael ducked back behind the tree. When he peered out, Enrico, having closed the front gate, waved and set off for the station. Michael swung his camera back towards the woman and managed shots of her front door closing.

He swore, grabbed his phone and booked an Uber for yesterday. It meant he was back in Enrico's street before the old boy even caught a train. Another call to Joseph meant the brothers rendezvoused in the pub midway between their homes.

'The dirty old man,' said Joseph looking at his brother's camera. 'I can't see the bitch's face.'

'He was standing in front of her.'

'Where is this?' demanded Joseph.

'East Camberwell.'

'Bitch! She told me she lived in East Malvern.' It was Chadstone.

'Maybe old Ric has more than one girlfriend.'

Joseph reacted with disbelief. 'So that's where I get my horny genes.'

'But what are we gunna do?'

'Pay the old bugger a visit and show him the bitch in action. It'll be the Christmas present he sure won't wanna receive.'

Chapter 34
Your girlfriend is a money-grubbing bitch who sleeps with men young and old.

That night, Pippa popped in to see her grandmother. Rosie told Pippa she was never so happy.

'Is he going to propose, Gran?'

Rosie struggled. 'I hope so,' she finally whispered, and the women hugged.

Next morning the Christmas couple found their happiness overflowing as Enrico and Rosie were back on stage together and back in love. Bev saw the striking change in Blackburn, and Russell observed the huge change in their behaviour on the set at Eastland. Enrico wanted to throw away his stick.

Sofia made her daily phone call nice and early to query his diet, medical requirements and private life.

'All the children are in love with Santa,' he said, 'and it's wonderful being back working with Rosie.' Sofia muttered. She continued to worry.

'I need to tell you something important, Sofia.' She held her breath. 'I've never been so happy in all my life.'

Sofia strangled a cry of despair. A psychologist would pinpoint the cause of her behaviour. She was the matriarch and taking control of her baby bachelor brother was a large part, the main part of her life. If this woman, any woman, took her place, what would Sofia do? How dare this Rosie creature usurp her role! Forget Enrico's happiness. What about mine?

At night Enrico would open the top drawer of his bedside table, remove the red felt-covered box and look at the engagement ring he bought with Beverley for his darling Mrs Santa. Beverley worried at the lack of an announcement, and her gentle prodding for news always ended with him telling her he wanted the proposal moment to be perfect. Okay, sure, fine, but when?

She wanted to tell him he was no spring chicken and at this rate might not last the honeymoon.

Sofia told her daughter she was certain Maria's uncle was about to do something disastrously stupid.

'You mean he's going to marry his Mrs Santa.'

Sofia nearly screamed. 'Don't even say that out loud, and if you think of a way to save him, let me know.'

Maria did what she always did and told her sons about their grandmother's concern. Their concern was a million times greater than hers. Their plan to show Ric photos of a naked Mrs Santa was brought forward.

Thomas Larsen hit rock bottom. Losing touch with his son broke his heart. He ignored all suggestions about hiring a lawyer and visiting medical professionals who deal with depression and other mental illnesses.

He took leave and planned to drive to an isolated spot. He kept thinking the darkest of thoughts. At night, he cried himself to sleep.

Lorna grew frustrated because her starring role in a TV ad remained unscreened. All her boasting in the storeroom wore thin. It was hard to boast about something which didn't exist. The fact that Enrico and Rosie seemed blissfully happy only made her anger more intense.

Lorna's love life produced nothing in the way of serious commitment. One night stands only increased her sadness.

Christmas Eve crept closer. The crowds coming to see Santa grew ever larger. Russell's photographs sold like hot cakes. Every grandparent in the area wanted a copy of their precious mite sitting on the knee of the old man in the red suit.

Big Graeme held the world record with five siblings, comfortably aboard his cavernous thighs.

Two nights before the big night, the great nephews bit the bullet. Michael had printed a few 10 x 8 photos of Lorna in all her glory. The shots they chose featured Joseph's back and backside with Lorna looking back at the hidden camera. Despite the faces she made, it was unmistakably Lorna and her juvenile lover.

'What if Ric recognizes you?' asked Michael.

'What, from my arse?' replied Joseph.

'Did he ever change your nappy or bath you when you were a nipper?'

Joseph raged. 'Who cares?' he snapped. 'All that matters is Ric drops the bird. Now let's do it and if you go all wimpish on me, think of the money.'

Enrico tried to relax at home. He worried about not asking Rosie to marry him. He kept procrastinating but so wanted the proposal to be special. He retired early and was in bed when his doorbell rang.

This was rare. He grabbed a dressing-gown even with the temperature being Christmas weather and opened his door.

'G'day Ric,' said Joseph in a stern voice. His brother looked equally serious.

Enrico jumped to conclusions. This was a rare visit, and they looked so solemn it must be shocking news.

'It's your grandmother? She's dead?'

The brothers stepped inside. 'No, Ric,' said Joseph now running the show. 'But we do have something serious to discuss.'

They sat in his lounge-room with Enrico on edge. His clasped hands shook.

'What's happened? Tell me.'

'It's your girlfriend, Ric.'

Panic set in. Enrico thought Rosie was injured or worse. Michael hated being here and forgot his brother's instruction to break the news gently.

'She's a slag,' said the younger brother.

Joseph dropped his head and whispered, 'Jesus, Michael.'

Enrico was uncertain about the meaning of the word or how it was related to Rosie but knew he wanted to be sick.

Three men stared in silence. The visit quickly became a disaster and still had the intimate pics to come.

Enrico stood. 'I want you both to leave.'

Joseph grabbed the envelope and, pulling out two photos, shoved them at his great uncle.

'You need to see these. Your girlfriend is a money-grubbing bitch who sleeps with men young and old. We're doing you a big favour, Ric.'

Enrico wouldn't touch the photos. Joseph held them in both hands. He nodded to Michael who picked out another two.

Shock gripped the old man's body. His blood boiled.

'Get out of my house,' he growled in a low and furious voice.

The young men were on a mission and wanted closure.

Joseph pushed for a sale. 'Can you not see this woman is a whore, Ric, that she's bleeding you dry?'

Enrico hated anyone disrespecting women and the volume of his voice explained his mood.

'Get out, now!' He shoved them towards the door. 'Get out,' he bellowed as they grabbed the photos and stumbled onto his verandah. They looked back at the old man in his dressing gown bought from London Stores in 1968. He didn't care who saw or heard him. 'And never come back!'

He closed his door with force and grabbed the door handle to stop from falling. He hated not having his stick because he would have used it to punish his wicked, appalling great nephews.

Chapter 35
The former barber sat there breathing long, slow breaths.

Enrico couldn't sleep and nor could his great nephews. The young men's plan to separate their great uncle, and his would-be bride crashed. His viewing of Lorna naked and behaving in an intimate way kept flashing through his mind.

The brothers discussed the event. 'He must love her madly,' said Michael. 'He didn't criticize her once.'

'I was sure the plan would work. And now we're stuffed. Instead of rejecting her, he'll forgive her, and she'll grab our inheritance.'

'She's so young she'll outlive him by twenty years.'

'Ahhh!' yelled Joseph having a Eureka moment. 'We've shown the pics to the wrong bloody person. We should have shown them to her.'

'Blackmail?' gasped Michael.

'It's our last chance. What's her address in East Camberwell?'

They set off and risked being pinched for speeding. They parked close to Rosie's maisonette.

'This bitch is a liar. East Malvern, my arse,' spat Joseph. 'This time she's gunna pay.'

The brothers approached the front door. Joseph knocked and waited. Both held two photos of the Lorna seduction.

'Knock again,' said Joseph, angry and desperate. There was still no response. 'Go round the side,' he ordered, and Michael obeyed.

He returned. 'No lights, no-one home except a yapping dog.'

Joseph grabbed a pen, held a photo against the door and wrote. 'Dump Enrico or these go viral.' He grabbed one of Michael's photos and repeated the scrawl then shoved all four photos under the door.

'This'll fix the bitch. Let's go,' said Joseph and they left.

Sitting alone and bored at home in Chadstone, Lorna's phone rang.

'Hi Lorna, it's Simon.'
'Simon,' she gushed, 'how are you?'
'Fine, darling. Look we've finished editing your ad.'
She glowed. *They're calling it "my ad".*
'Not sure when it's on air, but I'll send you the clip. Talk soon. Bye.'
She opened her ancient laptop and then Simon's email. The attachment took an age to download. She stared at the screen and hit the little white arrow.

It was the day before Christmas Eve. Big Graeme and Lorna knew nothing about certain photos recently in circulation. Enrico and Rosie knew everything, but both were so shocked they dared not mention it to the other.

Both arrived for their penultimate session. They greeted one another with suppressed warmth. Enrico had no idea how or when he might broach the subject. To him it was utterly confusing and devastating. Why would his great nephews have such photos, how did they get them and why would they show them to him? Was that Lorna or was it this thing called AI and fake photography?

For Rosie it didn't make sense. What connection was there between Lorna and Enrico? Was that Enrico in the photo? Having never seen him in a state of undress other than his shorts, singlet and padding, surely that was not him because from the rear, the male was much taller, slimmer and younger.

Start time arrived and they chatted about their second last show, the weather and Buster. They reached the door with the porthole, Enrico smiled, knew this was not the time and place to tell Rosie what he saw last night, and away they went. Being equally confused, she had no idea what to do. What should she do with those photos?

Their session turned fabulous. It was so close to Christmas, and both luxuriated in the happiness of the excited children. There was a moment when both were posing and fixated on Russell and his camera. *Oh my God! Was he involved? Did he take the photos of Lorna?*

She became the centre of their thinking as they returned to base. Soon Lorna would appear, and would that result in spectacular fireworks? Did she know what they knew?

Enrico and Rosie changed out of their costumes. Big Graeme bowled in causing the furniture to shake. No sign of Lorna. If he, like the others, had been privy to her saucy snaps, the world would have been told. He said nothing because he knew nothing.

Then it happened. Lorna arrived, late and angry. Enrico and Rosie watched spellbound waiting for her fury to explode. Which one of you bastards took those photos?

Yes, she was angry but apparently something more important than naked pics fired her rage. She stared at the three performers and hated herself more than anyone. Humiliation is a powerful weapon.

'Are you all right, Lorna?' asked Mr Polite.

'No I bloody well am not. That TV ad has me starring as an incontinent pensioner whose sole aim in life is to wear the appropriate waterproof undies! They used AI to add the diapers. Not happy, at all!' she yelled and disappeared to change.

Big Graeme worried while Enrico and Rosie looked at one another wondering why she never mentioned her naked pics.

Enrico accepted Rosie's offer of a lift. They talked about Lorna and those photos. Rosie pulled up outside his home.

'Last day tomorrow,' she said, and they looked at one another.

He decided to confess. 'Rosie, I must tell you something shocking.'

He struggled to speak. She interrupted.

'Does it involve revealing photos of the other Mrs Santa?'

He stared in disbelief. He explained the visit from his great nephews. She explained the photos under her door.

'But why are we involved?' asked Enrico.

'I don't think Lorna knows we received those photos. She may not even know they exist. But my granddaughter once met a young man who told her Mrs Santa was trying to seduce a Santa and scam him.'

Enrico's Italian heritage and his long hours gardening gave him a tanned face. It now turned white.

'This young man; what is his name?'

'Joseph,' she said. The former barber sat there breathing long, slow breaths. 'Are you okay, Enrico?'

'I'm fine. And tomorrow I will be even better when I work for the last time with my wonderful best friend and favourite Mrs Santa.'

He leant across and they kissed. He made his exit with extraordinary grace, blew her a kiss, waved and headed up the drive.

At last, Beverley could relax.

Chapter 36

The boy sat on his father's knee with Santa and Mrs Santa either side.

Enrico wrote a letter to Joseph and Michael. Apart from texts on his phone, handwritten letters were still his only method of communication. If a literary style could be attached to his missive, one might suggest brutal politeness. The opening kicked arse.

Dear Joseph and Michael
I know what you have done and as crude and appalling as it was, it failed and showed up your serious lack of intelligence. You two idiots have been targeting the wrong Mrs Santa. Now it's all over, Rover. You demean women and use crude language to describe them. Please allow me to lower myself to your level. You are both dickheads.
Your loving great uncle
Enrico

When the envelope addressed to her grandsons arrived at Sofia's house—he didn't know his great nephews' addresses—the matriarch could not wait to discover its contents. She told her daughter who sent her sons to Nonna as soon as possible, as in now.

Nervous, now panicking, the great nephews arrived, dreading news of their disinheritance. It was worse. They'd been sprung and made monumental fools of themselves. Sofia demanded to know what was in the letter.

'You don't want to know, Nonna,' said Joseph fuming not only at his failure to stop a possible marriage but at having spent so much time on the wrong Mrs Santa.

'Tell me,' the grandmother ordered.

Michael stepped forward. 'Ric has discovered we tried to stop his romance with Mrs Santa and has called us idiots.'

Sofia gasped. She ordered such action. Is she too an idiot?

Her grandsons left constantly wiping egg from their faces.

It was Christmas Eve and Enrico prepared for his final performance as Santa. Rosie sent him a text explaining how much she has enjoyed working with him and hoping they remain friends once their work together ended. He tingled.

As usual he arrived first and was dressed and exercising his special Santa walking stick when its creator arrived. He thought she looked even more beautiful than usual. Even if the storeroom had been filled with others—they were alone—she walked up to Enrico and kissed him strongly on the lips.

'Good morning, beautiful lady,' he said.

'Good morning, kind sir,' she replied then pointed at his mouth. 'Touch of lippy there Santa,' she pointed to the spot then left to change.

In costume for the last time, they walked along the corridor stopping at the exit door.

'Break a leg, good luck and thank you for being such a wonderful Mrs Santa,' he said. Rosie found a tear preparing for lift off, so Enrico pushed open the door, rang his bell like billy-o and called his greeting to the packed shopping centre.

Russell eagerly awaited his favourite couple. 'Morning Santa,' he called then, 'Morning Mrs Santa.' The spirit of Christmas, well Commercial Christmas was alive and well.

The problem the couple endured at the theatre company party, and the suffering both copped with the intimate photos' saga were both in the past. They were together, in love with their work and with one another.

At one of the few breaks in their session, Russell gave an order. 'Now you two, how about a photo on your own?'

They didn't need asking twice and Rosie sat on Enrico's knee. He put one arm around her waist and the other correctly on his knee. He would have preferred her knee. Both politely trembled.

'Smile,' called Russell and dozens of shoppers looked, pointed and laughed. The line of children busting to meet Santa meant the happy couple went back to work.

After the final little visitor met Santa, Russell set up the rope barrier and changed the sign to:

Meet Santa at 1.30pm

The couple gathered their belongings for the last time when a terrible scream filled the centre. It sounded terrifying and was so loud and continuous, the Christmas canned music and the hubbub from shoppers was no match for a distressed mother.

Enrico and Rosie exchanged glances and Russell interrupted. 'Sounds like a lost kiddie. Your presence may add to the confusion. I suggest you retire and thanks again for all your work.' They thanked him. 'Oh,' he said and stopped them. 'Have a look at your photos.' He showed them. 'You look like a lovely married couple.'

Their brains entertained dancing endorphins boosting their already excited moods. Russell put it down to the end-of-season performance and gave them the push to depart a shopping centre now filled with mayhem, cries and calls for a lost child.

Mr and Mrs Santa reached their storeroom and hurried inside. 'Let's change and see if we can help,' said Enrico. Rosie disappeared and Santa prepared to remove his cap and whiskers but froze when an unusual noise distracted him. He went to investigate behind boxes and fell back in surprise.

'Well, well, well,' he said in a loud voice. 'And who have we got here?'

Rosie heard the question and came exploring. She and Enrico, both still wearing their full costume, stared at a man and a small boy. Rosie held out a hand and drew the child to her.

'Hello and what's your name, young man?'

'Timmy,' he said looking bug-eyed at Santa and his wife.

She took him aside. 'I'm Mrs Santa. Have you come to meet Santa?'

The boy's eyes widened, and his nodding head answered the question.

As Rosie spoke with Timmy, Enrico struggled to kneel beside the man.

'How can I help you, sir?'

Thomas Larsen slumped. His exhaustion helped him surrender. 'I've tried to kidnap my son. My ex-wife has made my life a misery and blocked my access. I'm desperate and have done a stupid, stupid thing.'

'Well let's see if we can solve this little problem. Don't forget all's well that ends well,' said Enrico holding out a hand. 'I'm Enrico but you can call me Santa.'

The forlorn father whispered. 'I even bought a gun although it's an imitation.' He withdrew the weapon from inside his jacket. It certainly looked real.

'I can take that,' said Santa and the gun changed hands. Enrico shoved it inside his jacket pocket.

'I've ruined my life and now will never be allowed to see my son again.' He wept silently and without fanfare.

'Not necessarily. Do you want your boy to meet Santa?'

Thomas nodded as tears streaked his face.

'Dry your eyes and let's give your boy the best Christmas ever.'

Enrico moved to Rosie and whispered the story. She smiled, nodded and whispered. 'It's a wonderful idea from a wonderful man.'

Five minutes later as the lost child pandemonium continued outside, the quartet made their way out via the door with the porthole and into the frantic throng. People could hardly miss them. It was Santa after all.

He rang his bell and cried, 'Merry Christmas.' People stopped and stared. The lost child had been found and now was walking, holding hands with Mrs Santa and his father. Little Timmy's smile was infectious.

Like Chinese Whispers, the word spread. Timothy, who once was lost, now was found. His mother received the news and started running through the shopping centre to where people pointed.

The quartet stopped with a growing crowd of onlookers around them. Russell saw the situation and grabbed his camera.

Santa collected a gift from the set and handed it to Timmy. Thomas crouched and the boy sat on his father's knee with Santa and Mrs Santa either side. What a photo opportunity.

Stephanie and her friend Christine burst through the crowd. Stephanie went to grab her son but stopped. To do so would make her appear a terrible mother. The child looked blissfully happy with his father surrounded by Mr and Mrs Santa.

People snapped photos of the little boy who was lost then found by his father and Santa. What a tale for the local paper and, at this time of the year, it became a happy news clip for the TV news.

Thomas kissed his boy who turned and hugged his father creating more wonderful and moving pics. Holding back tears, Thomas turned his boy towards his mother and pointed. Timmy ran to her holding up his gift from Santa, then turned back and waved to his father. It was the best day of Thomas's life.

Russell stepped in and led the costumed couple back to their corridor.

'Great finale, Santa and I hope to see you back here next year.' The men shook hands. 'And you too, Mrs Santa. Don't let the old boy get away.' He kissed Rosie and left.

The Santa couple entered the corridor and embraced one another. They kissed with passion. Enrico broke free.

'I have a Christmas present for you, Mrs Santa.' Her heart rate took off. He reached into his pocket and touched the gun. Bloody hell. He searched further and found what he wanted. Now he faced the highest hurdle. How on Earth could he kneel in this relatively small corridor? How could he kneel anywhere? He slid with help from the walls. Rosie's excitement changed to fear as she placed her hands on his arms as if to guide him. He made it.

Once kneeling, he produced that little red jewellery box, opened it revealing that certain engagement ring.

'My darling girl,' he said, 'please will you marry me?'

She automatically put her hands to her mouth then came alive. 'What a silly question; of course I will,' she said and bent to kiss him.

He offered her the ring and helped slip it on her finger.

'And there's something else,' he said.

'Anything, Signor,' she replied.

'Can you please help me to stand?'

'Of course,' she laughed and soon Santa was back being vertical.

When they entered the storeroom, Big Graeme struggled with his costume with Lorna dressed and impatient. Her mood settled at dark and moody.

Enrico and his fiancée entered with smiles to light up the room.

'Oi, oi, you two look like your Christmases have all come at once,' said Big Graeme preparing to stand.

'They have,' said Rosie holding out her hand with her latest present. 'Enrico has asked me to marry him.'

Big Graeme lost his balance, and Lorna copped a figurative slap across her chops. She hated the fact others were happy and stormed out to start the final session.

'Well congratulations you two,' said Big Graeme. 'This is not an end of season joke I hope.'

'It's no joke, my friend. I even dropped down on one knee to propose,' said a grinning Enrico.

'I could never do that,' chipped the big man.

'You should never say never, Graeme,' said Rosie. 'Find the right girl and pop the question.'

'Yes but if I dropped down on one knee, I'd need a crane to get back up again.'

All three laughed. Big Graeme wished them Merry Christmas and a relatively long married life and lumbered out of the storeroom.

The lovebirds faced one another. Neither spoke. They held hands, two on two. The last month included a few adventures. The next month or months or years were waiting. What a day. What a Christmas. What a love tale.

Epilogue
Buster loved it.

Lorna wanted to scream but lacked the energy. Shattered described her well. Even her anger spluttered and died. It wasn't so much she missed the part in the movie for which she gave her all in the audition, the real pain came when she discovered there never *was* a movie. She joined the club for the scammed.

To rub salt in her wound, people recognized her as the lady in the ad, the woman wearing the adult nappies to keep her high and dry. 'Hello Grannie! Got your nappy on today?'

The one thing the great nephews hated was humiliation. Joseph, who considered himself one of life's winners, died inside. To make such a schoolboy howler targeting Lorna not Rosie was something he swore his brother, on pain of death, to never mention again—ever.

To make them even bigger fools, their mother later told them their great uncle and new great aunt decided to leave their wills unchanged, meaning everything the brothers did was a total waste of time. However, there was a new codicil in Enrico's document. Both brothers were required to work 100 hours a year for three years gardening in the grounds of a women's refuge before they would be eligible to receive their inheritance.

The humble pie was yet to be invented which could even remotely remove the shame the siblings endured. After the nuptials, the first meeting between Joseph and Pippa proved tricky. How embarrassing for the great nephew.

The publicity given to little Timmy, photographed and filmed looking so happy cuddling with his father, Santa and Mrs Santa, was so extensive, Stephanie came under pressure to give Thomas greater access to their son. The father, having surprised the boy, avoided a possible kidnapping charge by good luck and good people—it was Santa who saved the day.

The wedding of the New Year season took place in a marquee in Enrico's back garden with the clotheslines and garden tools tucked away out of sight. One tent peg barely avoided the biggest pumpkin.

The guest list was restricted. Pippa and her parents were there to support the bride with two of Rosie's best friends as ladies of honour.

The groom's sister and niece were there as was Alfrid with his fourth wife (common law) who helped the retired chef provide the catering.

Naturally the official photographer was Russell who provided his services free and gave Pippa his card if she ever wanted any photographic advice.

Miranda brought Sandra and like everyone, had a ball. Buster loved it and reckoned it was like all his Christmases.

The celebrant was the oldest person there.

The great nephews flew interstate to avoid having to attend.

Details of the honeymoon were not available at the time of going to print and the Pacific cruise holiday for the newlyweds was forgotten with Rosie now overwhelmed at having found her true love, her real-life Santa.

Meet the Author

Hello. I write novels, plays and musicals. I always enjoy hearing from readers.

You can read my play scripts online at www.foxplays.com.
My fiction and non-fiction books are at www.cenfoxbooks.com

I'll appreciate you taking the trouble to leave a review on Amazon or Goodreads.

Amazon
https://www.amazon.com/s/ref=nb_sb_noss_1?url=search-alias%3Dstripbooks&field-keywords=cenarth+fox

Goodreads
https://www.goodreads.com/search?utf8=%E2%9C%93&q=Cenarth+Fox&search_type=books&search%5Bfield%5D=on

www.ingramcontent.com/pod-product-compliance
Lightning Source LLC
Chambersburg PA
CBHW051937290426
44110CB00015B/2017